LOSS:
the doorway to new life

365 DAYS OF INSPIRATION

FRANNIE HOFFMAN

iUniverse

LOSS: THE DOORWAY TO NEW LIFE
365 DAYS OF INSPIRATION

iUniverse books may be ordered through booksellers or by contacting:

iUniverse
1663 Liberty Drive
Bloomington, IN 47403
www.iuniverse.com
844-349-9409

Cover Design: Lane Matthews
Cover Art: Frannie Hoffman
Cover Photo: Rob Matthews
Interior Art: Frannie Hoffman
Editor: Jodi Solomon

ISBN: 978-1-6632-5548-8 (sc)
ISBN: 978-1-6632-5549-5 (e)

Library of Congress Control Number: 2023915786

Print information available on the last page.

iUniverse rev. date: 02/23/2024

LOSS:
the doorway to new life

What people are saying about Loss: The Doorway to New Life

"Frannie's book is full of wonderful spiritual insight and wisdom, offering the reader unique perspectives and heartfelt guidance to help us all on this journey we call life"

John Munn
Amazon Best Selling Author of *Empty with Everything (A Memoir): Life affirming stories reminding us that we each have the inner power to transcend anything,* and Transformational Life Coach

"Deep grief has the capacity to either close us down or break us open. As much as anyone I know, Frannie Hoffman chooses the latter path. In her book, LOSS: the doorway to new life, the author shares her daily writings as she processed the sudden and tragic loss of her husband. Deeply profound and moving, Frannie shows us that there is new life on the other side of darkness, you are not alone on your journey, and when we let go of what was, we make room for a transformative awakening."

Beth Knopik
Author of *Beyond the Rainbow, A Mother's Journey through Grief to Grace,* and Life Coach

"Frannie's story of loss, grief and renewal has led me to a deeper place. Her book was a catalyst for growth, providing a path to profound personal release that revealed more of who I AM."

Lanee
Whispering Winds Yoga

By the sea
  By the sea
    By the beautiful sea
      You and me, you and me
        Oh, how happy we'll be…

Dedicated to my beloved husband
Steven Daniel Kaluza
5/5/1955- 6/10/2013

Acknowledgments

This book was spirit inspired as my husband, Steve, planted the seeds for these writings to become a book. When I asked Jodi Solomon to help me edit another book and assist me in all her talented and expert ways to bring this manuscript into life, she said, "I wouldn't want you to do it without me!" Her dedication to this project and loving friendship have been a true partnership.

My gratitude to my daughter, Lane, who used her superb design abilities to create the perfect cover and to add many inspired touches throughout the book. And to her husband, my cherished son-in- law Rob Matthews, for his steady confidence in and assistance with this book. Your knowledge and support were invaluable.

When I voiced my need for extra eyes to proofread the manuscript, my sisters Philomene Hoffman and Colleen Smith, along with my brother-in-law Bruce Smith, and lifelong friend Judy Totzke all stepped up. Thank you for your time, your amazing attention to detail, and all your wonderful feedback.

My appreciation to my brother, Phil Hoffman, who encourages and inspires me in his humble way. And a special shout-out to Sarah Painter who, at the beginning of this project, transcribed all my hand-written journal writings.

To my Angel Sisters, Ticia Cousy, Ann Besterfield, Sharon Salter, Liah Howard, Kathy Bliss, Azura Porter, Sherry Noland and Fran Kowalczk for your unending spiritual connection. Deep gratitude for my circle of women friends who bless my life with great love as you inspire me to soar: Lanee Brown, Di Stewart, Kem Lindsay, Debbie Dannheisser, Joey Schooley, Susan Powers, Marcia Lockie, Haike Vaudry, Twylla Gulley, Janet Riley, Cindy Phillips, Donna and Sarah Nicol, Brenda Atkinson, Janet Matthews, Brigitte Hamm, Joy Gardner (mother of my heart), Kristen Behlke and Jenny Blanos, and many other soul sisters. You acknowledge my writings and encourage me to keep rising up. To all my soul family, friends, and clients, I wish I could put all your names down. I honor you and acknowledge your presence in my life. I am overflowing with gratitude.

To Pat Grant, you are always there for me as a living example of love and acceptance. Cindy Waite and Terri Nelson, you listen with your hearts and remind me that it is always One Day at a Time!

And to all my men friends who have been a source of loving support for me, Rob Grant, Jim Riley, Max Powers, Don O'Keefe, Dan Dannheisser, and Christian Ulanch. Your tender hearts have listened to me through these times when I needed strength.

To Kristine Long and Jacques Gagne, your love and constant, unwavering support have again and again eased my burdens. My love and appreciation are beyond words. You are family to me.

Always, I'm humbled by the constant love and support of my children, Luke Andrews and his partner, Corin Finnie and Lane and Rob Matthews. You carry me with your incredibly big hearts. I bow to you. To my grandchildren, Theo and Milo, you fill my life with so much joy.

I offer my deepest heartfelt love to my family who held me through my broken heart and helped me in more ways than you will ever know as I journeyed through grief and transformed my pain into words to help others. Your love is unconditional: Philomene Hoffman, Colleen and Bruce Smith, Phil Hoffman and Janine Marchessault, Sondra and Dan Hirssig and their daughters Alicia and Amber, Mike and Julie Kaluza and their daughters, Amber and Ashley, Judy Totzke, Stephanie Noel and Chris Kraemer. My nieces, Lindsay, Lauren and Jessica and Jessie and their children Eli, Mattea, Bella, Ariana and River.

I bow down to the Divine as this Presence continues to give through this incredible life, I am honored to be a part of.

Thank you! Thank you! Thank you!

From the Author

Writing this book was an integral part of my grieving process. I wrote most days to help me feel and understand all I was experiencing. It is a way to honor my husband and to acknowledge all the lessons this life of loss has taught me.

I had almost completed the manuscript for this book when the pandemic hit our world. So much loss for so many. Our collective and individual hearts are broken. As we join here along this incredible journey called grief, I am grateful to now share my experience of healing through loss.

Grief is an invitation to sit in the pain and let yourself shatter. Let all that you were go. Grief can be scary as it pulls you into the darkness. But once there, you'll find that this dark hole is where you can empty, where you can release all that you carry that no longer serves you in this life to make room for something new to be born. As you give way to this rebirth of your true self, you will merge with the parts of yourself that are longing to live this life more awake and alive than ever before.

When Steve left, I repeatedly fell back into the dark hole of grief. Over time, it became familiar territory; you learn to live with it and that's okay. It's the new normal; life, as we know it, has changed.

This book is not a manual for loss but instead, a chronicle of my intimate journey expressed daily. It is my hope and desire that through my experience, I can help others feel their own grief. It's different for each of us. There is no right or wrong way to navigate this path but sharing helps us all know that we aren't alone.

Preface

Since before time you have been free. Birth and death are
only doors through which we pass, sacred thresholds on our
journey. Birth and death are a game of hide and seek. You
have never been born and you can never die.
— Thich Nhat Hanh,
No Death No Fear: Comforting Wisdom for Life

The early and unexpected death of my husband, Steve has forever
changed me. I understand so much more deeply now how precious life is,
and I do not take it for granted.

As a spiritual counselor, I have helped many work through
grief and other emotions that leave us feeling stuck, out of balance,
and disconnected from our true selves. Yet none of my personal or
professional experiences prepared me for what lay ahead physically,
emotionally, or spiritually in the wake of Steve's transition. Though my
many first-hand experiences have convinced me that there is life after
death, they did not diminish the depth of my grief.

It is truly one day at a time, sometimes one moment at a time.
Nothing in or of this world can prepare us or help us avoid this
experience. For me, tears easily fall one minute, then anger and fear
grip me the next. I do not judge these moments. Getting the tears and
emotions up and out cleanses our cellular memory, which opens new
doors for more life.

Some people try to bypass grief by keeping themselves distracted.
I have worked with clients who ran from the feelings that these dark
times can bring. Sooner or later, however, there will be a reckoning.
Eventually, the sorrow will come in one form or another.

Steve's death held up a mirror to my pain like nothing else could. His
death was also my death. When he dropped his body, he left me here to
face myself without him. I spiraled into despair. Who was I without him?

Lost in my darkness, I entered parts of myself that needed to be exposed. I couldn't blame him or project my suppressed emotions on him now.

I recognized that I had this work to do: another opportunity to go deeper, to look fear right in the eye, and let grief show me the way back to true freedom. It wasn't an overnight fix. This was my path to everything that needed my attention. I was blessed to already have a practice that included meditation, journaling, yoga, the 12-Step Program, and breath work. All these tools helped me listen to the guidance that wanted to bring me back home to my heart. It was broken. Yet, broken wide open, it gave me glimpses of heaven where love is Divine and holy, a mystical power that creates and sustains life. I had to learn my soul's lesson, which was to let go of my attachment to anything outside of me—including my attachment to Steve—giving me my worth and security. Slowly I confronted the truths that loss uncovered, which allowed my transformation to take place. By looking deeply at my shadows, I recovered and now live more authentically.

The moment Steve left his body, his mission on earth was done. Yet in his brilliant spirit, he found ways to communicate and remind me that we are one with God/Universe. That first night without him by my side, I felt Steve trying to contact me. I was resistant. I wanted to sleep so that he could come to me in a dream. But he wanted me to write.

Finally, I got up and immediately I could feel him communicating with me in my mind and in my heart. "I don't want to do this," I said to him. "It's all we have," he replied. And in that moment my computer woke itself up with a "ding, ding, ding!"

The words from Steve spilled out of me like water from a faucet:

My Darling, Sweetheart,
There was so much that was unsaid and so much to do. I tried.
I tried so hard to tell you all that I could. Part of me knew that our journey together in the body was complete, while another part of me was very resistant to it all. For months, I was getting messages that came in ways that I did not understand. So, my heart would close because I was afraid to leave you.

Maybe you thought I was your rock, but you were my float. You helped me so I would not sink. The tides and undertows of life were pulling me down—deep down into the despair and darkness that was underneath all that I was hiding. I tried to let myself rise through it, but all the beliefs of my past shrouded my sight and blinded me from the light. Just know that it wasn't easy for me to be up against all that I needed to see and release, but you were my line to the truth.

The light that lives in all of us was coming through in all kinds of ways. You did everything you could. You were the one that allowed the messages of true love to pass through your lips from the heart of the Divine. This was what saved me. This is what saves us all—the moments of realization that there is something so much bigger than this human existence.

You will always be taken care of. I am always touching your world. As I move through dimensions to find out more, I will bring it to you. I will make it all known so that the evolution of many is accomplished through our honest communication.

Now that there are no barriers, I am healing, too. This time is for us all to heal. Tell everyone that it is glorious here—like the beautiful sunsets. This world beyond human life is like one long sunset of lights and feelings of a love that join with all that we truly are.

God is so much more than the descriptions we humans try to capture in our limited vocabularies. As you leave the body, everything is shown. As I floated around the hospital room, a part of me was already receiving the higher truths as I tried to reach you. How could you hear me when all you could do was try to bring me back to our life together?

It is so freeing to leave the fears and the ideas of the life I thought was real. It was so hard to leave you and to leave my family and friends.

I am so grateful to have had the opportunity to watch all that everyone said and felt at the moment of my passing. It is like an infusion of love that fills you up with so much energy that we are always connected to.

I will be making myself known to you, sharing these notes of love that may help you understand, slowly, why I left when I did.

Know that leaving you was part of our contract and yet not what I truly wanted at the time. I am beginning to understand it all. Enjoy the moments when you can and try to rest in my arms, the ones that will forever be holding you.

I love you more.

While I miss his physical presence, Steve is more with me now than ever. Yoko Ono was once asked how she could bear to be without John Lennon, given that they had spent 90 percent of their time together. Her response was, "Now we spend 100 percent of our time together."

When I join with Steve in spirit, my misery fades. The death of the body is not the end of love. Steve's spirit touches us vibrationally from the non-physical dimension. His messages are precious jewels of love, gleaming in the golden light of the "I AM" Presence. In my grief, they help me return to my heart and respond to my deep longing to be in union with spiritual Presence. After loss, if we can open our hearts, we can partner with Spirit, return to the light, and receive the truth that wants to be shared.

Grief is not a fast process, and it will not adhere to any timetables. The experience has changed me. I'm no longer attached to my old life. This time of great sorrow also brings me greater awareness and transformation. My sadness—missing Steve and living a life without him—will always be with me. And yet I feel such awe and gratitude for the life we had together. As I look back at his transition, I appreciate how his path has led me back to my Beloved. Here we are never separate, never alone. Now I can see clearer, listen deeper, and receive the truth—that I am worthy.

Introduction:
Love Never Dies

The call of death is a call of love.
Death can be sweet if we answer it in the affirmative, if
we accept it as one of the great eternal forms of life and
transformation.

— Hermann Hesse

My appreciation for myself, my loved ones, and this world awakened more deeply in me during the fragile days, weeks, and months following the sudden death of my husband. It didn't matter how emotionally or physically fit I thought I was, Steve's unexpected death from an aneurysm shattered me.

While the busy world went on around me, I entered the valley of sorrow. There my children, family, and friends stood with me. At first, I was in shock. The trauma pushed me inside where all was revealed and uncovered. I allowed myself to move through the pain, without distraction, feeling sad, hurt, angry, and alone. There was no easy fix, no shortcuts.

No one can fix us or do this work for us. When I stayed in that space, missing and longing for my husband—and some days that was all I could do—I would cry buckets of tears. I was brought to my knees, to the very roots of the pain.

I had no one to blame and no choice but to face it all, but I was never truly alone. When I reached for God's hand, the force of energy that creates all worlds was there to participate in my creations. As I surrendered into the moment and allowed the divinity of the One to show me what I needed, I received assistance for every problem, every question, every task.

When I had the energy, I would pray, "Today let me touch these places within that call for my attention, for when I feel fear and resistance, I get in my own way. Let me trust that in God all things are possible."

As the anniversary of Steve's transition comes into the forefront of my awareness, I feel changed. This year of firsts—each holiday, birthday, anniversary; walking down the beach without him here with me in physical form, going into a restaurant that we loved to go to together—brought enormous pain and longing.

As I let myself move into all those moments of "life with Steve," I looked deeply into every part of myself to face all that needed to be released—all the attachments, all the love songs, and love letters. It chiseled away all that I thought I was with and without him. It unveiled me and opened me up like nothing else could and moved me deeply into myself where I experienced all my feelings and faced all that stood between me and my true source.

Here I am now—after a year of allowing moments to unfold and awaken me to more of myself. I am different. I am stronger. I am more open and loving. I care with greater compassion, and I will not put up with nonsense. This life is precious. Each person I meet is worthy of my connection. Relationships are richer and more authentic.

I live to connect to the Spirit that is within and all around me, the piece of heaven of which I am a part. Steve is right here, in all his glory, walking in Spirit and guiding my way, for he is now a part of the Divine. As I retrieve myself, as I awaken to what is true, God is moving into all that is reflecting around me. I have peace again. I can laugh and have fun. I can enjoy the beauty of this world. I can take the hand of Spirit and walk along the path that continues to unfold. It is lighted by the love of all that is. Here I am not alone, for inside our hearts, we are always in good company.

There is no turning back, for today I understand what grief has taught me.

How to Read the Book

When Steve left his body, it was a catalyst for me to come more into mine. For Steve, the transition was instantaneous; for me, it was long and slow. Allowing myself to feel and grieve and grow was a rich yet painful process, but that's the nature of birth. It's painful and messy.

My rebirth has been such a transformational time that I feared mere words could never truly do it justice. Nonetheless, I chronicled my emotions and experiences each step of the way. When I could, I allowed Steve to use me as a channel to bring in the wisdom of Spirit. Now I've distilled all my writings and all these messages from Spirit into this daily read. It's not dated because each of us must start where we are, which has nothing to do with a day on a calendar.

So, when reading this book, I invite you to let go. Allow the words to bring you deeply into all parts of yourself. This experience within is a beautiful journey, even when the suffering is so deep. We are one on this journey, and as we share ourselves intimately, we have nothing to hide, no secrets to hold us back. The longing for union with the Divine is calling us home to our hearts that remember everything.

On these pages, I share the feelings and experiences that helped me break open the hard shell that kept me attached to who and what I thought I was. From the stream of consciousness, I was able to tap into the energy that lifted me into being one with Steve in the light.

The "Spirit Speaks" sections in bold italic print indicate channeled messages. It is Spirit brought through me, often by Steve. But what's important is the message, not the messenger. So, for you, it may feel like wisdom from the Universe, loving guidance from God, your Higher Self, your spirit loved one, angels, or guides. I've also included meditations, insights and affirmations—all moments when we can allow Spirit to touch us in ways that free us to see beyond what is.

My healing and my transition progressed when I didn't get swept away by the busyness of life or the raging floodwaters of grief. Instead, I leaned into the forces that crashed into me and focused on staying open to myself and my connection to Source. When I could see beyond my pain and suffering, I was able to join with God, the Universe, the Light, where Steve's spirit lives.

I invite you to come face to face with your spirit as you navigate your journey through grief. It is my intention that by sharing my journey through these daily reads, I can help you to steady yourself and allow your humanity to bring you home to your heart where new life meets your grief. In time, you will have the courage to begin again. One day at a time.

Namaste,
Frannie

Prologue:
Our Last Morning Together

I remember the morning so well. The smell of coffee and the rattling in the kitchen as Steve cooked bacon in the frying pan woke me up. He loved Sunday mornings and even though I didn't eat meat or drink caffeine, I loved the aromas of both.

I turned over onto my side and grabbed the worn blue book that was lying on the cedar chest beside my bed. I love A Course in Miracles (ACIM). It's been my companion for over 20 years. Comfy in my bed, I lovingly use this time to read and apply the workbook lessons to my daily life. I was on the last chapter, "The Final Vision." I had read the last few lines over and over again. No matter how many times I read these pages of channeled words, I still feel like a new student of this course.

> "Thy will is done, complete and perfectly, and all creation recognizes You, and knows You as the only Source it has. Clear in Your likeness does the Light shine forth from everything that lives and moves in You. For we have reached where all of us are one, and we are home, where You would have us be."

These words were etched inside me as if scribed by Spirit just for me. As I digested the thoughts, the words fed my whole entire being. I began the day like every other day—in gratitude and excited.

I walked out of the bedroom into the light beaming in through the window shades. It was a clear day with bright blue skies and birds chirping their love songs. Steve was drinking his coffee and reading his book of choice. It was probably a science fiction or mystery novel. This was his morning ritual.

As I hugged my sweetheart good morning, loving the taste and smell of coffee on his mustache, I asked him if he wanted to meditate and pray with me. He said sure and followed me out to the lanai.

Sunday mornings we often had our church out there with nature surrounding us and the sounds of the busy world waking up. I opened The Promise of a New Day to June 10th, a daily read. The affirmation at the end of the paragraph said, "I go forth today alone and yet in good company. Everyone here in my life now is part of my destiny. Our trip is planned for today."

Then we went into meditation. The silence within brought us together, and I felt the light dissolve us into one. We stayed here for quite a while. I was remembering what I had read in ACIM; I opened my eyes as light illuminated us both. In the softness of the moment, I waited for Steve to open his eyes. He was at peace and so was I. I asked him what he received.

He was so open and filled with excitement. "I want to have a reunion here on Anna Maria Island with your family and my family!" "That would be great honey!" I replied. Inside I wondered where that idea came from. He sounded urgent in his delivery. Still, I welcomed the idea.

Soon we were off with our own agendas. Then he came out of the bedroom saying, "I just saw my first vision! It was so clear. I saw Lane holding a baby." He was grinning from ear to ear as he grabbed me. Looking into my eyes, He declared, "We will have grandchildren one day!"

Lane, my daughter, had just FaceTimed us two nights prior to announce her engagement. She showed us a room filled with rose petals and played the video that her fiancé, Rob, created for this milestone event. It was a compilation of short scenes from well-known movies each showing a man expressing his love to his woman. It was so well done, just as Rob would do. He made the proposal unique and special for his beloved. We watched the video and laughed and cried with them. I screamed with joy as Lane and Rob brought us into their special moment.

Steve wanted those grand babies ASAP. He had such a big grin on his face as he rushed around getting ready for his bike ride. He was so happy. We planned to meet at the beach after he finished his exercise and enjoy the afternoon together.

I went back out to the lanai and began editing my newsletter. He would be gone for a few hours, which would give me enough time to finish writing my story. Before leaving, he came out to kiss me goodbye. As he walked away, he turned around and said, "Thank you for forgiving me for any of my stupid behaviors over the past years." I looked at him with complete and unconditional love. Forgiveness is all about forgiving yourself I thought. "Of course! I love you so much. Till death do us part?"

Hours later we walked to the beach. He lifted his arm as if he was escorting me to a gala and we giggled like children. He spotted two woodpeckers on the tree. The male with its brilliant red helmet and the wifey, as Steve would say, were squawking at each other. Dressed in his favorite red biking shirt, Steve exclaimed, "Look at them! They are just like us. I'm trying to tell you something and you're not listening."

After lingering to watch the woodpeckers, we made our way into the Gulf of Mexico where we floated on noodles and discussed my upcoming milestone birthday. He wanted to have a party, and I finally gave in. He envisioned the whole affair in great detail. It seemed so important to him to make this plan.

Now I wonder if somehow, he sensed it all in that holy instant—had he glimpsed the future? Perhaps he saw this gathering, the birthday party plan that would be the reunion of our families on Anna Maria Island. But it wasn't for my birthday, it was for his funeral and the birth of his spirit. At that moment, he was so excited, he declared that today was the best day of his life!

When we got out of the water, he opened his arms with a big beach towel and wiped my body with every touch of presence and then held me in his arms. I wanted us to walk together but he said, "no, go and have a long walk, I'm going to finish getting dinner ready." I turned to walk away, and he called out my pet name, "Fancy Pants! Fancy Pants!" I turned to look at him. He pointed his finger at me and with great love beaming from his eyes he said, "You are so beautiful! I love you so much!" He said it twice. I turned and walked on. Those were the last words he said to me.

When I returned to the house, I could see Steve folding laundry with his back to me. I went into the bathroom to shower and get ready for the evening. I felt so happy and taken care of. My head was full of shampoo suds when suddenly all the hair on my body stood on end as I heard an energy like a train moving through me. It was an inner sound that brought doom and gloom into the moment. I jumped out of the shower, wrapped a towel around my body, and hurried out. There in the living room, my adult son, Luke, stood with his mouth open, paralyzed in fear. Steve's body lay on the floor. We called 911 and my son performed CPR until the paramedics arrived. Steve was taken to the hospital where later that evening, he died.

Like the oceans, our relationship was filled with unpredictability. One day was calm, another turbulent. Sometimes the undercurrents and rip tides took us into their grip, yet we always worked together to break free. This is what made our love so rich. We had grown deeply connected through all the tides of our 16 years together.

At times, I wanted to give up, but the voice of Spirit always showed me my way back to loving myself enough to stay and commit to our mutual growth. Forgiveness was something I learned through all the challenges of life. Then suddenly, without saying goodbye, he departed from his physical body.

Day 1

Truth: ...for the mystic, death is a doorway – the doorway to amazement.
Fear: It is the doorway to pain.
Truth: Yes, and the pain it brings fuels passion for life, for love, and for the expansion of beauty in the world. Until you can see the beauty of death, the illusion of death, you will not know who you really are.

– Tom Shadyac, Life's Operating Manual: with the Fear and Truth Dialogues

I entered the area of the hospital where his lifeless body lay. There was an energy all around me. I felt him; I saw his light. He was there, right beside me. There, in the silent room, I began to kiss him. I kissed his face, his lips, his hands, and I laid on his chest. He was still warm, but he wasn't in his body anymore. Gently, I removed his wedding ring from his finger.

His body looked perfect. There was no sign of sickness or even death. No longer in that body, his energy now filled the entire room. He is so much bigger than his body.

Soon we were escorted from the hospital by a policeman. Hand in hand, I walked with my son, Luke, along with Steve's sister Sondra and her husband Dan. We all walked like zombies, yet through our numbing pain, we could feel Steve's spirit with and around us.

As we drove over the bridge to Anna Maria Island, Luke and I saw a banner of golden light in the night sky. It looked like a doorway to heaven.

Once home, we moved like robots into the house and fell straight into bed. I laid on Steve's side of the bed, and Luke held me as we fell asleep, exhausted and in pain. In the next moment, I saw Steve in his brilliance and heard him clearly say, *"I am taking care of you. I am taking care of you,"* while in his hands he held a bouquet of lavender.

Day 2

Spirit Speaks

When you left the hospital that morning, after my body was laid under a sheet, and you said goodbye, I held you. I walked you out of the hospital; I guided you home; I held you in bed; I spoke to you and touched you in all the ways I could. Now is the place where I am with you. Feel the way you are held in a comfort that holds you up and moves you forward.

Yes, step by step you will move forward. Trust in how I am with you and that I will help you bring yourself into more life. You are a trooper. You always have been. You feel it all, the light and the dark, and then you are free to touch this world and receive its beauty.

It doesn't feel beautiful right now, but you will find your way back when you open to the idea that we will never be apart. You are a part of this incredible universe and as you allow it to be here for you, your life will become magical. Your life will become more conscious as you awaken out of the dream.

You did good—you have felt the pain of being stuck in the mud as you held what feels lost. Yet now life will bring more. All is well. Know that there is so much for you to experience now. I am with you all the way.

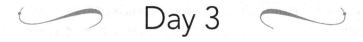

Day 3

I don't know how I stood in front of everyone gathered for Steve's memorial service. I had arrived at the funeral home heartbroken and weak. Shortly after, my niece Alicia came over to me and said, "Uncle Steve came to me in a dream last night and told me to give you this." In her hands, she held a bouquet of lavender.

I felt carried by a spirit of love. There was a Presence within and all around. Though sadness was inside of me and in the faces of everyone looking back at me, I could feel my love for him. It washed over me like a warm blanket. Not knowing what I would say, I opened my mouth, and the words came up from deep inside the well of grief. I was so empty, maybe numb, yet so full of an energy that I can only express as love.

He was in all our minds and thoughts. The feelings we shared helped me realize that he was still a part of us and communicating through each one who got up to share their stories and their relationship. Every hug, every tear brought more love from and for Steve.

As hard as the day was, it was also full of love and laughter. I received so much of him in all that was shared—a treasure trove of tales I had not heard before.

My memories console me as I rest in the stories of how life brought us together. While we weathered our share of challenges, those setbacks and heartbreaks brought us closer.

As I open to this moment, no matter how things seem, I couldn't be more loved than I am right now. I rest in the arms of God and in the ones that walk on this Earth with me. I look around and realize I am surrounded by soul family who wait for me to awaken.

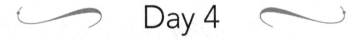 Day 4

Thinking that the death of a loved one is unfortunate, ill-timed, sad for the departed, or random is to deny the perfection and order that are otherwise so abundantly obvious throughout these magical jungles of time and space.
— Mike Dooley, A B, *A Beginner's Guide to the Universe: Uncommon Ideas for Living an Unusually Happy Life*

I am forever grateful for my family. As I walk on, yet not able to see ahead, I am steadied by the love that will hold me until I find my footing. Then in the stillness, I hear him whisper through the breeze.

Spirit Speaks

Baby Doll! Feel me here with you. Let it be okay, for now is an opening for you. Little by little, you will walk on solid ground again and find your way through it all. Changes in life will be uncomfortable at first, but soon you will rest again and know that life continues. No hurry, just be where you are, and many will surround you with what you need until strength comes back.

With every breath I take, every tear I shed, each mistaken thought or unspoken word, there are choices made and fears faced. I walk on as the veils lift, the layers dissolve, and all that I think I am falls away.

I breathe into feelings that take my breath away. I breathe into this moment where I lose myself in the pain of attachment. I let go into the loneliness and insecurities deep inside this unveiled heart.

The pain and suffering lead me to a mind of disharmony. While my weak and needy self drowns in my feelings, there is nothing for me to fix; I only need to remember that my happiness comes from within.

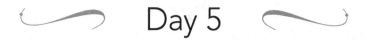

Day 5

Out of every crisis comes the chance to be reborn...
— Nena O'Neil

In the dark places of grief, I am in agony. My heart cries even when my eyes do not. I am breaking wide open. No words can soothe the wounds within. Everything in my mind—beliefs and ideas about life— is so shaky. I doubt it all. What I knew to be true is now filled with pain. I am fragile.

I am insecure and question everything. I feel discouraged as fear disables me at my core. Faith is all that can help me now as I am called to align with my heart. I grasp at a thread of hope and trust that it is all in Divine order. With patience, I stay with myself until silence brings a peaceful mind.

These times are most important even though it's intense and scary. It's like jumping off a cliff into an abyss with nothing to catch me. I trust that grace will come and mend this broken part of me that has fallen into deep despair. I hold myself gently until guidance comes.

These tears provide healing. As I let myself be held by others, they are free to cry too. I let myself release, no matter what is going on around me. No apologies.

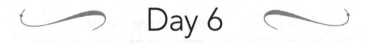

Day 6

I want to know if you've touched the center of your own sorrow, if you've been opened by life's betrayal, or have become shriveled and closed from fear of further pain.
— Oriah Mountain Dreamer

Early in the morning, the phone rings. I open my eyes in my darkened room, and for a moment, I forget that Steve had died just hours before. I force myself to answer the phone. With a trembling and weak voice, I say hello to Oriah, who is calling to share a vision.

Just hearing her voice brings me back into the reality that he is gone. She tells me that she saw Steve's spirit the moment he departed. "His soul looked back at his empty body and lingered for a while as if he was preparing a quote for a renovation job on a house. He pondered the situation for a moment and then said, 'I don't want to leave Frannie, but this body can't be fixed, and I can't be who I want to be in it the way it is.' And so, he was off on his mission without that body, which would have limited him."

Those words bring both comfort and pain. In my heart, I feel the truth she shared. Steve had always told me he wasn't going to live long into old age. He didn't want to be in a sick body.

The grief begins as I feel myself grasping for him physically. The heavy burden of loss pushes me into the unknown. As my weakened body sinks into the couch, this feeling takes over. I'm squirming in agony. With the blinds shut so no light comes in from the outside, I continue to shrink into my fragile and insecure self.

God, help me accept this overwhelming pain. Help me surrender and trust that how I feel is ok.

 # Day 7

Winter falls upon us so spring can bring new growth...
Cry the tears! Allow the longing! Sadness brings surrender
and a deep desire to be free.

—Rumi

I cry out to Heaven as I deeply feel my brokenness, my emptiness. I don't think I can go on. I pray for the healing of my mind that is stuck in thoughts of suffering. "Please! I cannot bear this pain of missing and longing. Where are you, my beloved?"

Exhausted, I wait for something more. I know this pain is breaking me open so that my heart can receive the truth. Yet I am scared.

I breathe into the yearning and sadness.

I meet myself here, in all the misery with unconditional acceptance.

Every cell of my body confronts me as I sit at the bottom of this well of despair.

As I listen to the voice of my higher self,

I feel a presence that warms me from the inside.

I am tired of being in this barren land where nothing quenches my thirst…hunger leaves me empty and weak. I cannot stay here, for the needs cannot be met with you gone.

I must search deeper and move through the valley of sorrow where I can dream of my dance with the Divine.

Day 8

Spirit Speaks

I am here in this moment now with you. It is painful when you hold on to what was. Surrender into the sweet moment that is here. Then the bridge between worlds becomes clear and steady. Grasp onto the gentle hand that reaches deep within your heart to have and to hold forever and eternity. There are no words here, only the sweetness of a moment of connection to all that is real and all that continues to grow into the fruits of a life lived fully.

I am here, amongst it all, waiting for you to see that you are never alone. Take the moment and be free from the world that was us. New life gives to you with ease. There are so many tears flowing yet when they pass let the peace abide and listen to what is being given to you.

Day 9

I said: What about my eyes?
He said: Keep them on the road.
I said: What about my passion?
He said: Keep it burning.
I said: What about my heart?
He said: Tell me what you hold inside it?

I said: Pain and sorrow.
He said: Stay with it. The wound is the place where the Light
enters you.

— Rumi

With the funeral over and life—for everyone else—getting back to normal, the reality of being alone without Steve is quickly setting in. I go to bed only to wake up in the middle of the night forgetting he is gone. When the temporary amnesia lifts, I spiral back into grief.

I do my best to stay with all my feelings. When I am open and empty all the tears, there's room for Steve to enter. He walks so close these days. No body, yet, somehow, I see him with my mind's eye and experience him with all my senses.

A force reaches into my body and mind, opening me. Even as my pain and fear disorient me, I can sense the guidance gently encouraging me forward. I do my best to embrace this unknown place within. I feel it all without trying to fix anything. It takes great effort to allow my God to take the lead in this new dance and carry me into a silent mind.

Holding the space for myself can be brutal. I am terrified to let go. I fear the thoughts that tell me I am alone and left behind. As I remind myself to breathe, I empty and deeply take in the words I hear whispered from the heavens, "I will not leave." My breath affirms this truth; I will not leave me.

I rest in this quiet space and let this inner something—God, Universe, Presence—help me go on. All I can do is keep breathing.

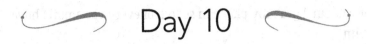

Day 10

Meditation

If I could tell you what I feel,
I would cry the words out loud,
Lost in my longing for your touch.

My heart feels empty without you here
Yet full of sadness that spills out
in an endless river of tears.

You are gone yet never closer.
My every thought is of you.
Grasping onto memories that pour through me,
I try to remember every part of you.

Don't leave me, not for a moment,
Lest I forget you, my precious love.
Please don't fade away like an old dream.
How could I live without you?

You will live within me
As everything I do.
I will live my life fully
And feel grateful for this new life
That was birthed because of you.

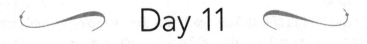

Day 11

The dead are not far away; they are very, very near us.
— John O'Donohue

I wake up in the middle of the night with a panic attack. As I bolt
up in bed trying to catch my breath, I urgently cry out desperate to hear

his voice again. I grab my phone in search of every voicemail I have from him.

Listening intently, I hang on to all the ways he speaks my name and says I love you. I want to burn it into my mind like tracks on a CD. As his voice rings softly into my heart, it pulls on me like a string reaching down from the heavens. I cling to my phone while I reach out into the beyond, calling him with my longing heart.

Spirit Speaks

I am here with you, never leaving you, so drop the notion that what was is gone. Know that the evolution of soul is why we came together. Allow Spirit to fully guide your way as you let go of the doubt that in any way you are not worthy.

Day 12

Disbelief becomes my close companion, and anger follows in its wake. I answer the heroic question 'Death, where is thy sting?' with 'It is here in my heart and memories.'
— Maya Angelou, *Wouldn't Take Nothing for My Journey Now*

My family and friends are taking care of me until I care again. I can't fake it. I have fallen into a deep, dark canyon of suffering. It doesn't matter how spiritual I am or how much I know about the other side; it all just sucks.

My chest is full of fear. This death was like an explosion, and I am brought to my knees. I feel like a child who can't take care of the littlest things like taking a shower. My will to live feels fragile and weak.

I must go through grief like everybody else. Even though I can connect and feel Steve beyond his body, I want him here in the physical. I stay in these feelings until I can open and allow in something that isn't this pain. The peace may only last a moment, but the moments do come when I am willing to let go. And for a little while, the heaviness of this black cloak of grief softens.

I accomplish my greatest task when I let myself go into the pain without judging it or holding back in any way. This pain is my entry into Spirit, into truth, into the reality of being connected to all that I am. I am learning to trust this journey I am on.

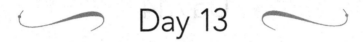 Day 13

The sun's still shining in the big blue sky
But it don't mean nothing to me
Oh, let the rain come down
Let the wind blow through me
I'm living in an empty room
With all the windows smashed
And I've got so little left to lose
That it feels just like I'm
walking on broken glass.
— Annie Lennox, *"Walking on*
Broken Glass"

On my last morning with Steve, I opened the cupboard door and a dish fell out, smashing on the floor. It was a special dish; Steve's mom made it. I picked up the pieces feeling remorseful and fearing Steve would be upset.

When he returned from a bike ride, I broke the news with great trepidation. He responded by saying, "It's only a plate and it was an accident," his happy mood unshaken.

A few hours later, Steve, like the plate, fell to the kitchen floor, irreparably broken. Everything shattered—our life together, my illusions, my ideas, and beliefs. And me. I'm shattered, broken into a million pieces that I am now trying to put back together.

I can feel the trembling inside. As I look around the room, everything that once gave me pleasure is now a source of pain. I breathe in and feel the sensation. I allow my emotions to run deep as I hold myself with unconditional acceptance until I settle inside.

In the arms of the angels, I feel the tears wiped from my cheeks. Even in the darkness, light peeks in through the window. It feels like grace is winking at me through the blinds. Comfort comes in all kinds of ways.

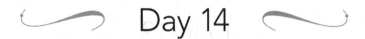

Day 14

Not long before you died, death scenes crept into my life.
We watched a course of events that cast me as witness. Each
encounter making death less strange.
I wondered why this was happening.

— *What the Ashes Wanted* by
Phil Hoffman, Canadian filmmaker

As I look back on the days before Steve's death, I realize that I was being prepared. I didn't consciously know that he was going to leave, yet I now see the many moments that led me to his departure.

It is these moments that my filmmaker brother, Phil Hoffman, explores in his film, "What the Ashes Wanted." There, he examines "the death scenes" before his partner Marion died of cancer.

These moments reveal how rich and connected this time was. Maybe we can't always listen to these promptings. Yet I see that it made me aware and more present.

For example, a few days before Steve died, my client Robert died of a heart attack and connected with me through a dream. He spoke to me, and I woke up thinking he was bringing me a message for his wife. All I remember hearing was, "Keep your heart open." I said to Steve, "I know he told me a lot more in the dream, but I just can't remember."

Throughout the morning, I felt anxious. I told Steve about Robert's heart attack and asked Steve to get a checkup. Still, this nervous feeling wouldn't go away. Feeling my uneasiness, Steve assured me that he would get checked out when we came back from our trip to Canada the following week.

I had not worked with Robert long. After his first session, he said he felt so open-hearted that he wanted to come to my workshop. When I gave him my book, he said he was looking forward to doing his work with me.

He didn't make it to the workshop but called to apologize and explain that he had had a medical emergency and was at the hospital waiting to get an angiogram. He also thanked me for my book, which he felt had helped him heal his fear of death. Soon after we spoke, he passed.

And now he was bringing me a message, "Keep your heart open." This message was an important reminder to connect back with my heart. And when I did, I moved out of the nervous feeling of fear and into the expansive feeling of love.

I'm glad I didn't stay in fear because Steve and I had such a romantic weekend. The trip to Canada was not to be. Instead, family and friends came to us to celebrate Steve's life and mourn his death.

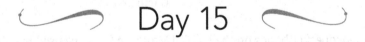

Day 15

Grief pulls me away, ever so abruptly, from life as it was. All the attachments that used to seem important don't have much meaning anymore. This time of loss is wiping away those desires, peeling away what used to matter.

The ordinary ways I'd get on with my day-to-day living—like putting on makeup or fixing my hair or deciding what I was going to wear—take too much effort. It feels so hard just brushing my teeth. All the little ways I filled up my moments, like taking vitamins, doing yoga and meditating. I don't have the energy to get on my mat to do child's pose. I'm of no use to anyone, not even myself. It's like a mountain has been placed in front of me, blocking me at every turn. The idea of communing with the Divine holds no appeal, no hope, no relief.

I know some people judge me. They believe I'm staying in grief too long. Yet there is a gift, a richness in this experience. No matter what I am feeling, I do not abandon myself. And as I stay, I access an inner strength beyond my imaginings.

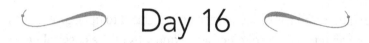 Day 16

"The Dance"

Looking back on the memory of
The dance we shared beneath the stars above
For a moment all the world was right
How could I have known you'd ever say goodbye
And now I'm glad I didn't know
The way it all would end the way it all would go
Our lives are better left to chance
I could have missed the pain
But I'd have to miss the dance

— Garth Brooks

A woodpecker bangs on the big Old Man tree (as Steve used to call it) that lives in my backyard. The bird pecks loudly until I acknowledge Steve's presence. I hear him say, "It's going to be hard, but you have to let me go. Let go today and you will feel lighter. I will guide you."

Today we are going to spread Steve's ashes. Everything is flowing just like he said it would. My son, Luke, and brother-in-law Dan ready the boat, while Steve's sister, Sondra, my friend Judy, and I put the ashes in the car and drive Steve one last time around beautiful Anna Maria Island that he so loved. We stop at the ice cream shop where we honor Steve by having his favorite treat and celebrate the motto he lived by, "Dessert first!" We move on to the house where we were married, conduct a little ceremony, and sprinkle some of Steve's ashes under the big old oak tree there.

We launch the boat into the water and as we get underway, my son asks, "What channel do you want on the radio?" In my mind, I see 106.3 and when he turns to that station "The Dance" by Garth Brooks begins to play. This was the song we played to end Steve's funeral. Amazed, we all cry and sing along. As I hold to my chest the carved box that houses Steve's ashes, I take a moment to acknowledge the Divine plan unfolding.

We set anchor at Steve's favorite fishing spot—the 3-mile reef—the sacred space where he caught his fish and communed with nature. This was his meditation practice. There is so much love pouring out of us all as I release the ashes into the sea along with a lavender bouquet. I feel Steve in the sun's rays that reflect off the water like crystals.

It hurts too much to stay attached. Calmly I listen to what grief is telling me. I am ready to let go so I can begin to join with life again. Life has sent me an invitation to dance... and I said yes.

I will never stop feeling this loss, but now I am learning to dance while holding it all.

Day 17

No coming, no going, no after, no before. I hold you close,
I release you to be so free, because I am in you and you are
in me.

— Thich Nhat Hanh, *One Buddha*
is Not Enough: A Story of
Collective Awakening

I sit in my garden surrounded by all that is alive and giving. The flowers touch me with their beauty. As the sun peeks over the top of the houses in the distance, I hear sounds of banging hammers from the new house going up across the street. A gentle breeze moves the leaves of the plants and trees. I am caressed by nature.

As I look around and see life, I know that pure joy is right here to grab and allow in. Yet the weight of my grief holds me back. I feel like these emotions will swallow me up. I don't have the strength to reach out. The heaviness of this sorrow is normal and necessary. I feel broken and I need help through this time.

I miss him terribly and as I lean into that feeling, I look around at the flowerpots Steve had set just weeks ago. I remember the special way he touched each piece of pottery as if it was a sacred and holy task. He knew how much I loved this garden.

This is how he lives on. He is in everything that is left, and the energy fills me up. All his love for the earth and for me feeds me this early morning after my heart has once again let the slow ache of grief float up. I begin to fill up with this feeling that continues to give life as a memory of him so real and so here with me now. Steve is connecting with me in all these ways. I open to this new relationship with my beloved.

Spirit Speaks

There are so many tears flowing, yet when they pass, let the peace take hold and listen to what is being given to you. The other side of this world of sadness is full of life and promise. It is all here within you.

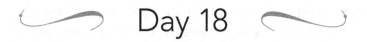

Day 18

Some changes look negative on the surface, but you will soon realize that space is being created in your life for something new to emerge.
— Eckhart Tolle, A New Earth:
Awakening to Your Life's Purpose

One day seems to blend into the next. How do I bring myself back? Surrounded by so many who love me, I feel alone. I have no energy, and I don't want to do anything. I feel guilty; I tell myself I'm lazy.

Death stirs up these shaky and unsettled feelings. It consumes my attention, even though a part of me wants to avoid it. Yet I know that every tear that falls from my eyes helps to open my heart. I choose not to numb out. I let the sorrow have its way with me as I sit in the emptiness.

The heaviness covers me up as I watch my moments through the eyes of the observer, the one who sees it all without judgment. I watch the world around me from the center of it all, not separate from anything. My world has been turned inside out and upside down. It has broken wide open. Or maybe I am broken wide open to witness who I am, merged into all that is around me and all that is inside of me. Everything is as it should be as I watch and listen to the truth that rises through my heart.

These emotions are important. Through them, I am fully and intimately touched by that which participates in my spiritual growth. In the stillness, I know God loves me. This journey I am on is to love myself that much until I am ready to live life fully again.

Day 19

When I touch the excruciating pain of this human experience, when I open to the agony of my longing for Steve and breathe into all that feels broken, initially I feel disconnected from the Divine. But as I surrender into the pain of losing what was, I find that slowly and gently Spirit embraces me like a fresh, warm breeze caressing my skin. Amidst this anguish of missing, I soften. I stay in the deep pain, even though it is messy. Like childbirth, bone-deep pain and great effort are interwoven into this miracle we call life.

I feel cracked open, and I feel fear and doubt. Yet the sacred sound of my beating heart is becoming louder overtaking the noise of all my cries. Grief has forced me to the edge of the cliff, and the pain of wanting what can never be—having Steve back here with me—beacons me to jump. But that constant, soothing drumming of my heart guides me back from the precipice.

When grief begins knocking at our door, we can take a step back and choose to sit out the dance.

While I have chosen not to dance there still is movement. Now I can stay within it all. In my own time, I turn the knob and open the door that reveals the light that illuminates and shines inside.

I allow all that life is bringing me to help me release, and as I let go of the past, I can rest in the peace of the present moment.

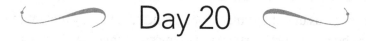 Day 20

Meditation

Sorrow

In the center of it all,
It's here for you and for me
To see how precious this soul is.
I listen to the whispers in the wind
That say you are me and I am you.
I am shattered yet open to this mystery called death.
Why did you leave?
I wasn't ready to feel so much.
You offered me my freedom
But the constant song of your name continues
Underneath this great current of memories
That loudly calls me to go deeper into myself

As missing you settles into the softness of my body.
I ache for you.
I long for me.
Part of me left with you and that's the pain.
Part of you stayed with me and that's the love.
Spirit, hold my hand so that I can be with it all –
No yesterdays, no tomorrows, only today.
This suffering brings me closer to the Divine.

I celebrate the life of my loved one. It is a sacred ritual that helps me process my grief as I help myself and others let go and remember the love. I receive all the ways this suffering brings me inside where I feel deeply. This aching heart is held in this precious moment of now.

Day 21

Spirit Speaks

    Trust yourself as you allow the tears to flow and the pain to go so that there are openings for my spirit to come in and share this love that never dies. Our love is the doorway, and we, on the other side, are your angels. Believe me, my sweet, there are many angels around you...many, many angels. Everyone has their own angel since birth. So, feel yourself held in this grace and know that slowly your own wings will spread out again and one day you will feel the freedom fill your days.

    There is no time here, just as you always speak of. There is just one moment, filled with so much love and appreciation for life itself. This life continues beyond the body. The forms that our spirit takes are just a shadow of what becomes more when we join with Source. There is so much to share. I am adoring you as I always did and yet, of course, now it is without judgment or control.

Take each moment as if it were the last. Receive its gifts and allow the energy to fill you up. All your tomorrows will come from this act of kindness; this simple way to be while you are living.

Day 22

Learn to get in touch with the silence within yourself and know that everything in this life has a purpose. There are no mistakes, no coincidences, all events are blessings given to us to learn from.

— Elizabeth Kubler-Ross

I go through the motions of being here while the real me watches and waits. It's all just a dream, so why can't I wake up? Over and over again I say, "I can't wrap my brain around it." He's dead. He's never coming back. Yet inside I am crying, "Come back! Come back!"

I kneel yet again on the cold terrazzo floor of my bedroom. Anger rises up in me as I hit the bed, "Why did you die? Why didn't you take care of yourself?" I feel my judgment. I want to blame him.

The anger is there. I feel it, and I want to release it. I touch these feelings and let go once again so I can feel the silence within. There I can forgive him for leaving me here all alone. I know I am surrounded by many, but still, I feel the loneliness without him.

Now leaning over my bed with my hands over my eyes, I pray: "Oh God, let me feel the truth of who I am. Help me trust that as I fill up with your love, it doesn't matter what I'm doing or where I am. I am in this vast ocean where compassion tears down the walls that block my inner world. This love that I choose more consciously frees me to live life fully."

All that matters is that I offer this goodness that lives here in my heart right now.

Day 23

Spirit Speaks

You are free to choose to be anything you want to be. If you want to stay in bed and be sad, that is your choice. If you choose to get up and share your light with the world, that is your choice. There is always an opportunity that awaits you as you listen to your heart.

The mind may take you on a roller coaster ride of fears and doubts that hide in the darkest parts of you. The body is not a prisoner of these thoughts if you just allow yourself to be quiet for a while. Then you can rise above the pain and allow love to overcome but only when you have allowed yourself to feel what is there.

The truth is that even in the most painful times of your life, good will rise to the surface, and the light will shine again. And when it does, you will see the plan. You will understand more deeply that love prevails and manifests in ways that serve and nourish the soul.

Meditation

Breathe deeply into the center of being here
Without letting your thoughts distract you.
Allow yourself to rest inside your heart
As parts of your vulnerable self begin to be revealed.
Open to seeing these parts of you in others.
Your healing is theirs
As the same truth touches the world.
Accept it all
As Spirit's voice speaks softly.

...if you are alive, if you have a heart, if you can love, if you can be compassionate, if you can realize the life energy that makes everything change and move and grow and die, then you won't have any resentment or resistance.

— Pema Chödrön, *The Wisdom of No Escape: and the Path of Loving-Kindness*

As I muddle my way through another day, I open myself to learn once again the lesson that this life brings me—to be present with my human self. When I am in my feelings, I am in misery until I sense Spirit calling me. The pendulum swings, and I allow guidance to remind me of the truth. I let go of judging myself. When I am in this pain, my ego always wants to blame me. What a tremendous opportunity when I realize that my anger, sadness, and grief can move me into my higher self. If I can accept it instead of resisting it, I don't have to call this discomfort suffering.

In the Presence, the joy of being alive is more real than the pain of being a victim of this lonely life without Steve. I sit in this experience that is now flowing, allowing it all to be still inside me.

Step by step I walk, looking inward as I move outward in a world that continues to change. Life goes on.

It's not easy to choose to be happy. First, I must choose to connect within to a truth that will set me free. Life is difficult, yet when I accept this, it becomes easier. With the suffering, I can grow into more self-love and feel a deepening sense of security. In every moment, I am here, calling on Spirit to show me the way back home inside my heart where I evolve and the pain of living fades.

Day 25

...being left with the dread of sadness and the hollow
feeling of unwanted new beginnings, it has finally dawned
on me that if I build a home within myself, a palace of peace
created with my own awareness and love, this can be the
refuge I have always been seeking.
— Yung Pueblo, *Clarity & Connection*

Meditation

As I sit inside of me, I look deep within
to touch the parts of me that feel uneasy.
It's not unfamiliar to ask the question—
"What is here for me to see?"

I listen to the stillness that is under the surface
of my turbulent thoughts.
I listen as I sink slowly—
falling into more of me.

The way into this unknown place brings me the awareness
of everything that is nudging me forward.
I do not resist.
I do not try to change my mind.
I listen to it all like an "Unchained Melody,"
the song I played on the piano when I was young.
I practice, over and over again until it flows like a stream.
I become this stream of consciousness.
I hear the stillness in the center of my being
And I let the stream take me.

I sit right here inside your heart. Never have we been this close, joined in the union of pure light. This is the light that birthed you into form, and this is the light that carries you into the realms beyond your death of the body. The light is everywhere like a vast ocean. Here there are no shadows, and every moment is one touching the next. Where you are, there has to be the darkness and the light as the calm waters turn into storms. The light is in everything, just let it all bring the richness that is deep within. It all needs to be turned upside down so you can see inside where all the hardships bring light. All pain is a temporary state. The new consciousness awakens and expands your perception as you create in a new way, illuminated from the inside, you see life as opportunities for growth.

Day 26

Trust ourselves and the grief process. We won't stay angry forever. But we may need to get mad for a while as we search over what could have been, to finally accept what is.
        — Melody Beattie, *The Language of Letting Go: A Meditation Book and Journal*

My sister Philomene brings me to the doctor to treat my frozen shoulder. The procedure is excruciating. It breaks me down. I feel weakened; I'm lost in this battle with my inner pain.

I respond to the injections like an animal. On the ride home, I begin to scream and yell out the anger. Philomene lets me go into my insane ranting. I'm safe to scream and cry without holding anything back.

Now is the time to be with my rage, and it is so necessary. Like it or not, this anger begins to show itself. I don't like it, yet I welcome it. It must come up and out otherwise it sits in the body, inside the cells creating disease.

Through the prism of anger, I see pictures that come into my mind's eye of unpleasant moments with Steve. As the images flow through me I yell, I scream, I call him names. I am a raging lunatic. I let out the rage—it's just a projection of my mind. I pound pillows, I move my body, I make all kinds of sounds. It isn't pretty, but I know I must let the pain out. I am not afraid of this dark part of me that has been hidden inside.

When I am tired, I rest in the fetal position, holding myself as if I'm holding a child. I breathe consciously, forgiving him, forgiving myself, forgiving my past.

This anger, these feelings are not just because Steve transitioned. They have been stored within my cells from years, decades, perhaps lifetimes ago.

The false core belief that I am not worthy or of value is a negative belief passed down through generations. The insecurity of living in a world without Steve brings me to the biggest lie—that I am not good enough.

I forgive myself for the countless times that I have forgotten my true nature. I am a child of God, worthy to be loved. Loving myself through this darkness is the greatest gift I give to myself and to others. This is the doorway to heaven. In my healing, I can walk through with the love of self. Maybe this is the freedom that Steve felt when he dropped his body, along with all his false beliefs, and connected to what he truly is. I can join him in this empowered mind that is full of infinite possibilities.

I am grateful for this lesson that is being shown to me again and again. When I let go of the anger, hurt, pain, and loneliness, the love is always there within my heart.

Philomene lets me be in this healing space. As I breathe in the calmness of my surrender, she wraps her arms around me. I let go once again and arrive inside the silent place within my heart where love, as always, is waiting for me.

I hold myself now and take in the truth that sets me free. I am worthy to be loved. I did nothing wrong. I am innocent, and I am good enough.

Day 27

*Someone I loved once gave me a box full of darkness. It took
me years to understand this, too, was a gift.*
— Mary Oliver, *"The Uses of Sorrow"*

Sad and weary, I shrivel up inside my shattered heart. Left to pick up
the pieces, I feel myself sinking deeper and deeper into the fear. I touch
parts of myself that I never knew existed.

This journey through the valley of sorrow seems endless, yet
somewhere deep inside, I trust that the experience will lead me back to
my heart. As broken as I feel, there is a strength inside that holds me and
moves me forward.

I must find ways to cultivate what I need. Through all this suffering,
I don't want to forget who I truly am.

Spirit Speaks

*I hold you as you cry those tears of agony and pain. As others hear
you, I am also with you. Take these words and trust in the knowing
that life goes on living as you are pulled along by the energy that
brings you forward.*

This human experience is the highest spiritual path I have. Every day
I am given challenges to overcome and walk through. It is not easy to
receive myself fully on any given day, yet I am all I have. No one can do it
for me.

Day 28

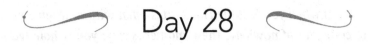

Meditation

I'm trying to find my way into this moment.
I have lost my way but the sounds,
Like whispers in my ear, call me home.
It's in the moments, daily, sometimes minute by minute,
That I reach for you with my mind.

The trees I pass invite me to walk on by.
They show me it's possible
To drink that dark, muddy water
That is full of misery.
I turn and there is another offering
As I wait patiently for the morning light.

My sweet love, I will dip into your ocean
Where I am lifted into the endless blue skies.
It reminds me that my salty tears are worthy to be kissed.
There must be a reason for it all.
I won't leave for a moment.

Here's where I open to the present.
I am glimpsing the fullness of Presence as I Am.

Day 29

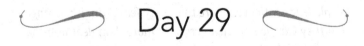

Spirit Speaks

Whether you are in a body or not, being here is the sum of all parts. You are the center of it all, observing all the aspects of yourself, playing all these different roles, and finding the way back to this moment where all is perfect!

Yes, even when you feel the floodgates open within, when emotions seem to come out of nowhere, these moments shift your whole reality if you allow it to move through you. Sometimes you are the channel of these emotions that need to move, not just for yourself but for all who surround you. You let it all go and then, voila, you become the space that brings more love into the world.

I am lost in my suffering, yet these self-criticizing thoughts bring to my attention the feelings of unworthiness that need my acceptance. This path of aloneness gives me more space so that I can commune with all that I am. Here I am conscious of my heart and that becomes the opening where I can access and uncover more that needs to be let go of.

Maybe now I can shift my reality and change the script so that my intuition inspires me to follow my heart. I can put the key into the door and free myself, ready to live in my highest self for the greater good of humankind.

I am seeing the truth and understanding that loving someone is a Divine gift. Thank you for helping me awaken to more of myself. Everything is love, and my soul is the vessel.

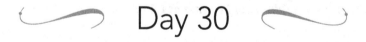 Day 30

People fear death even more than they fear pain. It's strange that they fear death. Life hurts a lot more than death. At the point of death, the pain is over.

— Jim Morrison

I find comfort in the arms of others who have gone through loss. My brother Phil lost his partner Marion to cancer. His words console me. He understands what I am going through. These moments on unsteady ground are a bit easier to navigate when the one comforting me has gone through it, too.

Sometimes I cannot ask for what I need. When I feel dead inside, I call for help without a voice, and people still show up. They cook for me and answer the phones. Some friends leave food on my doorstep. My neighbor fills some empty pots from my garden with plants for the next time I feel strong enough to look out. My daughter, sisters, and close friends stay with me. My son sleeps in the spare room, so I won't be alone. They sit with me in the silence. They hold me when I cry. They let me scream and be angry.

No one can make it better and yet all their love and support hold me when I need to be held. We grieve together. When friends and family show up, it's all a blessing and never taken for granted.

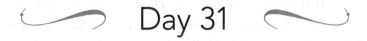

Day 31

When the heart weeps for what it has lost, the spirit laughs for what it has found.

— Sufi Proverb

I weep and I mourn for what was and what could have been; what should have been. My sorrow sits heavily upon my heart. I feel squeezed between what was and what will be. I am constricted by the misery of being in this world without Steve's presence physically wrapped around my daily life. I weep as I pass through the storm—unchartered waters where I am tossed underneath the darkness of all the yesterdays and tomorrows.

I catch my breath—the breath of God—and it begins to flow through this instrument, my body, as life goes on. I must move forward; place one foot in front of the other and remember who I am and why I am left here to find my way without him.

I weep as I long for the comfort of you.
I weep with tears that love you so.

What seems like a mistake in this seemingly timeless death is but a moment of renewing a love that will continue to lift you all even in the darkness. I can only bring to you the light, for that is where I am, and as I share with you, your lives will be seen with more clarity and understanding.

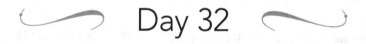

Day 32

Shattered Heart

I'm spending time with family in Canada. For a moment, as I have breakfast with my sister Colleen on her balcony, I am free from my constant sadness. But then I feel guilty for having this short reprieve.

While we chat, a truck that looks like Steve's comes around the corner and jolts me back into the reality of this dark night of my soul. My sister is speaking but I can't hear her. I'm triggered and this charge of energy rises through my solar plexus.

As the anger takes over, I feel selfish and vulnerable. Without warning, the anger bursts out of me. All the stages of grief—shock, denial, guilt, anger, depression—collide and come crashing in on me all at once. I scream of my broken heart and let the pain spill out. Colleen pushes me back inside (I think she was afraid I would jump). I scream and scream and then cry and cry. I feel lost, alone, angry, and hurt.

I let that raging, wild, and hateful part of me come up. Will it end my suffering? Probably not. These raw and overwhelming feelings occupy everything in and around me. When this mood comes without warning, it's hard. Really hard. This too will pass, however easier said than done.

Later that day, the neighbors came home to find the glass partition between their balcony and Colleen's shattered with broken glass all over the ground. To our amazement, we see that all that remains in the partition is a piece of glass in the shape of a heart.

Today I stand at the threshold of a new day as I patiently allow it all to just be.

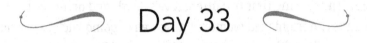

Day 33

You may not control all the events that happen to you, but you can decide not to be reduced by them.
— Maya Angelou

I breathe into the sacred and holy mystery called life and receive the blessings that are here. My family, my friends, and my community are here to hold my hand until I am steady and balanced. I walk on, shedding the garments of my past yet seeing that every layer of myself is worthy to be held sacred. I have been brought to this place where I am okay and no longer drowning in the tears of grief.

I must continue in this dream called life, my precious life, until I meet my beloved again. My beloved wants me to be happy and to enjoy this short life in a body, for it will go by in the blink of an eye. We only have a limited number of moments to experience life and well-being. Let's begin now by breathing in the best that life is here to offer. As nature reveals to us that we are not alone, we see that we are given a choice in every moment. Choose life, for life is worth living.

I am grateful that I have been given this day to be alive. How worthy I am!

Day 34

Prayer is the intimate language of the Universe, the holy voice through which we co-create the world.
> – Caroline Myss, *Intimate Conversations with the Divine: Prayer, Guidance, and Grace*

I return from my first trip after Steve's death and arrive at my home airport a frightened woman. I'm scared of going back to a lonely house where life without my husband is unbearable. So many times, Steve was here at the airport, welcoming me home with open arms. Our homecomings were like honeymoons, the rekindling of our love.

Now alone, I must find my way back, but I don't know where I want to be. I can't go back to the life that was. Moving on with my life is my only option. So, I pray as I share my thoughts and talk to God as if I was communicating with a friend. I have learned to align my inner world with the familiar company of my higher power, guides, or angels. I share my feelings and all that seems so hard to face.

In the next breath, I feel a peace come over me. It is as if a veil lifts and I can see everything as it truly is. Facing all my fears, sadness, and anxieties becomes the bridge to the Divine. My soul calls for the soft voice of Spirit that waits for me until I am ready. This moment, like many others, is necessary as I traverse into the unknown. I see Steve's spirit in my mind's eye, beside me and around me. We are in this together. The window to the world he is a part of opens, and I receive his presence.

Spirit Speaks

Drink in the truth as you reach inside to what our lives have brought us from the past and now like a doorway opened into many experiences that are anew.

I open to the truth that whispers through my heart. I am the suffering, and I am the grace. I am the darkness, and I am the light. I am everything that is and ever will be. I am a part of all that is. I can be happy, for it is my birthright. My spirit loved one is with me all the way.

Day 35

Spirit Speaks

You know that the sun is shining somewhere but can you trust that you, too, will feel it again? During these dark times, it is important for you to connect with what is inside. In this re-connection, you can let go and let the Universe take care of the problems at hand. If you are willing, you will be lifted into the light that begins to shine in the darkest moments of your life. Little by little it takes up the place inside where despair and fear are lurking. This is not who you are. It is a cover that sooner or later will be released as you take the hand of Spirit that always waits for you. Surrender to the place where you feel powerless and alone. These are not easy places to be yet there is richness in a life that can hold your humanity with faith. This can be where you begin to look more honestly at the mistaken beliefs and flaws of character.

This is the beautiful gift of self-acceptance or a more beautiful way to love yourself unconditionally. This is how God loves you. It is the doorway to life. Take a leap of faith and trust that who you are becoming is happening because you have not lost anything. You have gained a better understanding of all the mistaken beliefs you have about the world. Here, life can be an experience that passes through your higher thinking as you remember why you came into this incarnation—to have and to hold, the beauty of everything that exists as the whole.

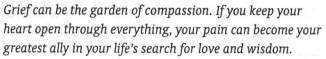

Day 36

Grief can be the garden of compassion. If you keep your heart open through everything, your pain can become your greatest ally in your life's search for love and wisdom.

— Rumi

This road I am on is challenging. As I experience the pain of loss, I stand in two worlds—the physical world outside of me and the spiritual world I access from inside. My five senses tell me the frightened part of myself is lonely and depressed. When I remember that I am more than this mind or body, I have a different perception. My soul is the bigger part of me that will never die. I am not separate from the Universe.

At times my little self needs my compassion. So, I care for myself the best I can and let others know I need help. These actions reveal my emotional awareness.

Through all the pain and suffering that grief brings me, I am supported. I take care of that little self by loving my saddened heart that aches and throbs. Others around me reach out and wrap their compassionate hearts around me with words of comfort, pans and platters of food, and so many prayers and thoughts of love.

I feel loved and cared for by those who have suffered loss before and those who love me in their unique ways. Even the ones who left my side to take care of themselves bless me with their choices. I am embraced by this incredible world that knows suffering.

Spirit Speaks

Do you know what I mean when I say I will take care of you? I am a part of the non-physical world that comes and holds you. I am in the painted skies and sunsets. I am in the people that bring you messages from their hearts. I am in the birds that caw and the ones that fly in front of you. My voice speaks through this world as it whispers to your heart and tells you this love never dies. It will show itself to you when

you are ready and then the pain of letting go will be the birth of more life, more love, and more joy.

The whole world joins me in sorrow, for through lifetimes we have all endured this universal experience.

 Day 37

> *Your sacred space is where you can find yourself over and over again.*
>
> — Joseph Campbell

When we feel unsure of ourselves, can we remember that who we are is of great value? By reaching inside and lifting our minds and hearts to join with the mind of God, we also receive support from our spirit loved ones.

Now, as we take the hand of the Divine, we reach out with the other to hold the hand of humanity. We walk on, our focus within so that the chaos of life can be seen with the eyes of the soul. Here we have an opportunity to move from the inside to the outside because we are deeply connected to the Source that lives and breathes through our very being.

This inner strength gives us confidence as we accept that we are not alone. Together, we can rise, awakened from the dream of separation, and join with all humanity as we listen deeply to this guidance that comes when we are open to receive it.

Meditation

I am free in this moment to choose life.
I remember the truth that we are all born equal.
No one is separate from this incredible power
That lives in all creation.

Together we join in this love that creates worlds.
Our world will be a peaceful, healthy, incredible place.

We are safe and held in the knowing
That we awaken in greater compassion.
Be the lover for every human being and creature
Of this place we call Home.
Blessed Be

In my connection to self, I settle deep inside my breath where there is nowhere to go but here. There is nothing to reach for and nothing to long for as I wait for this moment to unfold. This endless love feeds me.

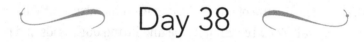

Day 38

> *Grief, I've learned, is really just love. It's all the love you*
> *want to give but cannot. All that unspent love gathers up in*
> *the corners of your eyes, the lump in your throat, and in that*
> *hollow part of your chest. Grief is just love with no place*
> *to go.*
>
> — Jamie Anderson

I grieve the loss of my beloved husband, Steve. He was taken too early. We had so many dreams to fulfill. Yet this great loss brings me back to myself as I allow myself to feel it all fully. I allow the waves of grief to come and go like the tides. There is an ebb and flow to life.

I can't change the fact that he is gone from his physical body. No more touches or kisses that used to come as naturally and predictably as the sunrise each morning. Though the sun will shine again, Steve will never walk through the door and call out "Sugar Lips," "Frannie Love," or "Fancy Pants." No hand to hold, no toothpaste on my toothbrush, no tea in my grandmother's china. No arms around me, no whisper of sweet nothings. Our romance in the physical is over. Crying won't bring him back and longing keeps me in suffering.

I know that the stages of grief have their own timing. As memories flood my mind, morning awakens me into a kind of acceptance.

I accept my mourning today. As I embrace my brokenness and move through the suffering, I know I am on the journey towards my wholeness.

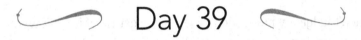 Day 39

For the flower, it is fully open at each step of its blossoming.
— Mark Nepo, *The Book of*
Awakening

As difficult as the grief has been—to wake up in the morning without him, to go to sleep at night alone in our king-size bed—these days have pushed me into the reality that he is not coming home. I walk the beautiful beach at sunset. I sit on the chair in our front yard. I gaze at the stars and listen to the silence of the evening, and inside I feel alone and not myself. It all looks the same on the outside, but I will never be the same.

People say, "Call me if you need something." I don't. They say, "Call me if you need to talk." I won't. They don't know how hard it is to pick up that phone. When I am in this grief, I am paralyzed with emotions. Wide-open and vulnerable, I protect myself.

Without saying a word, I call for help. When I'm ready, Spirit shows me what is there inside it all. Until then, with every conscious breath, I wait.

Day 40

*Opening to the possibility that you can change your life for
the better by paying attention to your inner experiences—
such as your emotions—puts you on the spiritual path. The
more aware you become of your emotions, the more able you
become to shift your experiences from Victim to Creator.*
> — Gary Zukav, *Universal Human*

Moving forward is possible. You can step into infinite possibilities
when you're not stuck in the past. Of course, that is easier said than
done.

I don't judge my pain. I don't even try to get rid of it. I allow it to just
be and do my best to carry on with life as it is. These devastatingly hard
times will eventually provide more compassion and understanding for
myself and others. We are here to share what we learn through life's ups
and downs.

Sometimes I just want to drown in the pain and sorrow. Yet the
moment I let it go, I feel him in everything. It is two sides of the same
coin. Both existing and both needed. You can't bypass the pain. You
can't remain in denial forever; sooner or later you must pass through
the valley of sorrow because that is part of this journey with grief. The
journey is so personal; no one can tell you what it's supposed to look like.

Spiritual gurus say that our grief is the loss of our connection to
Source. We feel so awful in the pain of loss because we are lost and
disconnected from who we truly are. Then one day we let go and align
with our Source within. Or, like Steve, whose soul returned to non-
physical reality, we align once free of the body.

I am taking this moment to feel the sweetness of acceptance. Will the
pain of loss go away for good? I don't know. I just know that when I can
expand around it, it's no longer my focus.

Day 41

On the bridge between me and me, I find my imperfect human self. I am humbled by the spacious emptiness. Resting inside this opening, I witness my obsessive mind. I wander back to myself and feel how this presence sustains me and gives me life.

Here, inside I open and let love take up room in my heart.
I rise through my awareness of what is,
Not leaving myself but allowing the truth in.

This is well being.
This is my ability to love greater
And to appreciate these moments as I move through my senses.

It's so beautiful
As I arrive here amongst the conditions of my world
And lean into me.
The external world brings me more in touch
With the hidden parts of myself.
Everything and anything become the passageway to life.

I open to the emptiness that seems to house my soul
And begin again through the transformation
That is taking place.

I rise and connect with the Spirit of God's love
Which bonds me to everything.
All is possible here.
All is received in this sacred encounter within,
Where the Divine energies of Spirit serve me and all humanity.

Everything I seek is inside.
Love is the medicine.
This love is always waiting for my return.
Alas, I come into myself.

*I find this compassion for all I have been through
and the qualities of my inner being shine!*

This loss has now built a strong fortress around my inner being. Not to stiffen me or make me rigid but to help me stand strong.

 # Day 42

Sometimes I touch the things you used to touch, looking for echoes of your fingers.

— Ian Thomas

Letting go is a process. I force myself to empty Steve's closets and sell his truck and boat. Little by little I let go. Taking his voice message off the answering machine is the beginning. I am sure it is a shock for people who call to still hear his voice on the other end of the receiver.

Sometimes I call my home number just to hear his voice again. I play it over and over. I don't want to forget his voice. I don't want it to fade away, yet how could it not? All the hanging on is the ego needing Steve to give me security. Yet expecting him to fill my needs is an impossibility that keeps me in suffering. The pain comes when I cannot have him. Living without him seems impossible.

The way of the human world is to get our needs met. Steve has no needs where he is. He's my cheerleader on the other side waiting for me to let go of the past and encouraging me to open to how I can address my needs now.

These times are lonely, and I feel like I am in limbo. The days go by spilling one into another. Some days all I can do is the essentials—brush my teeth, make a smoothie, walk the dog, and feed her. Perhaps throw the toys around for her.

I begin each new day with acceptance—even if all I do is breathe deeply and take on one project, like paying the bills, cleaning out a drawer, taking a walk, or picking up the phone. I give myself permission to just be, to meditate and connect with my inner light.

As the dim light appears, I receive and trust that it will show me the way to feeling at home inside myself. So much is shifting inside of me. I trust that through this deep loss I will one day be strong enough to re-engage with the world and serve humanity again.

Day 43

I miss my husband, and as I sit here on his favorite chair, I see him sitting across from me shining his light across the living room and gazing at me with sweet affection. I allow his presence to join with mine, and it gives me comfort. Listening to the humming of the air conditioner, I allow the peaceful surroundings of my quiet house to open me up to the way Spirit will speak to me today. Here I am connected to all of life in this world and beyond...

Spirit Speaks

It is so wonderful to sit here with you. So many days before my transition you sat here writing loving expressions. Now I am right here with you bringing more light to the world. The most incredible way to touch the world with this love is to be fully yourself, to allow your honest-to-goodness you to begin the day. Your true nature is given and when you have aligned back to the Source inside of you, your open heart expresses your love—just like in your dreams. You don't have to physically take action until you are ready or when your inner guidance says yes. Until then, your open heart is hugging the world because you are in your true natural state of openheartedness. It is the ego that needs to confirm what is right or wrong. The heart knows that right now in this very moment you are the giver of life. It all spills out from your fullness.

The other side of this world of sadness is full of life and promise. It is all here within me. I appreciate that the Universe continues to fill me up. This feels good. Gratitude is love.

Day 44

As I walk into the garage and make my way into the laundry room, I look at Steve's fishing poles hung perfectly at the top of the shelves; his roller blades lined up beside mine; his work boots, worn out from the many days on the job. I see his bicycle, the one I bought him last year for Christmas. Each day he rode it, he would say, "Did I tell you how much I love my bicycle?"

He is everywhere and nowhere. As I step through this garage, I feel so many emotions mixed into the waves of grief crashing inside me and tossing me around like a small ship in a large storm.

Mindlessly, I fold the warm washcloths and pillowcases and speak out loud to Steve: "I miss you so much. Please come to me. I know you are here, please show yourself." As I weep over the folded laundry, I steady myself but can't stop the tears. They rip through me pushing me down, down, down.

As quickly as the cries come up, I feel a gentle calming down. I walk back into the kitchen and, forgetting my plea to the ethers, stand in front of the sink, wipe the counter, and put away the glasses. Lost in the moment while present with the tasks at hand, a sudden energy comes into the room sending a card off the baker's rack and onto the floor in front of my feet.

I gaze at the card. It's from Steve. There is a heart on the front, and it says, 'I Love You.' As I pick it up, chills make the hair on my arms stand up. He heard my call and in response, shows me he is still so close.

The new relationship unveils in ways that catch me off guard. These little moments of communication touch me deeply.

Slowly I let go of the human relationship and open to the ways he now can share with me the love that will never die.

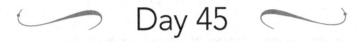 # Day 45

There has never been a time when you and I and the kings gathered have not existed, nor will there be a time when we will cease to exist. As the same person inhabits the body through childhood, youth, and old age, so too at the time of death he attains another body. The wise are not deluded by these changes.

— *Bhagavad Gita*

Spirit Speaks

Happiness is all around you when you find it in yourself. I know you understand all of this and yet isn't it amazing how when life threw you the curve ball (meaning my transition from a body) you lost your footing and allowed yourself to feel the deep grief of loss.

There's nothing wrong with feeling it so deeply, for in doing so you have paved the way to what you truly desire. When you leave yourself, I mean your true self—the one that knows that there is no death and that you are worthy to have what you desire—then the suffering, when felt, causes you to move into the reservoir of all that you truly are wanting. Now you have every moment of every day to choose again.

Life continues to push you off balance until you are so willing to anchor in who you truly are. This authentic self is living in your heart, knowing that right here, right now, life is flowing fully taking you anywhere you desire.

I wait as if I am in a cocoon, wrapped in the arms of all who love me. Love is wrapping itself around me, keeping me safe and holding me in complete oneness until I fly again. Happiness is all around me, waiting for me to let go of all I think I know.

Day 46

Anyone who has lost something they thought was theirs forever finally comes to realize that nothing really belongs to them.

— Paulo Coelho, *Eleven Minutes: A Novel*

As I let go of things—clothing, tools, and other possessions—all that defined Steve's enormous and adventurous life here on earth, I create a bit more room inside to bring myself more here. Little moments bring me into a knowing that we could never be apart.

I roll over and as I awaken into the early morning, I touch the light inside that calls me to join where he is. He is on a journey to fulfill his soul. How easy it is for me to dwell in the missing of my physical relationship with him, this past that truly has nothing for me but the pain and suffering of grief. Yet I do not judge my way. I allow it to bring me to wherever I must go to open myself up into the sea of my emotions. Each smell or touch of his things brings memories of a beautiful and fine life that has become the doorway into this moment where the light greets me with open arms.

The light lifts me into so much freedom. I settle into the choice of being here, right now, held in a love that continues to feed me. It fills me up and gives me more—more hope and trust and commitment to walk into my day.

Day 47

*Such growth will move humans into ever-higher energy
states, ultimately transforming our bodies into spiritual
form and uniting this dimension of existence with the
afterlife dimension, ending the cycle of birth and death.*
— James Redfield

I sit deeply inside my heart, missing Steve. The tears well up in me,
filling the empty hole where he cannot be touched.

*Where are you my sweet love? You are beyond this world, reaching
into my heart from the unknown place called heaven. Take me into
your world so that I can see all that is, for now, my life feels forgotten. I
am trying to find my way back to being here in this heart that longs for
your touch.*

I receive a vision that gloriously opens me. With my inner eyes, I
see myself so vast in bright, calm waters—a huge ocean with light
reflecting off it. I know that it is a glimpse of where he is and what we
are all a part of. I continue to rest within and cherish these peaceful
feelings that engulf me. I feel myself again. Perhaps I feel more of myself
than I have known. His spirit is with me as I travel today and every day.

Day 48

Spirit Speaks

**Oh, sweet love! There is no separation and there is no time in this
world of connection where everything that seemed lost is now found.
Can you begin now to realize the perfection of this plan that is beyond
any of your human thinking?**

Can you, for this instant, touch within yourself that feeling of

*sweet love that has no conditions? Can you allow yourself to trust
that in every moment of your living, there is a choice to be made? It
comes easily when you have returned to your heart where all is being
received!*

*There is only one moment that moves into the next. When you
rest and go to sleep, you are fully aware of this state of being that
replenishes and allows you to move beyond any conditions of the mind.
The truth that lies within is always telling you that life, as it is right
now, is okay. All you have to do is participate with yourself and join
your heart with the heart of all creation.*

*Listen deeply to your heart beating, and there you realize that
there is a power that is running the show, and it is you recognizing
yourself as whole and complete. The work in progress is the realization
that who you are is enough in every aspect of your life.*

 # Day 49

*It's impossible to live or die without God, but it is not
impossible to think that you are.*
                                — Neale Donald Walsch,
                                                Home with God

It is so hard to open my eyes to the daylight. I feel like I'm
underneath something so heavy that I struggle to breathe. The pain of
my thoughts shoves me deeply into the abyss full of soundless cries of
longing for Steve. I am crushed under a wall of grief that has fallen on
top of me, and now I'm like a shattered piece of porcelain, broken into a
million pieces.

Where am I? I am lost in the valley of sorrow. It hurts so much; I
want to die. As I move into the grief and all that it is bringing me, I pray
for help.

I need courage to let myself go into the sorrow without judging it or
holding it back in any way. This pain is my entry into Spirit, into truth,
into the reality of being connected to all that is.

I am walking on shaky ground and it can be difficult to trust this journey. And yet, I am learning to embrace the depth of who and what I am.

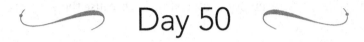

Day 50

I open my eyes, look up at the brilliant sky and see white streaks of clouds from the jets passing by overhead. They form an X. To most people, this design is random, made of contrails. For me, they are kisses from Steve. He always signed his cards and notes to me with big fat Xs and Os. Now he is reaching from wherever he is, still sending me kisses. I feel the warmth of the presence of God holding me and filling me. This connection lifts the veil and shows me that Steve is right here waiting for me to open to the only way he can connect with me now... through this magnificent world.

He is not gone; his presence continues to show me he is still here. If I can bring myself into a peaceful state, I will not drown in the suffering, grief, fear, or despair. I see Steve as part of this world and not separate in any way. My attachment to his physical form keeps me hooked to the past. When I let go of what was, I touch his presence in other forms of manifestation.

There is a knowing that shows its face when I surrender to the place within. I let go of everything that I think I know and open to this space where my loved one is waiting to share in it all.

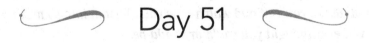

Day 51

Behind your image, below your words, above your thoughts, the silence of another world awaits. A world lives within you.

— John O'Donohue

Sometimes I think I will never feel okay again. This longing I feel for my old life will be my burden for the rest of my days. Friends say that they miss me. I reply, "I miss me too!" I feel like a mere shell of my old self. I am like a vase that is filled with grief and all the emotions that weigh me down. Then the vase cracks and the tears, the anger, and the pain all spill out. Once empty, I can rest inside because there is more space.

Time and time again, I empty, only to fill up and empty again. I am desperately trying to find myself. Who am I now? Who will I become now that I am alone?

I allow myself to enter the vastness that calls my name as I Am. Here I listen to the silence as I commune with the voice of Spirit.

I let myself be here in all my feelings until I soften and open to a peace that truly is beyond any understanding. The serenity comes and how long it'll last is anyone's guess. These moments of stillness come when I am willing to let go of everything I think I know and allow the present moment to be what is real.

Day 52

Spirit Speaks

You are not lost without me! You are moving forward and finding out more about yourself. I always said you were the strongest woman I know. Trust in yourself and watch how you blossom into so much more than you ever thought you could or would be.

Your body is strong like a huge oak tree. All that you have released, all the tears you have shed have watered this tree and have helped you to grow the deepest roots and strongest limbs and branches. This growth is needed for you to move into this spectacular life that will hold the wisdom of all the ages.

As the months of inner hibernation help you let go of what was, you will begin to blossom. The fruits of your labor will bring aliveness and delicious parts of you into the world. Your body is the vessel of this infinite life that will continue to give to the world.

Day 53

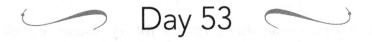

A single act of kindness throws out roots in all directions and the roots spring up and make new trees.
— Amelia Earhart

Loss is the way back to the heart. Now I am making choices that are for my own sake. Can I love myself enough to cook for only me? Some days it's a big effort just to get out of bed and face the day.

I gaze out of the kitchen window as the colors of the sunrise peak over the trees. The bright orange brilliance calls me to enjoy its beauty. Oh, how I love to listen to nature's calling. When I am present without my focus on my chattering mind, I can hear nature speak. How great is that?

It's so easy to be taken away by the loss. It's so hard to let go and trust the moment. Sometimes I want to stay wrapped up in the misery and despair. It seems to be a way to touch Steve. Missing him keeps him alive in my mind and for a while that was okay.

Sometimes all I can manage to do is breathe. Lost inside myself, I call on Steve to help me. He is beyond human needs, and I'm a scared little girl wondering how I will go on and take care of all the responsibilities of this human existence.

As life goes on, post-traumatic fears after the death of loved ones can keep you from embracing life. It is a process that is individual and necessary. Grief will show us the way back to who we truly are. We are never the same, yet we can rise through the mud that grounds us here and respond to the light from within and without that forever calls our name.

We can choose to take the hand of a power greater than our little selves. Slowly, as we unveil, we become a part of the living world once again.

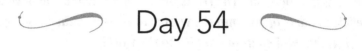

Day 54

Spirit Speaks

It all began the day you surrendered, fell to your knees, and asked for help. Slowly you entered back from the painful attachment to what was as you loosened the grip that bound you to grief and suffering.

Good Grief! It is needed. It is necessary to walk through the valley of sorrow. And when you do, your grieving heart breaks wide open as the tears wash you and cleanse you of all the pain of losing what or who you love. A common metaphor for loss is the doorway back to the one that never leaves.

You are here, the you that is forever a part of an unchanging constant light. You are forever joined with Spirit where I am always with you. Here there are many—all your beloved spirit loved ones, all who walk before you and after you. Here the strength is within this magnificent love where you gather, alone yet in alignment with the bigger picture.

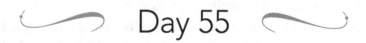

Day 55

When Steve died, I wanted to run away to Bali like Elizabeth Gilbert did and wrote about in her book "Eat, Pray Love." But God has another plan. I fell and broke my arm, leaving me home with all the triggering memories of life with Steve in this house and on this island.

Luke is auditioning for *America's Got Talent* and asked me to come along. The night before his audition, we stop at a store with puppies. I walk directly to a tiny, 3-pound shih tzu, and she leaps into my arms as if she picked me.

As she nuzzles into my chest, I cry happy tears for the first time since Steve's passing. Without blinking an eye, I decide she is going to be mine.

When we pick her up the next day, a family of 5 Swedish girls, ages 3 to 9, encircle me. "What will you name her?" they all seem to say at once. As I look into the eyes of the middle child, she raises her right hand to the Heavens, and then bringing it down, as if she is anointing my new puppy, she declares, "Her name is Mollie." Energy moves up and down my spine.

On the way home, I can't get the name Mollie out of my mind. Then I realize that my grandmother and girlfriend Debbie, both in spirit now, share birthdays this day. My grandmother had a shih tzu, and Debbie had a dog named Mollie!

Through this child, Spirit touched me deeply, with this message received loud and clear. This guidance reaffirms the path I'm on as my spirit loved ones help guide my way.

Recognize the tremendous courage you show every moment of every day, with each breath, you reaffirm your decision to embrace and learn from your own challenges. Within that recognition, you will find your soul.

— Robert Schwartz, *Your Soul's Plan*

 Day 56

From a spiritual perspective, from your spiritual, from your soul's point of view, all of these things are offerings being made to you, to give you the stuff through which you can grow clearer and stronger and emptier and more available to your heart.

— Ram Dass, *article "Truth of Grief"*

I bike down to the beach, excited to finally return to this place where the sea meets the sand and sky. My heart expands as I park my bike between two trees. I am pulled by a force that feels like a magnet. That's what it feels like to surrender completely to this Presence that knows what I need. I am being guided as I'm pulled into the stream of consciousness where all that exists is filling me up; I'm in the flow where the veil lifts.

I fall onto the towel atop the powdery white sand, and as I merge deeply inside myself, I let out a sigh of relief. I am here fully, free of all burdens. Even though the beach is full of people, I feel totally alone, basking in the magnificence of this day.

I breathe into my body, letting go of everything I think I should do, and I melt into the warmth of the sun. I fall into a deep sleep and wake up completely rested. I hear Steve's voice in my inner ear, **"Hello Baby Doll, it's good to have you here."**

It is not a foreign feeling to be in this place with Steve. Sometimes I wander off into the valley of sorrow or disappear into the busy mind of unwanted chatter. Sometimes I stay away, not because I consciously choose to, but because I am pulled in the direction of doing and that's okay. It's part of living in this human world until I find balance. The balance is within, and it is always my choice to find that center again.

When I choose to pay attention to what matters, I will be led by my heart like I was today.

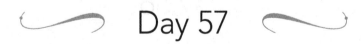 Day 57

The spiritual path wrecks the body and afterwards restores it to health. It destroys the house to unearth the treasure and with that treasure builds it better than before.

— Rumi

Some days I kick and scream and want to leave. Those times, I wish I had died. Yet what truly has died is the falseness and all that can no longer live in me. Going through this experience is very painful. The suffering seems endless; these days, weeks, and months feel like eternal moments.

I reach inside and allow the tears to wash away the hurt and pain of life lived honestly and lovingly. That's when it hits me—this relationship was a success! Steve and I had lived well and worked hard together. Our mission has been completed. Yet letting go is the hardest thing we ever do. Life goes on and sooner or later we must, as well.

I acknowledge my progress, and I am grateful for it. As I let go, I can see more clearly, and the future looks less scary. I can feel peace in being here as I resume my mission with focused energy.

Day 58

Meditation

There is a grand plan that must unfold.
As I wake up today, I practice again and again
Letting go of my resistance to the present moment.
I reach into the silence of my open heart.
I breathe deeply into this moment
that wraps me up in a comfort
That is beyond my relationship with my loved one.
No matter what is pushing against me,
I receive my own humanity
with compassionate understanding.

Judging myself only keeps me suffering.
I accept my weak and vulnerable self.

The self-imposed boundary softens as I let go.
I dissolve into the ocean of this devotional love.
I bask in this timeless moment to remember what is real.

This love that feeds me merges with my God
that has no image or likeness.
Silence and peace now take hold.
I am in total acceptance of being here now.
Separation is gone.
In oneness, I share in this love that has no conditions.
Fear and judgment fade away.
It all happens within.

Day 59

Enlightenment is intimacy with all things.
— Dogen Zenji

Of course, there are regrets. I remember the last day Steve was alive.
I was so upset with him because he did not meet me at the beach when
he said he would. I was hurt and I wanted him to know and feel it, so
I said something mean. I was feeling my stuff about him not coming
home on time. But then I took his arm and we walked down to the beach.
Fortunately, I let it all go and enjoyed every step of what would be our
last time there together.

The guilt from that moment still shows itself. When these feelings
come to me, I say, "I'm sorry, deeply sorry." I know I am not perfect,
but sometimes it is hard to forgive myself. That's when I reach inside,
breathe, and hold it all without judgment. Then I can feel myself expand
and become a part of something much bigger than my little human self.
There is no more thinking, just an open channel for Spirit to light up my
heart and bring me the wisdom I become part of while immersed in the
light.

Everything around me begins to soften and merge into oneness as I connect deeply inward. The light within, along with the light outside, is illuminating and reflecting everywhere. I feel whole here, not because I have left my physical state but because I have held my physical self so honestly without judgment.

If I am calm and serene, this energy flows into every part of me. I feel fully connected to everything and everyone around me. I am in the oneness. It is both grounding and expanding.

I'm okay, even when I feel like I'm not okay. When I forgive myself, my mind is at peace, free to feel the gentle stirring of love.

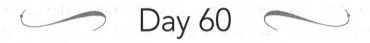

Day 60

For life and death are one, even as the river and the sea are one.

— Kahlil Gibran, *The Prophet*

I miss Steve so much and yet that seems selfish. He is so free, unshackled from human existence, while I'm here, chained to a life of doing dishes, paying bills, and getting groceries. He is beyond all these human acts and actions, happy in the world of Spirit.

I look around this place I call home, and my head fills with memories of us. These memories crowd my mind and pull me into sorrow. Tears run down my face as I let myself be here in all these emotions, thoughts, and feelings. They pass like clouds, and when they clear, I move into the quiet space within my heart and merge with the Presence.

Thank you, God, for today you will guide me and move me into the unknown place of living without my loved one. I trust in you so that I may join with him as his spirit continues to walk with me in this beautiful world where life is one experience after another. With courage, I let it in and allow my spirit to fill me up and bring me more here.

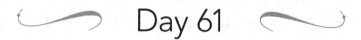

Day 61

My friend Judy and I are at my family's cottage in Canada talking about the last time I was there with Steve. I ask her, "What would it be like if Steve walked back physically into my life?" And to our surprise, Siri responds by saying, "No, that will never happen!" We both feel energy fill our bodies.

Steve isn't ever going to walk back into my life in the physical, yet now his spirit is walking with me in all kinds of ways. He brings me into the deeper understanding that our spirit, who we truly are, never dies. We become so much more than we were within the limitations of our physical form.

Spirit's communications always bring me into conscious awareness of the union between the physical and the Divine. It doesn't matter when it happens, I allow the moment to open me. Like when I look in the eyes of my niece's children who light up when they talk about Uncle Steve. Their love brings me back into the present moment, which reflects the beauty of being here.

I am so full—life is right here, telling me the secrets of all my tomorrows. I listen. Tell me more.

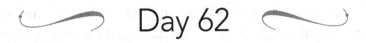

Day 62

Spirit Speaks

You are healing. You are remembering who you are. There is only this love that will continue to hold you and form you into more. Let the light in and merge with the energy that fills you up like nothing else can. Here you are making love with the world, and it will spill out of you when your heart holds more than you can contain.

This time is for you. Drink it all in and let it open you into more life. You will be held by the sweetness of this world and beyond. You will know when it is your time to enter back into life again.

Remember that you are guided by your heart, and here, Spirit will always take your hand and show you the way. Let the hand you hold be mine as I walk in the light with you for always.

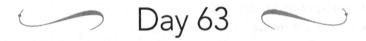

Day 63

Solitude has soft, silky hands, but with strong fingers it grasps the heart and makes it ache with sorrow.
— Kahlil Gibran, *The Broken Wings*

I walk on, my eyes clouded with tears. I walk on, though I can hardly see the path before me. It is so hard to move forward without him. Everything is unfamiliar. There's so much movement around me, like a merry-go-round. I watch it like a movie. I'm trying to find my way through the empty places that used to be filled by my beloved Steve.

I am scared and alone, yet I know it's another opportunity to face myself and all the masks I might have worn to cover up my fears. My body continues to signal me, and intuitively I know that the knot in the pit of my stomach will bring me to my heart. So much heartache and pain are buried inside of me. As I face myself and acknowledge what is here, I soften the grip that protects me from these false beliefs that are at the core of my being.

I breathe in as tears spill out. Again and again, I breathe into myself and say, "I am afraid, I'm really afraid." Taking off the mask by being honest, I crack through the hard shell of my self-protection. No more excuses. I'm not hiding behind the belief that I know anything. I feel insecure and alone, but I will not abandon myself.

Life has brought me to my knees and the practice to be faithful to my inner journey helps me accept where I am. I become my own lover, and inside my heart, I take the hand of Spirit as I blindly walk into my life. With a compassionate heart, I begin to resonate with a higher truth that who I am is worth holding just the way I am.

Day 64

Meditation

Enter the flow of love with a quiet mind.
See all things as a part of yourself.
Rest right here and receive
As you let go of your attachments.
With loving-kindness, you move
From your head to your heart.
The light enters as you see clearly
And trust that it is all perfect.
You are the opening
To this new relationship with your spirit loved one.
Speak from your heart
As you silently share your thoughts.
Feel their presence.
Listen deeply to the message.
The message of the soul may come
As a song, a butterfly, a rainbow, or a bird.
The world becomes the vessel
For this love that never dies.
There is nothing separate from you.
Love is everywhere.

Day 65

*If we limit life only to opinion—which we do—then there is
no forgiveness in it. When your forgiveness is genuine you
will see how you can alter opinions. You become energized
when you do that. You will see beauty in another that
you never saw before because you have put away your
resentment and all your "knowings" of yesterday.*

— Tara Singh

My human imperfections show themselves and keep me feeling
stagnant. The tension that builds up harms my body and keeps me
unproductive. I feel consumed by this resentment and anger that gets
triggered by the least little thing. I get irritable and can easily bite
someone's head off with my answer to a simple question.

I let the thoughts of the past be my focus, and before I know it, I have
given my power away to experiences that aren't important anymore.
Why do some of the things Steve said still hurt me? We were different in
our thinking. So what? Fighting for my opinions keeps me in suffering. It
pulls me out of balance.

Endings and losses happen every day. We all have the same pain and
struggles. It's not easy staying with our human frailties. But when we
recognize our own precious human life and do the inner work to touch
our anger, misery, resentments, and betrayals, we can one day see that if
we do not give up, life can and will inspire us.

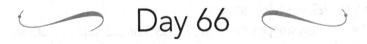

Day 66

It's impossible to answer some of the questions that come after the
death of a loved one. I walk around the house saying, "How could you
have gone so quickly?" "What were you thinking the moment your sick
body was incapable of speaking?" "Did you know that this was going

to be our last day together?" All these thoughts cannot be soothed by a rational mind.

It's a still night. The stars are shining bright enough to guide my way on my walk along the beach. As my mind revisits these questions that have no answers, I look down and written in the sand I see, "I love you. Steven."

Energy flows up and down my spine like I am plugged into an electrical outlet, and I feel my lips turn up in a smile. I answer, out loud, "Thank you for loving me. I love you too!"

In the center of my being, I feel the call of my spirit loved one who continues to whisper sweet nothings into my heart.

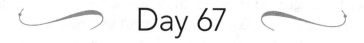 Day 67

To be broken is no reason to see all things as broken.
— Mark Nepo, *Inside the Miracle:*
Enduring Suffering, Approaching
Wholeness

The trauma of this experience pushes me into the darkest, most painful well of despair. It shatters all my beliefs and ideas about how I have lived—dedicated to helping others and serving God in a very conscious way. In one holy moment, my world was turned upside down when Steve left our life together.

The pain has stopped me in my tracks. I have lost my creativity, and I don't know how to get the passion back. This time challenges me to listen, truly listen, to my inner guidance. Can I be that honest with myself?

I feel broken, and it isn't easy to be with this feeling. I want to fix it, make it go away. I must drop this idea that I am a wife (I was but now I am not), a counselor (How can I hold people in their pain when I'm a mess?), and an artist and writer (I feel no creative flow moving in me). I am in limbo. There is nothing to do and nowhere to go. Being here is enough.

Steve's death changed the landscape of my inner reality. God is right here in the pain and in the opening. Finding the rhythm between the two is my work now. Just as Steve's transition has moved him to the next part of his journey, this loss opens me to the next part of mine.

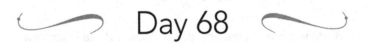 Day 68

In the flush of love's light, we dare be brave.
And suddenly we see that love costs all we are and will
ever be.
Yet, it is only love which sets us free.

— Maya Angelou

I slip back into bed; the darkness of early morning surrounds me as I snuggle with Mollie. Her warm body gives me the comfort I long for. As I breathe and begin to move into my meditative state, the lamp on the other side of my bed turns on. Steve is making his presence known by turning on the light. Peace fills me as I allow his presence to make contact.

I acknowledge Steve's presence, then expand into the softness of the loving energy that bathes me in this eternal light. I hear him speak in the silent space within my mind and heart. I am filled with the energy and align myself with it.

It is as if he is speaking inside my head. **"Baby Doll,"** he says, **"you are okay."** I feel his energy giving me encouragement as I move into my inner strength, which I know is always there. It's a mystery why I leave it at all. Or maybe I am in it as I allow these feelings to have a place. Just as Steve has transitioned into his light body, I can feel that I have, too.

The greatest choice for me now is to make my intentions clear as I choose love over fear. This transition brings me to my purpose to create a fulfilling life. This is my responsibility as a powerful creator with the Universe.

Day 69

"When you lose a loved one, you suffer. But if you know how to look deeply, you have a chance to realize that his or her nature is truly the nature of no birth, no death."
—Thich Nhat Hanh

In this moment there is so much light making all that feels good so beautiful and all that doesn't feel good easier to endure. I can allow it all in—the easy and not so easy. This acceptance is important because it allows me to enter the sanctuary of peace and harmony. Here I regain balance as my mind sees and accepts change as the most natural part of life.

The range of human experience—the good, the bad, the ugly—is all needed to create the real me. When I do not cling to the past or grasp for the future, in the neutral state of being present, I can choose to be here where everything exists.

The past doesn't have to be repeated through my reaction. Instead of being stuck and stagnant, I can enter the flow of life, allowing the creative movement of energy inside where it encourages movement towards becoming.

Letting go of what I think I know seems to be the ticket home. Let it go, allow it all to unfold, and recognize how my attachment to the outcome just keeps me suffering.

I don't know what the divine plan is for me, but I can't move forward if I'm grasping or clinging to the past. Life is a constant state of impermanence, which means that everything changes.

Steve's death has influenced everything inside and around me. Life pushes for change, and I am changing.

As the days move me through the seasons, they help me touch the small gap within the moments where magical imaginings open my heart.

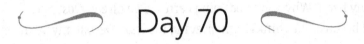

Day 70

It takes strength to face our sadness and to grieve and to let our grief and our anger flow in tears when they need to. It takes strength to talk about our feelings and to reach out for help and comfort when we need it.

— Fred Rogers

It takes courage to step into unknown territories with hope. I try to see the truth and recognize the impermanence of suffering. I remind myself that everything is temporary in this world.

As I lay in bed with my sad, sick heart, I am aware that there is a deeper meaning in it all. Grief has brought me to the edge, helpless in this place of human suffering. In my humanness, I must ask for help. I have let myself be seen so vulnerable and weak.

Nothing seems important, yet I feel loved; I feel peace. I open myself up like a baby bird that opens its mouth to be fed by its mother. I know I am cared for.

I let Spirit in. I don't have physical strength, but I have an inner strength. Life brings me to the very edge of the abyss, and I must trust that every step of the way, I am guided by something bigger. The Universe knows what I need. It's up to me to stay open, to let new life in, even when it looks like it's all falling apart. When I let go and let it take me, then the opening becomes the perch from which my spirit soars.

Day 71

*...And in her silence, intuition will whisper to you through
a stillness that only befalls upon souls before life and after
death—and say, "Be here, my love. All is coming."*

— Sez Kristiansen

Sometimes I criticize myself because I just want to pull the covers over my head. Why can't I be doing better? I've already lost one friend because she thinks I am grieving too long. Despite my years of meditation and spiritual practices, some days my inner serenity eludes me. I can't fit into a mold of how to grieve. I must trust myself and have the courage to let the grief flow. I surrender completely to it. I let go of all of me that existed before he fell on the floor and died.

Spirit Speaks

***I'm here in everything that exists—seen and unseen. Take this
moment to receive this life, for you do not have to die to know the
truth that the next moment is a step through the doorway of the
unknown. This life is waiting to come alive with your connection to it
as you witness all that is experiencing through you in this moment.***

I can't go back. I have to surrender so that who I was can be transformed.

Day 72

*Say not in grief 'he is no more' but live in thankfulness that
he was.*

— Hebrew proverb

Today is the first Thanksgiving holiday without him, and as I pray and meditate this morning, I ask for all my spirit loved ones to help me move through this day with grace. This day was so special for us. Every year I would get up early to prepare the Thanksgiving meal, and then I would go down our street to the thanksgiving yoga class.

It's a wintry day—cold and windy for Anna Maria, Florida. I walk into Island Yoga Space feeling vulnerable, so I lay my mat down in the back corner, away from the crowd. As I settle into the restorative poses, I focus on my left arm, which I broke a few months ago. I am mindful— no weight-bearing poses.

Present and awake, I move into myself, into the heart-opening place, and settle in. Soon tears uncontrollably well up inside. I try to let myself into this sad, sad space without Steve and the love we had for each other, but the feelings overwhelm me. I am going round and round in my mind of misery.

Seized once again by my grief, I get caught up in a turbulent cry. I leave the quiet space of the room, hoping to calm down, but I can't stay. I am gripped by my pain of loss. There is no gratitude on this day of thanks. Only the pain of loss and loneliness without him. I can't stop the tears—as I try to muffle the sounds, I feel exposed.

Blown wide open, I return to my empty house and life without him. I have no turkey cooking in the oven, nothing resembling the past. How can I be grateful for this piece of life that sucks and leaves me missing him so much? How can I fill this day—a day where family joins together, filling their hearts and tummies?

Yes, my mind can say, "I am grateful that he didn't suffer. I am grateful to have had him for all the years." Yes, there are all the lovely memories that I have of a man who loved me so. But today, right now, I am angry, hurt, and scared. And yet I must get through this day— because it is all I have.

I go to dinner with family, look around the table at the smiling faces of my son, my sister- and brother-in-law, and thank our God for them.

Underneath the surface is a torrent of feelings ranging from suffering to brilliance. There is great complexity in this human self.

Day 73

Shatter my heart so a new room can be created for a limitless love.

— Sufi prayer

I feel my broken heart as I touch the profound feelings that are so raw. This ache draws me back into myself. Even though there is pain, I meet it with compassion as I forgive myself and others for all the hurts experienced and caused.

We are all human. Sometimes we miss the mark, other times we downright fail. But we don't have to be perfect to be worthy of love and forgiveness. In this moment, forgiveness is letting go of what was so that the ending can be a new beginning.

This dark night of my soul illuminates my path on this sacred journey of self-love. Along the way, even my most petty and trivial ideas can illuminate what keeps me from my true self. My wounds can have a deeper meaning that can bring healing.

No one is responsible for our happiness. In fact, when we allow ourselves to be dependent on anyone or anything, it can turn into deep sorrow, shame, or regret. Then our weaknesses and our intolerable guilt will prevent us from taking responsibility for ourselves. It obstructs our ability to see and face our fears. When we become fearful, we can run, or we can face the darkness and rise up.

Blaming another for our pain takes us away from the truth that can set us free. We aren't here to be saved, nor are we here to save anyone else. Every part of our humanness is part of the whole that is humanity. Accepting it all is easier said than done, yet taking personal responsibility is necessary. When you meet yourself here, you'll find your true power.

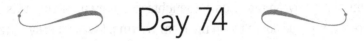

Day 74

It's an honor to be in grief. It's an honor to feel that much, to have loved that much.

— Elizabeth Gilbert

As I reach deep inside the canyon of this dark moment, I feel my broken, shameful self, the child inside that cannot save anyone. I accept my vulnerable, scared little self who forgets I am worthy to be held. I reach inside my pain as I unveil myself, nothing to hide. I am not perfect, and I do not know it all.

As I arrive at the place where everything has been shattered, I feel the light of a love that is always waiting for my return. I am worthy to be cared about, even when I'm in my pain.

I wake up in the early morning with the vision of Steve's body lying lifeless on the hospital bed covered by a sheet. I touch his still warm skin. As tears flow out of me, I kiss his eyes, his ears, his nose, his mouth, his arms, his feet, and then sink into his chest. I take his hands into mine and kiss each finger as I remove his wedding ring.

Touching his body for the last time, I thank him for all the gifts his life brought me. I thank him for the love and the pain and everything in between.

I wish I would have kissed his feet while he was alive and told him all that was beautiful and all that was true beyond the darkness of our human frailties.

Owning my shame is so powerful! We all have shame! As I receive myself authentically, the light shines on the darkest moments allowing my true self to remember how worthy I am. I am good enough as I choose to live fully today.

Day 75

During these months, it feels like angry black clouds follow me every moment of my day. So many dark thoughts cloud my mind. But this gut-wrenching rage doesn't stop me from writing. I write. I pray. Often I weaken and crumble on the floor. Yet, I keep moving inward. I scream and cry, swallow my tears, and pray some more.

If I keep breathing, if I keep moving forward, if I can just place one foot in front of the other, I trust the light will make its way to me. Sometimes it's just the light shining through the window onto the fruit bowl in the kitchen or a smile from another dog walker. This unsure footing reminds me of the awkward and insecure young girl I was as a teenager. I stumbled through this time. I was skinny with thick glasses and braces, wishing I could be confident like my two sisters.

I realize that right now, in this awkward stage of grief, I am shedding this skin again, this feeling that I am in between who I am and who I will become. It's shaky to move into this unimaginable time—this phase of life. I am gripping to the past knowing full well that letting go is required, and then I turn on the music.

The Supremes' "Ain't No Mountain High Enough" gets me off the couch. I pick up my puppy and we dance in the kitchen. Tears turn into a smile as I remember that silly, funny girl who just wants to laugh again.

The music gets me dancing but the courage to let go reminds me that I have done this before as the life behind me gets smaller and what is in front of me seems almost too big to take in. I'm growing into this new normal. This garment truly is ONE SIZE FITS ALL!

I am like that skinny, scrawny, little adolescent with arms too long and legs even longer. As I clumsily trip into the next moment, I realize that it's not easy. But I do it because the music is striking a chord within my heart that calls me "Fancy Pants." I wiggle my way through this tunnel where light is at the end and I don't have to die a thousand deaths, just this one moment when I step into the overwhelming bigness of a new life being born.

I pray—God, help me through the agony of this labor of loving myself in all my pain. I sing at the top of my lungs. I sing the songs that moved me through those awkward years of my self-abuse. I remember that the journey to self-love is a love affair with myself. I begin again.

Every part of my life has helped me to know who I am. It is this dance with the dark and the light that has allowed me to meet myself. This romance with myself has grown to be my truest love and I know now that wherever I am, that love and energy are always available for me.

— From Modeling Clothes to Modeling Self by Frannie Hoffman

Day 76

Spirit Speaks

Oh, sweet love—know that these days in a body are only moments joined together to remember who you truly are. You, a Divine being of light. You, a child of God, always cared for.

You, my sweet beloved soul, are loved beyond words. This world is filled to the brim—all the way—for you. The sun warms you and guides your way back.

Through this challenge, grief has taken me to my knees. The wisdom of these days teaches me how to move through pain and suffering and out of fear. I will help others face the hardships of loss. With compassion, I allow love to transform my separateness.

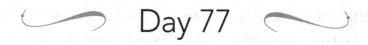

Day 77

...now is where love breathes.
                 – Rumi

I am intuitive. I believe everyone is intuitive. And though we all can access our higher self, most of us stay stuck, held prisoner in old ways of thinking that keep us believing in our false self—the little self that is rigid and resistant to change.

We all get hunches, truth chills, and feelings right before phone calls. We all receive information, feelings, or impressions that sometimes are called your "6th sense." That's what it is, another sense that we all have, just like the other five that we are already familiar with. We are more than these five senses. As children, our brains are not as fully developed, so we rely more on other senses—our instincts—to understand and comprehend what is taking place around us.

So now I consciously take a breath when something gets my attention. Then I can look at myself intimately and feel worthy of what life offers.

The quiet voice of my soul gets my attention and nudges me to partner with this amazing Universe, my loved ones in spirit, angels, or spirit guides. It's all love, no matter what you call it!

Truth chills move up and down my spine as I align with this powerful Presence once again. My intention to choose love over fear allows another voice to speak to my heart.

Today, God answers as I am taking out the garbage. I hear whispers in the wind that urge me to let go and just be in the present moment. I answer the call and feel my heart expand.

I am beginning to see the Divine everywhere!

I breathe into the now and appreciate this love affair with myself that continues.

Day 78

The things that frighten us just want to be held.
— Mark Nepo, *Seven Thousand*
Ways to Listen: Staying Close to
What is Sacred

When I am locked up in the fear and darkness I feel around Steve's death, I get stuck in pain and suffering. When I allow it to pass through me by writing, screaming, crying, and just feeling it all, the acceptance of where I am in that moment softens the hold that my mind has on me.

Slowly I expand, and inside a space opens up as I am more present and aware of the moment. I walk on. Sometimes it feels mechanical, putting one foot in front of the other. Then as I open my eyes, I can see this world around me. I can receive the moment as I discover who I am without my partner. As I walk through the darkness of loss, I am finding more of myself and slowly coming to life again.

I can now see and accept that a part of me died with him. As I shed these parts, I connect with the wisdom that shows me the way back to the beloved—the one who has never left and is always here. This feeling asks nothing of me but to be present. As the gift of life consciously flows again through my veins, I now feel more connected to Steve than ever before.

In this open heart that I choose to be, the whole world looks different. My inner sight and other senses are showing me the pathway back to my soul. It is a knowing that has never left me and is speaking louder within my silent mind.

With fear absent from my mind, the greater power of love shines through as the Universe shows me what I need to change. I can stay here more easily when my mind is quiet and not hooked by the pain created by fear. Then I become the compassionate heart that is aware of what frightens me. I can consciously choose to stay connected in the Presence. Here I am walking with Spirit and taking the hand of my beloved. Steve walks ahead of me now and knows what my heart is asking for. As he uses this world to dance with me in this new partnership, I trust that God is leading the way.

I am open to the Universe, and it is changing me for the better.

 # Day 79

> *When we pass away and leave our bodies, only fear is lost. It takes faith to believe that there is anything beyond our body and this world of perception. Once we believe in the next phase of existence, we stop dwelling on fear. We feel good and right. It satisfies a need that we have more meaning. I believe when we pass, we become aware of Reality. Our knowledge is more complete and we are ready to help those who are still in this world. We inspire them to choose love instead of fear. We reach them through love. This is why every time we love we are extending creation infinitely. It's love that is eternal and is connecting us from this life to eternal life.*
>
> — Jim DeMaio, *Helping not Fixing*

Today, I'm in this familiar place within where I long for Steve's touch or at least another visitation from the other side. I yearn for a sign—a white pick-up truck passing by, lights going on and off, or a fish jumping out of the water.

There are so many signs, simple gestures from the other side that appear on our path and touch us. Some may call them coincidences, but I call them messages from the heavens. They ground me and keep me here in the present moment.

The signs of love are messages I receive in my heart, which drinks them in like sweet kisses. For me, it's a moment when time stands still, and I can meet him once again as he opens me up to this new relationship.

A card from Steve falls out of my book—it has a puppy on the front underneath which he wrote, "bad dog!" Inside he added, "Thank you for being the one who sees the best and the worst of me and doesn't leave or shut down. I was wrong in the way that I let my feelings out, and I am very grateful for your strength in bearing it with me. I will do better.

Something clicked in my head, and I see that my actions are not what they should be. You are the best thing in my life, and I love you so. Love you always, Steve."

Yes, yes, yes. I needed to hear those words again. Steve is here with me. He lives in my heart. How blessed I am that I was able to spend those days and years with him. Our love wasn't perfect. It was conditional. It was the human dance of our insecurities and doubts. It was the relationship back to our own selves that woke us up to true love. Steve's life was his to live. His choices were his to make.

This loss has moved me into higher consciousness and when I remember to merge with my higher self, when I relax into this space inside, I become the space and settle into more of myself. When I surrender, I am that peace.

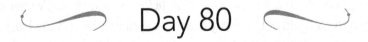 Day 80

It's the great mystery of human life that old grief passes gradually into quiet tender joy.
— Fyodor Dostoevsky

There is no control when someone you love transitions. There's nothing you can do to stop it from happening. And when it does, you can't get them back in their body; you can't get them back into the life you had together. It doesn't matter how many tears you cry, how much you scream, or how many promises you make. The mind can go over and over all the things you should have done differently—all the 'if only I had done this, said that...'

Nothing will bring them back to you. And yet, knowing that they have now joined with all that is, you realize that they are with you in every way but the physical manifestation of form. Now they are much more and can join you in every moment of your existence if you want that.

Day 81

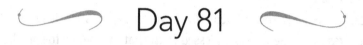

No matter where life takes you, the place that you stand at any moment is holy ground.

— Susan Vreeland

The trauma is still energetically stuck in my body. Just to speak about it pulls me into intense feelings as if it just happened. I am stuck in the pain and unbelievable shock of his sudden death.

Today I let go. I go through these feelings—all of them—and allow myself to step into the experience. After releasing the tears, I see the gift of Steve's death. He didn't have to suffer, and he didn't leave me. His body died, yet his spirit is with me always. I know this intellectually, but I couldn't fully accept it. So many deep, difficult feelings.

Even though I am a healer and have helped so many people over the last 25 years, I could not save my husband. I know it wasn't my job, but in some ways, I felt that my love should have saved him. I'm not mad at God anymore, I just thought Steve would come back, that our love could keep him here. Why is it so hard to let go?

I've read countless books about near-death experiences and I believed he would come back because of our love. But he didn't, and now I feel left behind and left in this pain. To come to terms with this trauma, I need to find a way to listen deeply to the pain that is calling me. I need to let the voices that keep crowding my heart open me to the voice of my soul. I am accepting all the voices of my pain yet the layers of letting go continue to be uncomfortable.

I want to let go. I want to trust. I want, I want, I want! Maybe, for right now, I will just sit on this holy ground and nudge my attention back to my breath. As I trust more, I relax and sink deeper into myself. I feel content.

I want to live for myself now. I want to truly listen to the voice of Spirit and let it guide me.

Day 82

Spirit Speaks

This is a transition time for you too! You just didn't have to leave your body behind. I know that you are in pain when you think of the past when I was with you. Now let go of it and venture into this moment where life is full of newness. Here you begin to feel yourself again. And as you nurture this feeling of love, there is a dream that holds you in a vision of complete oneness. You have been shown this time and time again. When you stay here, your whole being merges with what is true. Here there is clarity. Here there is a depth of peace and understanding that is beyond your wildest dreams. It's pure magic living where your inner light is more real than anything the optical eyes can see.

In the physical, it looks like I am not here. These four walls only show you emptiness and loneliness. Yet when you choose the true vision, your inner sight, you feel the presence of the love that has never and will never die. Allow your senses to live fully in the acceptance of all that nurtures and heals you. The pain of loss is the gateway into all that we are beyond the body.

Day 83

Authenticity is a collection of choices that we make every day. It's about the choice to show up and be real. The choice to be honest. the choice to let our true selves be seen.

— Brene Brown

It really doesn't matter how I feel—terrified by what is going on in my life or content that everything feels okay—the sky continues to be the backdrop of clouds or sun. Rain or shine, the birds still sing. I can trust this day or wake up with my stomach in a knot. The choice is mine. When I set my intention to show up and be real, then I find myself at the doorway that unites me with my true self.

Today I open my eyes and allow the lessons of my past to bring to me the wisdom that these experiences have shown me. I need to relinquish my old ways of being in the world and follow the truth of my heart. I want to align with love and choose to not be distracted by others' dramas. I must trust that everyone is where they are supposed to be. My job right now is to go inward and focus on myself. This part of my journey presents a crossroads for me spiritually and physically.

On the surface, my choice feels selfish—will I help myself or continue to help others? Caring for others has always been the right choice for me. But the truth is I can know my worth and love myself while having compassion for others. Every part of me has to trust completely that everything is in Divine order—for me and my life, for my family, friends, and clients, even for Steve and his death. In this acceptance, I step onto a new path, a new dream without Steve's physical presence but always, always joined in Spirit loving and guiding me.

These amazing experiences help me trust that I am growing. With patience and focus, I have the commitment and courage to see these experiences differently. And so, I pray. And as I do, I feel all that is inside where my emotions help me receive the gift that compassion brings.

Great Mystery,
Teach me how to trust
My heart,
My mind,
My intuition,
My inner knowing,
The senses of my body,
The blessings of my spirit.
Teach me to trust these things
So that I may enter my
Sacred space,
Love beyond my fear,
And thus, walk in balance
With the passing of each glorious Sun.
— Lakota Prayer

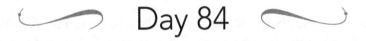

Day 84

In my first book, *From Modeling Clothes to Modeling Self,* I unveiled the deepest parts of myself, and I told the truth about my insecurities. Now I am going even deeper, and I understand that I can't abandon myself anymore. I reach deep inside to embrace the parts in me that I judge. As I grieve, I feel angry, selfish, lazy, and weak. I become controlling. And yet, I do not resist it. I allow myself to be real. The power comes from facing the truth that nothing has to be hidden, not even my brilliant and beautiful self.

I look deeply into the places within where I am afraid that I'm not strong enough to take care of myself. Voices of my past tell me that I can't make enough money to support myself, that my frail and sick body will take me down and make me dependent on my family. I see my abused, frightened, victimized self who believes I must prove I am worthy, and I allow myself to be that needy little girl. I don't hide her. I don't suppress her. I listen to what I need. I am okay, even in this fear of the future. I began to forgive all my human conditions.

I look in the mirror at my aging self and notice the wrinkles and my sunken eyes from crying. I breathe in. Life is giving me this chance to hold my weaknesses and behold, here lives my strength. When I open to myself with compassion, I can love others and live free.

As I touch my darkness, it shows me the way to bring unconditional love and self-acceptance to my entire human self. I am becoming more transparent as I blend all the aspects of who I am—the positive and the negative. In all that is flawed and imperfect, I Am BEAUTIFUL!

Day 85

Life, as it unfolds, can shake us out of the mundane, repetitive daily ways we shut ourselves off or numb out. We become robots and forget that at any moment we could die.

When I stay in fearful thoughts, I lose sight of who I am as soul. When I consciously shift back to my center, I get myself out of the chaos that is stunning my senses. I go deeper into myself as I choose to be aware of the unconscious intentions that cause me to contract and feel lost. Here, the answers come to me in so many ways. I don't want to miss it, so I choose to be more present in even the smallest moments of this rich life. I choose to be courageous as I act from a loving place within me by allowing the most loving part of myself to compassionately be with all the fragilities of my deeply flawed self.

In my mind, I see myself walking in a forest that has been destroyed by a fire. Yet amongst the ash and burnt timber, I see new growth emerging from a dead tree.

We are magnificent beings who walk through fires that destroy so much of what we hang on to. Then when the calmness returns and the sun shines again, we can see that we have grown.

I need to be clear about my intention of what I want in my life. I know the Universe will support me. I'm responsible for my life now. I need to make choices that are for me.

I want to live for myself now and truly listen to the voice of Spirit guiding me.

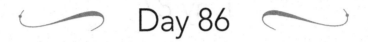

Day 86

Death is a gift meant to wake up the living, to nudge us toward a life of purpose and intention.

— Alicia Keys

So many mornings I wake up and find myself weighed down by the heavy feelings of dread. It's all I can do to get myself out of bed. Then it seems like all I do is cry. Grabbing what I can—tissues, toilet paper, my sleeve—I cry like a child, snot running down my lips and chin.

When anxiety captures me, I wake up feeling worse. I have no will to live. That scares me the most.

Today I go back to bed. In the darkened room, I curl up in a ball and cuddle with Mollie while trying to shut out the entire world.

I hear banging on the screen outside. It's so loud, I must get up. I hear seagulls screeching and see a flock of them dive-bombing the screen that covers my back patio. Mollie joins in the chaos, barking like she's yelling at them to stop.

It's so disorienting, I have to sit. And the moment I do, it all stops. The birds stop squawking and Mollie stops barking. Soon the gulls fly away. Now all I hear are the sounds from the palm fronds and leaves rustling behind me, and then suddenly everything is still. My mind is quiet, too.

My heart opens and lets in the stillness as I settle into myself. I settle into this heart of mine and feel the aliveness of everything around me. I don't feel dead, numb, despairing, angry, sad, or afraid. I just feel like me again, like I'm back on track. I didn't have to do anything or figure anything out; this alignment just happened.

Still, I am human, and life just sucks sometimes. But no amount of crying is ever going to bring Steve back. Why did it take Steve's death to wake me up to the truth of who I am? He saw it the moment he left his body, and he was overwhelmed with the reality that he was loved completely and unconditionally.

Day 87

Spirit Speaks

Today, in this very moment, you can rest in the Presence that fills you up. Your ego will distract you or spiral you into the false identity that feels powerless and alone, while the heart will bring you into the oneness where peace abides. Life will unfold with or without you being here. So, stand strong within yourself and allow life to show you the way to a world within that has no conditions.

Be free to be just as you are, and in self-acceptance, the opening within gives birth to all that spills out of you without effort. All that you have control over is your ability to be happy. Your happiness is the medicine that heals your heart and in turn, heals anyone who walks with you.

Breathe into this presence and let life take you for a ride as you hold onto your hat and let the wind blow through your hair and tell you the secrets of the Universe. Life is for the living, so you might as well allow it in. Through you, many hearts remember why this beautiful world is a playground for each to join in and be merry.

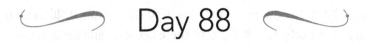

Day 88

We can't selectively numb emotion. Numb the dark and you numb the light.

— Brene Brown

Worthiness to be loved is at the core of so many of our impulses to numb out with some substance, to shop for things we don't need, or to eat when we're not hungry. I watch myself wanting to run from this feeling of not being good enough. When will it disappear from my consciousness? Why do I want to keep it as my truth when it causes me to spiral down and feel alone and unworthy of a life filled with joy?

At times, it can be hard to recognize that I have choices. Some days it's harder than others. Some moments are unbearable. But as I take my power back and take responsibility, life can be filled with opportunities that create more life. When I choose to be connected, I find that the past holds the wisdom that brings a glimmer of light within my heart. There, I clearly see the truth that brings me some freedom. I am changed.

When I am knocked down by all the demons of my past, I choose to get up. It only takes a moment to go inside and tap into the resources that are waiting to flow through me. Here, I choose to live in authentic power as I move toward the love and light, which is infinitely bigger than the darkness.

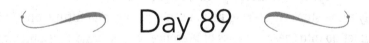

Day 89

This heart aches. It grieves for what is lost and never will be again. It still hurts like a wound whose scab keeps getting ripped off. As I catch these feelings that come like waves, I try my best to surf them without getting pulled under. But these inner waters can get turbulent. Patiently, I climb back up and ride these waves that, like the tides, have an ebb and flow.

I breathe in and out and trust myself to stay deeply inside. I do not fight it. I do not attach to it. I accept these negative emotions instead of reacting or suppressing them. I let go of the habit of engaging and just let it be. I am committed to this mindful practice.

Meditation

Breathe in as you take your focus inward.
Sitting still brings you closer to yourself.
Look at your life as if you are gazing at a canvas.
Remember who you are
And let the falseness fall away.
You are free to just be yourself.

It doesn't matter where I am on this journey, these feelings will come and go. Eventually, they will pass through me like waves in the ocean. It doesn't matter how many times I fall; I will rise again and again.

Day 90

As I look around my house, I feel an urge to do some decorating. Maybe I'll paint the walls. I will definitely get a new bedspread for this way-too-big bed of mine. Perhaps I am trying to distract myself. Or maybe I'm trying to muster up some creative energy.

My mind stops chattering its nonsense of past and future, and I feel myself let go into the sweetness of Presence. As my mind falls quiet, my body expands into the soft energy. There is space inside, and I feel a little lighter. It only takes a moment; the field of consciousness is right here, not in some faraway place.

As I imagine myself changing the inside of this house, I feel something stirring in my belly. I take a deep breath and without asking a question, I listen to the whispers in the stillness...

There is new life for you to receive. Fixing your home is giving you more aliveness. This is the time for you to create and to feel the beauty of being here in your world. You are listening each moment to what your needs are. Step by step, you awaken more deeply in self. This is your home where all your humanness exists.

When you accept yourself fully, you open your heart to receive your life with unconditional love. There is nothing that is new to you. Yet when you awaken a little more, the light infuses everything from the inside. You see clearer and with all your senses, which expands your thinking to encompass all ideas and beliefs. It is all here in the whole of everything. You begin to watch the world with the eyes of soul, inhabiting this body for a short while until you understand the bigger picture.

In my mind, I repeat the quote from ACIM like a mantra:

"In the quietness are all things answered, and is every problem quietly resolved."

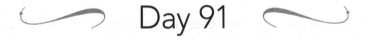

Day 91

Grief is not a disorder, a disease, or a sign of weakness. It is an emotional, physical, and spiritual necessity, the price you pay for love. The only cure for grief is to grieve.
— Earl Grollman

A siren blares and the sound brings me into the moment when Steve fell to the floor. It all happened so quickly, this dreadful experience that threw me into the darkness. Again and again, my thoughts are accompanied by the sadness and pain of living without him. The terrible pain of needing without getting. This ache for love moves me into myself.

When will I be filled with the joy of our lovely memories? Sometimes they come and bring a smile to my face only to lead me back into despair and loneliness. This journey to heal my heart is filled with all the emotions. Like everything else on this journey called life, it is all an experience, and I can open myself up or shut myself down. Consciously I can help myself by allowing this compassionate love to change me.

Then I slip into the quiet of my mind where the light enters and holds me tenderly. Peace begins to rise from the ashes of my past. I'm just being me, for that is the only way back to my heart. I allow Spirit to show me the way back into being with myself.

Life has taken a turn—
There is an opening somewhere—
Right here in the center of my being.
Here I look at everything.
As I sink into myself, memories come and go.
Sometimes they are accompanied by emotional pain or just a thought that bursts into more.
Forgetting and remembering.
Contracting and expanding.
Opening and closing like a door
But a door that swings both ways,
Allowing this new life to enter from either side.

It's hard for me to believe that life is beginning again. Yet as I accept it, as I choose to align with Spirit, I feel empowered.

This power that anchors in love and peace grows within me no matter what has been triggered.

I'm beginning to see that my yesterdays can give way to even richer tomorrows.

My cries for my loved one are natural. The loving memories will come again as my heart continues to heal. I am held tenderly by the love that continues. I welcome anyone who comes on my path today.

Day 92

In the end these things matter most:
How well did you love?
How fully did you love?
How deeply did you learn to let go?
— The Buddha

Letting go happens naturally when I acknowledge and welcome what is here instead of resisting and withdrawing. Wishing for life to be different than it is keeps me suffering and living outside of reality.

My life right here, alone with my dog in my little beach house, is where it's happening. It's where love can grow if I let it. When I let go of everything I think I know, I let go of all that is in the way of my serenity.

When you accept where you are and stay right here, you can choose a different path. Your return to your loving and joyful self will come after you have prepared yourself.

Breathe and allow all that is to bring you into alignment. Stay here and fall back in love with yourself. Choose to sustain this good feeling that gives life as you live fully as your true self.

Clearing my resistance is my responsibility. When I stop judging—myself, anything, or anyone—I soften and expand around what is. It's how I prepare my own temple for Divine energy to arrive. I sweep out the cobwebs of the past, dust off the surface of the mind, and let go. Again and again, I allow the flow of life to begin. I invite it in and it comes.

This journey I am taking beyond my limited five senses can open me to my bigger self. Here I am one with all that is beyond my thinking. Here I can rest in the arms of love.

Day 93

Spirit Speaks

You are freed once again when you awaken to this new moment when you are released from the ego. Take the hand of Spirit and become the peaceful warrior, the one who has joined forces with the Divine. Captured in the light that takes you into the oneness of creation, you can create a new moment, one that is filled with the promise of new life.

It is your opportunity to again rise, clear your mind, and re-emerge into the feelings of this beautiful life that continues to give. It is all right here, nothing at all has changed yet inside there is a shining light, a flicker of a flame that has never gone out. This spark is your true self, the one that knows that you are enough, just as you are, a pearl amongst the stones.

You are here to show up for yourself and to choose to be happy. Let go into this timeless moment and listen to your innermost truth. Your spirit loved ones wait patiently for you to awaken to who you truly are. You don't have to drop your body, just choose to be the receiver of this life. Open to more love and joy. This is creation at its very best, always creating more life.

Day 94

It is not impermanence that makes us suffer. What makes us suffer is wanting things to be permanent, when they are not so.

— Thich Nhat Hanh

I am beginning to wake up out of the nightmare. I have trekked through the valley of sorrow, scared yet comforted by many, supported by all who love me, held in the arms of my beloved spirit. As tears flow through my broken heart, I move on without knowing where I am going.

Throughout each day, the challenges and difficulties stab at my heart. Sometimes the negative states of my mind keep me filled with criticism. There is no peace here.

As hard as it can be to hear, I know I am being guided to receive the infinite possibilities of the future. If I hang on to the past as my source for affection, I will suffer. When I open to who I truly am, worthy of life and worthy of connection, I will blossom and become more.

So, I pray the Sanskrit Buddhist prayer:

May everyone be happy.
May everyone be free from misery.
May no one ever be separated from their happiness.
May everyone have equanimity free from hatred and attachment.

Day 95

The day Steve died his spirit began to share his personal demons. What I saw was a battlefield, of sorts, covered with the heartbreaking remains of his fight with himself. Steve was showing me his shadow— his fears, his doubts, his insecurities, his regrets, his self-loathing, and self-judgment. He has no ego anymore, so telling the truth was easy.

He is free, nothing to hide. I am left with it all and it also frees me. The burden I carried is now shining with light. With this understanding, more compassion moves through my heart. Oh, how I wish he could have told me the truth when he was alive. I now see the pain of all he carried in his shame.

Steve is gone. I can't project my inner darkness on him. I can't blame him when I feel like I am not good enough. Sometimes it feels like a wild animal is lurking inside me. While I feel ashamed of this part of myself, I know that it can't be denied or ignored. Grief helps me embrace it all.

It leads me on the journey to uncover my deepest fear, so I can allow my darkness to come into the light.

I am born worthy, and any thought of unworthiness is a lie that cannot bring me peace. Right now, here inside myself is the truth that will set me free. I give all the false ideas away to the Holy Spirit and line up my thinking with the mind of God. God is my healer. God sees me as perfect.

Day 96

Meditation

Listen and you will hear the truth
That resides inside the silent center.
This opening is like a vast field
Filled with nothing but the loving breeze
That envelops you and welcomes you back.

As you allow yourself to be held by this Presence,
You realize that you are a part
Of everything that exists—now and forever.
So sweet is this lesson you have come to learn.
It is not for the meek.
It is for the brave
Who venture into unknown territories.

This place holds nothing to feed the ego.
Only the heart remembers.
Clear yourself from these unwanted feelings
That cloud your vision.
Let go, and as you soften,
Turn your gaze inward.

You are an opening
For love to enter.
This love quenches any longing.
It is the experience of returning
To whom you are,
Worthy to be alive.
When you live this life fully for yourself,
You share yourself without conditions.

Day 97

Goodbyes are only for those who love with their eyes.
Because for those who love with heart and soul there is no
such thing as separation.

– Rumi

My mate in Spirit continues to show himself to me in so many ways that comfort me. I don't have to live without him. He is here with me without his body. He is in all the knowledge and light of consciousness. Once I have released my anger, I can sink even deeper into my body. There I am filled with that same knowledge and light that he is. We are one, joined in the heart of God, who loves us all unconditionally.

My life has been a series of experiences that bring me into greater awareness. Steve's death is just part of these myriad moments that unfold so perfectly. As I continue to let go into myself, I allow these higher forces to take over, and Steve is part of it all. I can stomp my feet, resist, and suffer, or I can let him in and trust in how he will guide my way.

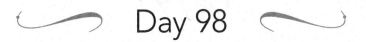

Day 98

It's holiday time. Christmas music is filling up all the stores and restaurants. I can't get away from this life that continues to move on and on. So, for today, I will let it in, even if songs like "Santa Baby" make me crumble and fall apart. I will let the tears come until they stop, knowing there will be more.

This first Christmas without him, I remember that he is with my mom and dad, his mom, and so many others. They are our angels, bringing more joy as they send love through our world.

When I line up with this image, peace comes into my heart. This peace permeates my being as I join with all my spirit loved ones. Here I am held in a love that continues to give peace on earth, focused within a moment of acceptance. Here I join in harmony as I am part of a bigger plan that is bringing us all together as one heart.

May today there be peace within.
May you trust that you are exactly
where you are meant to be.
May you not forget the infinite possibilities
that are born of faith.
May you use those gifts
that you have received
and pass on the love
that has been given to you.
May you be content knowing
you are a child of God.
Let this Presence settle into your bones
and allow your soul the freedom
to sing, dance, praise, and love.
It is there for each and every one of us.
– St. Teresa of Avila

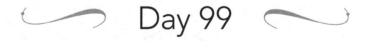

Day 99

There is a Secret One inside us; the planets in all the galaxies
pass through his hands like beads. That is a string of beads
one should look at with luminous eyes.

    – Kabir, "I Have Been Thinking"

We can start each day contemplating the different choices we have before us. Then moment by moment, breath by breath, we string them together, like a jeweler transforming precious stones into jewelry. Co-creating with the Divine, we fashion a design for this life that is of our own making.

Today, I choose to connect inward and listen to Spirit calling. Consciously receiving guidance from my inner being, I make choices and cherish life.

In the moment of inner quiet, as nature makes its voice audible, I hear Spirit. I am pulled inside to listen, to feel, to touch the Divine. There is a moment just before I rest in the abyss when I have a choice to react outward or stay inside. Today there is no turning back. Spirit has me lying down in the lush green grass of unconditional love. Here there is nothing to forgive as I am enveloped in the gentle caress and sweetness of God's love.

Sometimes words cannot fully touch the way I feel when I let go into the softness of acceptance. While thoughts come and go, I rest in a feeling of peace beyond my thinking mind.

The One that is creation is tapping me on my shoulder, calling me to let go into this soft bubble of light. It is so freeing to let go of it all and just be. I feel more alive as I pray for others and let myself be the instrument of peace. Steve's presence is so inviting. He says, "I am here. Right here." I, too, am here. Right here.

Spirit is in all things. I have the help I need to walk on my path today and every day of my life.

 Day 100

The best and most beautiful things in the world cannot be seen or even touched. They must be felt with the heart.
— Helen Keller

I did not realize it until I left my body and floated around watching and feeling it all. Wow, Baby Doll! You get to do it now in your body, and all the while I will be with you watching this great life you are creating. Then, and only then, can you share all that has been given to you. You have the ability to bring unity consciousness to the world by trusting all that is coming into you, infusing you with incredible love and light. It really is simple, and believe me, you will stay fully present in each moment.

Nothing is left by chance. It is all a Divine plan and perfectly woven for you. And when you allow yourself to breathe in the love that is all around you, it will pick you up and move you forward with ease. Let these days to come show you the way to be inside, dwelling in this perfect place of serenity.

Day 101

The daylight peeks into my awareness while feelings of depression move me into a dark hole. As I start my life over again, fear speaks to me every day. It can paralyze my heart and stop me from taking action if I let it. I can get stuck in grief, mired in thoughts that bring more pain and suffering. I feel disconnected and alone.

Today the sun touches me like my mother's loving glance. Oh, how I miss her and my dad. My body still cries, and my mind still spirals into thoughts of despair, making my heart beat faster. Yet I resist the urge to crawl back into bed. I thank myself for choosing to get up.

We can always choose another path. Despite the fear, we can take a risk and leap into life again. When you put your toe back into the stream of life, you will find the gentle current lures you back in. The part that is led by grief will eventually surrender to your determination to live again and experience joy. All it takes is the courage to make that first move forward.

That is what my life has taught me. Whenever I have encountered challenges—from health problems to divorce and death—I respond once I am able by taking the risk. Determined to keep my heart open, I make my way back to that stream, and I move into life, knowing it means I will face loss again. There's no quick fix. It is not an overnight process. Slowly, moment by moment, step by step, you find your way back to life.

Shying away from death and the ever-changing nature of things stops us from fully living. With awareness, we can face the reality of death. Then death can become our ally. Instead of avoiding pain and suffering, we embrace these opportunities to heal our emotional body.

Life is flowing. I enter my inner world—a place where no one takes up room but me. I take this life by the reins as my soul steers me in the direction of love. I open to the pain and the joy that allows me to live and love more fully.

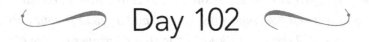 Day 102

When finally we find within ourselves courage and compassion enough to traverse the fault lines of the past, sit with our grief, our pain, our might-have-beens and trust in selfless grace, we will have the strength required to turn the page of rebirth and breathe the Universe anew.

— Linda Maree

There is nothing more fulfilling than staying with ourselves and our feelings. We stay and gather up the pieces of our old life that were left like raking leaves into a pile and placing them in bags. It's time to toss out all that is not needed anymore.

How wonderful it is to look at the job well done and sit with your tired body that has worked so hard to clean up your backyard. Sit in the garden as the flowers blossom and the birds sing and discover the sweet songs of your soul that are becoming the songs of your heart. How beautiful it is to stay with yourself as you let all that has been left behind take you deeper into the truth of all that you are.

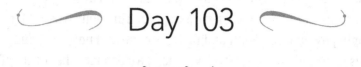

Day 103

Spirit Speaks

Feed yourself with this light that fills you and illuminates from the inside to the outside as you see what is real. Here we are forever joined, and the lies are dissolved and forgotten. What is true is that this life is yours to live and to bring forth to others through your connection. This cannot be held back, for when it is, you will feel resistance and pain. This freedom is in all when allowed to flow through you into the heart of another.

In the expansion, you sit in the center of everything that is alive—jumping with joy! The bliss of being here becomes heaven on earth. There is only a veil that separates us now, and as you lift your eyes to the light, you will receive the knowledge that continues to give life.

Even though I am no longer in a body, we still can dance and twirl and walk together joined in God's love that knows everything. Go now and see with every cell of your being how beautifully this world can reflect the heavens.

Day 104

Meditation

The sounds of the outside world
Take me inside
Where there is nothing

But the breath.
I return for no other reason
But to be in my own company.

I don't always like it here.
With all my self-talk about suffering—
I feel it.
Nothing to do
But accept this human frailty.
I grasp for a lifeline
That might come in a whisper
Spoken in the silent place
Called nowhere.

I come to this sacred, holy moment
That holds nothing and everything.
I stand inside it all
As if I was the center of the Universe.
"Welcome home," I say to myself,
"Welcome home."

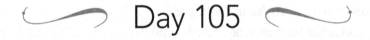

Day 105

Suddenly you're ripped into being alive. And life is pain, and
life is suffering, and life is horror but my god you're alive
and it's spectacular.

— Joseph Campbell

A squirrel creeps slowly along the telephone wire above my head, tightly gripping its path from one side of the yard to the other. I watch with amazement at its focus, balance, and confidence as it traverses this tightrope.

Mollie barks, yet this critter doesn't take notice, it keeps looking straight ahead as if the vision to get to the other side is all that matters.

How easy it is for me to lose my footing when I stray from what is important to me. Why is it so hard to follow my intention and to listen to my heart as I hold my vision for my future sacred within my mind? How easy it is to lose myself in my cell phone, other people's dramas, fixing or wanting to be fixed.

I take care of my inner chaos so I can make room for the unmanifested to come forth. As I enter meditation today, can I listen to the whispers of my brave heart as it encourages me to take refuge inside?

I take it all in. Even though I am all alone, I'm not depressed, just quiet. I sit in this refuge where I find peace in the Buddha mind, in serenity, as I allow the sweetness of the still calm waters to bathe me this early morning. I glance over at that big old tree. It's not the Bohdi tree that Buddha sat under, but it's my canopy, my sacred holy temple. My garden lights up the dark; its sounds spark my heart and enliven my spirit.

This love for myself, this kind gesture, helps me feel connected and grounded. From this space, I can move to the edge and leap. I can take the risk to jump because of the work I have done. Each day I let go a little more and make the choice to love myself.

I become the warrior who trembles and fully feels my human fears. As I look at all the obstacles, I breathe in and walk this tightrope like my teacher the squirrel.

I have the courage to be me as I leap once again into the unknown. If I stop before I jump, I can choose to leap into another day!

Day 106

Meditation

I choose to be happy
To connect within
And hold all of myself
Without judgment.

I am, in every moment,
The silent observer
That accepts where I am
In all my feelings.

Here I stay conscious and awake.
Here I am out of my insane thinking.
Here I am inside my heart
Feeling the oneness.

Day 107

Spirit Speaks

This way of being assists you in living your days detached from the many dramas created by the ego. Instead, each moment becomes another experience to remember who you truly are. You are not the one that lives in suffering or longing.

You open yourself up to the day, looking forward to what is unfolding for you. Yes, you still feel the heaviness of grief pushing on your chest like an elephant that won't get off you, but you can feel the vastness of the energy that is all around you. When you choose to swim in these delicious waters, they expand you into more Presence.

Then you look around at what is familiar—like your puppy Mollie sleeping by your body—and relish in the softness of her presence joining you in acceptance of what is real.

It doesn't mean that the experience of grief is not real, it just doesn't have to be all-consuming. You acknowledge the sadness of not being able to snuggle my body but now you have this warm ball of fur that melts into you and allows you to feel the unconditional love that exists so fully in this moment.

You see, my darling, that's what it is like to be a sage. You can choose in every moment to dwell in this love that is everywhere and in all things. When you allow it to be your connection to this moment, then much, much, more begins to be a part of you. You breathe into your heart and without much effort, you realize that the elephant is no longer sitting on your chest. You are filled with a peace that is beyond any understanding and you begin again to welcome more of yourself here.

That means you welcome anyone who comes on your path today and together you feel the magnificence of a beautiful day created for all humanity. When you do not shy away from what death brings you, you do not shy away from life.

Day 108

The deeper that sorrow carves into your being, the more joy
you can contain.

— Kahlil Gibran, *The Prophet*

At first, the moments were hell. I could not see anything good because I was lost in all the missing and longing.

This house was his before we met, and every part of it reminds me of him and that he is no longer here. I feel it all so intensely until I go inside myself and connect with the pain. After the tears flow, after I touch the anger and despair, I hold it all with compassion. Then a peace comes over me. In the safety of my inner chambers, the Divine meets my humanity. I expand into a stream of consciousness where light fills my entire being.

It is the practice that I know so well. My breath brings me into the body. Truth fills my heart as I let go of Steve again and again. He was not my Source, yet he was the one who led me back to all that I am. All of me is shown in this sacred place of my aloneness. Steve has become the voice in the silent place within my mind, and as I let go of who he was, he helps me align back to my true authentic power. He comes in all his brilliance and through this world, he shows me the way back to what is real.

Love has found me again. My ego softens when I arrive safely in my heart. This is a moment-by-moment journey as life as it was falls away. With my trust in Spirit, I am guided.

My heart is opening to the guidance that is always there as I begin to trust myself to step into the next moment. God reaches for me like rays of sunshine touching the petals of the flowers that grow upon the earth. Love has found me again as I soften and let go.

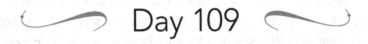 # Day 109

Were it possible for us to see further than our knowledge reaches, and yet a little way beyond the outworks of our divining, perhaps we would endure our sadnesses with greater confidence than our joys. For they are the moments when something new has entered into us, something unknown; our feelings grow mute in shy perplexity, everything in us withdraws, a stillness comes, and the new, which no one knows, stands in the midst of it and is silent.
— Maria Rainer Rilke

I breathe into my life now, acknowledging the newness and the feeling of acceptance. Yes, he is gone physically. Yes, he was ripped out of my arms, and into the arms of God he went. The light called him, and he chose to let go and move on. He dropped his precious roles of husband, father, brother, son, friend, contractor, artist, lover, diver, fisherman, and so much more.

He let go because something greater was in his plan. Now I am here to let go of the man he was. A good man. A great man. A loving and kind man. He had shortcomings like all of us and so many endearing qualities, too. He was filled with questions about God and life after death. Now he knows what it is all about.

As I join with him in the light, I am shown some clips, some precious pieces of heaven, for grief has its own way to unveil all that needs to be taken away so that one can step into the Presence. This new life continues to be full and rich and opens me to this mystical experience.

Things will never be the same. I realize that I am different in so many ways, and maybe that's a good thing! This experience has brought more wisdom and compassion.

Mother Teresa said, "We cannot do great things, but we can do small things with great love."

Today I choose to go deeper and bring myself here, where nothing is guaranteed. I must trust in the unknown, even if it seems scary! I hope my life is headed in the right direction. And this little thought makes me feel happy.

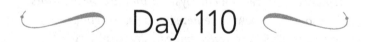 Day 110

I learned this, at least, by my experiment; that if one advances confidently in the direction of his dreams, and endeavors to live the life which he has imagined, he will meet with a success unexpected in common hours.
— Henry David Thoreau, *Walden*

There is no place that I am not. As you walk into your moments, know that this world within you is reflected onto that which you see. When you are filled with love, you see it all around you.

It's right here in this holy moment where, breath by breath, you surrender completely to Spirit. The path you walk is lit up by your conscious connection to the Divine. God places you in the moment to communicate this love—you need not speak—just be the receiver.

Your heart is healing—you can feel the sadness rising up and yet your choice is to hang out with God—love—Presence. It's all the moment of choice. Then you look around and see yourself in all your fellow human beings upon the earth. All roads lead back to love.

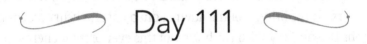

Day 111

The days of absence and the bitter nights
Of separation, all are at an end!
Where is the influence of the star that blights
My hope? The omen answers: At an end!
Autumn's abundance, creeping Autumn's mirth,
Are ended and forgot when o'er the earth
The wind of spring with soft warm feet doth wend.
The Day of Hope, hid beneath Sorrow's veil,
Has shown its face...

— Hafiz

I put down the dish towel and choose to sit for a while on the beach under the night sky. Letting go of things I think I need to do can seem hard. But I do let go, and I take in the sounds, the smells, the touch of this beauty that arrives in this moment as I enter the center of my own expansion.

I look at the stars that fill the darkness tonight. I close my eyes and listen to the sounds that fill me with this feeling that expands my heart.

This subtle, sweet moment always waits for my return. It makes me wonder why I forget to reach out for this lifeline of hope. Why does it seem to be hidden from me when I am lost in fears or feelings of deep sadness? This limitless wisdom fills my heart in these moments when Spirit expresses itself through this world of form.

When we allow ourselves to stay distracted by all the chaos and busyness of life, we miss the moments when nature surrounds us with complete perfection.

I have challenged my fears and welcomed my emotions and experiences so that my highest potential could move me into transformation. I am present with all that I am because I choose to let go of the struggle and live in this precious moment. I am home here in this incredible body that serves my soul. Here I become the flowing water, the sunrise and sunset, the birds, the wind, the smell of salt air. I am a part of the process of evolution as I shift into an expanded perception where the Universe is the bringer of the dawn. I am a hopeful heart reaching out to the Divine. I cry with the beauty of this ever-present energy that gives life.

Meditation

Stillness brings me
Out of distraction
And into a quiet mind.

Life is fleeting.
From this sacred place,
More is revealed,
And it is shared so intimately.

Nothing is hidden.
With this limited life,
I can live and love more fully.

A full life will have pain,
And it will also have joy.

In the center of my being
I have hope.

This hope seeps into all aspects of my life.

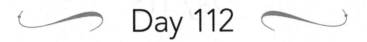

Day 112

The grave itself is but a covered bridge, leading from light to
light, through a brief darkness!
— Henry Wadsworth Longfellow

Be the sweetness of a love that loves another without conditions.
You cannot deny who you are, for that rejection keeps you stuck inside
the well of grief.

Take your breath deeply inside. Return to the empty space that
reminds you that there is no greater moment than this one. You have
returned to the fullness of being you. You have touched your fears,
hurts, anger, and resentments and wrapped yourself up in the Divine
embrace of the Universe.

This meeting of self has bridged the separation where all is part of
the whole. You are the bridge when you do not leave any part of your
humanity. Your perfect human self as woman, child, mother, daughter,
sister, and friend has been held in the arms of acceptance of this
journey back to the truth that brings you out of delusion and into the
reality of what is.

This day is for you—to be yourself without hiding any part.
Nothing to reject—only to be the receiver of everything that illuminates
the dark.

This light is you because you have met your highest self-reflected in
the eyes of Spirit.

I face my shadows as the light of truth brings me deeper into the space
between my thoughts. The pain is not for me to hold on to. It is not mine

to keep. It only reminds me that I am not alone as the sun warms me and touches my deeper knowing.

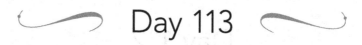

Day 113

You cannot prevent the birds of sorrow from flying over your head, but you can prevent them from building nests in your hair.

— Old Chinese proverb

I am weakened by grief, a paler version of myself. Grief robs me of my power and leaves me with a huge space inside that needs to be filled with a brand-new identity—one that is unfamiliar to me. It takes effort to get up each day and get into this life that I am left with without Steve. Clearing the garage, getting rid of yet more stuff is hard. Still, I do it, and little by little the space inside of me gets bigger.

After each step, I feel my legs give way as I collapse into a puddle of tears and heartache. Stuck in the heaviness of my emotions, the days come and go while my progress feels like I am moving through mud. But each time I feel myself here, I let go a little more.

Day 114

To everything there is a season, and a time to every purpose under the heaven:
A time to be born, and a time to die; a time to plant, and a time to pluck up that which is planted;
A time to kill and a time to heal; a time to break down and a time to build up;
A time to weep, and a time to laugh; a time to mourn, and a time to dance;

— *Ecclesiastes 3:1-4*

Losing my husband was just the beginning. I lost friends. I lost the life I knew. I lost a part of myself. Parts of me have come back but not the "me" I knew with him. For example, cooking with Steve was always so much fun. He had this way of making dinner magical, like when he would make a salad and cut up the red peppers into little hearts. And when we ate, at first bite he would always say, "This is the best (whatever he just tasted) I ever had!" Then he would pull me into the living room, and we'd dance to one of our favorite songs.

Now I am alone and trying to allow this loss to show me the path back to myself. Loss brings us to places inside that need to be found. That's the journey now—to be okay alone. Eating with just myself, sitting alone with no one beside me to validate my existence, being with myself again without distraction. It's not that I am afraid of being alone—I like my own company—it's just that I miss Steve's companionship.

My needs aren't being met and that's sad. I love sharing my life with a partner. I am lonely, yet I am learning lessons that help me re-enter life once again. In the meantime, I dance alone which is ok—I am good at that!

There is a time to let go and a time to receive. I can look back and see more than the pain of what I lost. I can appreciate the life we shared.

 Day 115

The moment you become aware of the ego in you, it
is strictly speaking no longer the ego, but just an old,
conditioned mind-pattern. Ego implies unawareness.
Awareness and ego cannot coexist.
　　　　　　　　　— Eckhart Tolle, *A New Earth:*
　　　　　　　　　　Awakening to Your Life's Purpose

When we are in the storm of life, when challenges come upon us, we can reach inside to touch that part that never leaves us—this force of light that brings calmness and serenity amid the dark night of our soul. It can be so easy to forget that we are not alone, that our higher power is right here. We merge or at least touch this Presence when we remember to breathe into the stillness of the moment. We have a choice whether or not to listen and trust in that which continues to guide our way.

This guidance can be from an earth angel, someone who is there for you through times of great challenge. Or you can reach into your heart and witness your spirit loved ones who wait patiently for you to acknowledge their presence. How sweet it is to hear them speak or show you that they are here.

It can be as simple as watching a butterfly or listening to the wind move through the trees. In that quiet moment, Spirit speaks in all kinds of ways to let us know that we do not walk alone. Here we are taken into the holy instant where Spirit joins us because we are willing to let go of the past and receive what is real. Love is right here, guiding us home to our hearts where all exist, and we are free.

Life beckons us to rejoin the stream of consciousness and allow ourselves to be carried in its ceaseless flow. Every part of this journey is for the evolution of soul.

Day 116

Spirit Speaks

No one can force you into this moment of pure essence. It happens when the ego has no power, and you choose to live in your heart. This is the beauty of being home wherever you are. All of it is within you, and nothing keeps you separate from this power that creates worlds.

Your love is expanding you into the next moment where you are like the sun. Your connection to your true power lights you up and melts you into all that has emerged through the igniting of this fire that unveils you. It moves you into sharing this radiant light, love, and joy with all who walk with you.

You reach inward and the whole world is touched, for it is both inside and outside of you. Here there is only one as God expresses and shares this love through your beautiful and ever-expanding heart. Together you create a world that gives life from all that seemed to be lost, for now, everything joins back into the ever-flowing river of life.

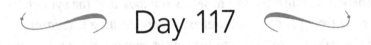 Day 117

Clouds come floating into my life, no longer to carry rain or usher storm, but to add color to my sunset sky.
— Rabindranath Tagore,
"Geetanjali" (Song Offerings)

When a loved one dies, it's so difficult to accept. Perhaps with all the lost plans and forgotten dreams, we can find a moment when we feel an opening inside.

It slips in and out of the shadows. Something unexpected happens and instead of sadness, there is a feeling of joy that opens our heart. We feel a sense of our loved one participating in the moment. We begin to remember the happy memories with an energy that lifts us up instead of pulling us down.

As I walk down to the beach, I see the sky light up like a Maxfield Parrish painting. I smile knowing that Steve might have painted that sky for me tonight. And as I receive my loved one, I feel him smiling, too. I am so blessed that he shares the things that lit up his world as I continue to walk on in mine.

I rest in the Presence as I allow this perfect life to show me the way to every sunrise and sunset. Life is for the living, so I might as well allow it in as I remember the love.

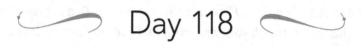

Day 118

Spirit Speaks

There is so much for you to see as you look into the eyes of humanity from your true awareness, where nothing is separate from you. Like the sunrise and the sunset, you are the one who waits patiently for your awakening. You do not have to fall asleep again when the world around you is unconscious. In your heart, you can choose to be fully aware of who you are as you stand in the center of yourself. And in each moment, as you look at past events, you would find the wisdom that helps you to see what is true.

Look at everything in your life as temporary. This changing world will continue to do so, yet the changeless self continues to connect you to what is true in every moment. The way you choose to trust yourself completely in life allows you to be in every moment without judgment. Judging is seeing things as right or wrong, good or bad, black or white. Be the witness of this ever-changing life you are a part of and know where you want to hang out.

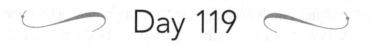

Day 119

The privilege of a lifetime is to be who you are.
— Joseph Campbell

Life goes on and now I feel I can grieve Steve without being stuck in the trauma of this death. My soul chose this experience, and now I will move forward in the light that has awakened me because I have gone through this pain of losing my alignment. I transition into the truth that I am worthy to have life. I don't have to dwell in the past. Today I choose to surrender to God's plan and trust that someday I will see it all.

I am alright. As the cloud lifts, I can return to my true self. I have compassion for my self-judgments as I make discoveries that help me evolve my soul. The deeper truths are inside as I am guided through life to be the best version of myself. I have faith in who I am.

I don't have to be afraid of being myself. I accept all of me, and I allow my true nature to come into the rhythm of my soul. I can feel my growing desire to begin again, to restart my life. God shows me the way and opens me up to this mission.

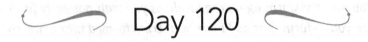

Day 120

The Well of Grief
Those who will not slip beneath
the still surface on the well of grief,

turning down through its black water
to the place we cannot breathe,

will never know the Source from which we drink,
the secret water, cold and clear,

nor find in the darkness glimmering,
the small round coins,
thrown by those who wished for something else.
                                            – David Whyte

I awaken to my darkness where I don't deny my ego while I take responsibility to feel my vulnerable heart. As I put my mind aside and choose to trust life, I let the projections dissolve and merge into the light that is always inside.

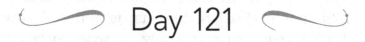

Day 121

Out beyond ideas of wrongdoing and rightdoing there is a
field, I'll meet you there. When the soul lies in that grass,
the world is too full to talk about.

— Rumi

As I move into my day, I am grateful for all that surrounds me. The sun gleams its brightness, and it is up to me to let it in.

Spirit Speaks

You are transforming on the inside as you wait patiently for it to change you in form. Just as I have been transformed into more, so are you. It doesn't have to continue to be so painful, even as the birthing of all forms stretches and expands your entire being.

These thoughts, ideas, and beliefs cannot live inside your head anymore. Here in my world of Spirit, they hold no validity. Let go of these beliefs that do not serve you. Allowing the mind to miraculously shift you is the most enlightening experience. Choose from the comfort of past ideas that are helpful and allow the light in. The love of your very being will shine around you as it becomes your power and your future.

Before I left my body, I was afraid of death. But when I first left my body in the hospital room, I walked around it and saw how damaged it was. I then went to the next level looking at all my mistaken beliefs that I was so caught up in when I was in physical form.

That's what meditation has taught you to do. You hold it all and

breathe in the spiritual Presence that gives you that calm feeling that
everything is okay. Everything is okay.

I let the light shine in on all that I am grateful for. Beyond all the ideas
and beliefs, I rest in the field where everything is okay.

Day 122

Some days I can barely get out of bed because the grief covers me
up and holds me prisoner. But most days I do something to move myself
forward.

Sometimes it is all I can do just to answer the phone. The phone that
now hardly rings. People get busy with their lives. I am sure the thought
of me passes through many minds, but life goes on.

How easy it would be for me to stay inside my house, shut the blinds,
and feel sorry for myself all day long. I try not to spiral into the big hole
of darkness.

If I feel like I'm heading that way, I call someone. In a holy instant,
the love of my children, sisters, and girlfriends helps me move through
the pain, tears, and heartbreak.

With constant awareness, I can face reality. Instead of avoiding suffering,
I seek to heal my emotional body. By feeling this suffering and accepting
where I am, I can live life to the fullest as I welcome the unseen.

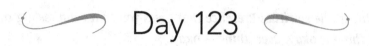

Day 123

Life goes on and even though Steve's death rocked me to my core, I don't have to dwell in the past. Today I choose to surrender to God's plan because someday I will see it all.

My Sweet Crushed Angel

You have not danced so badly, my dear,
Trying to hold hands with the Beautiful One.
You have waltzed with great style,
My sweet, crushed angel,
To have ever neared God's heart at all.
Our Partner is notoriously difficult to follow,
And even His best musicians are not always easy
To hear.
So what if the music has stopped for a while.
So what if the price of admission to the Divine
Is out of reach tonight.
So what, my dear, if you do not have the ante to gamble for Real Love.
The mind and the body are famous for holding the heart ransom,
But Hafiz knows the Beloved's eternal habits.
Have patience, for He will not be able to resist your longing for long.
You have not danced so badly, my dear,
Trying to kiss the Beautiful One.
You have actually waltzed with tremendous style,
O my sweet,
O my sweet, crushed angel.

— Hafiz

Day 124

It seems like a dream, very surreal at times and yet probably the most precious time of my life. I am moving through the darkest parts of myself. I am left alone with it all, even if there are others around me. I do not want to get out of bed, let alone make decisions about the house, bills, my life. I feel overwhelmed. Slowly, one step at a time, I muddle through the day gathering information and finding ways to get through it all without him.

It's not easy—but I do it and now my eyes are wide open. I see the strength that is given to me by all the angels on this earth and beyond. I learn so much about myself and grieving. I do it the best I can, trusting in all that is leading me from the inside. I allow Spirit to show me the way through this labor that truly births me into more consciousness.

I realize that I am awake right now. I am not separate from this living Presence that is within my awareness. My intuitive nature moves me into this limitless well of creativity. I am clearer. As I choose to partner with this energy that creates worlds, I unlock the door to infinite possibilities.

I appreciate all the moments that have brought me here. Now I can let go and open up to the brilliant life that is offered to me daily. I do not feel lost anymore and maybe that is because I let myself be in the valley of sorrow without being distracted from any of it.

Today I feel reborn and grounded with Spirit as I embody more of myself. I am willing to let God lead my way and partner with me fully. I choose to go out into the world to teach and share all that has been given through me and allow it to spill out in my daily living.

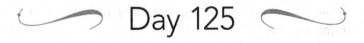 Day 125

At our death, all the defensive barriers that separate and exclude us from our presence fall away; the full embrace of the soul gathers around us.
                                        — John O'Donohue, *Anam Cara*

I am always walking beside you. I watch and I try to guide you in a way that might inspire you to think of me—never apart but free to let you be yourself. That's the way to live in heaven and on your beautiful Earth.

How wonderful that life was, but here you can't even imagine the beauty and the depth of the love that is always giving without conditions. It's so amazing how wise you become when you drop the body and the personality.

Here there is no ego, and every part of your life is shown to you like watching a great movie. It seems endless because each moment is like a hologram, and you get to choose to see different facets of it. Everything is shown to you by your guardian angel, and you get to learn from the choices you made.

There is no judgment or remorse. It's all like one great moment of healing. You realize all the moments were just for love—when you didn't get love, or you didn't give love. You have plenty of moments to learn about who you want to be the next time the choice presents itself. I didn't do so bad—I saw the good in all my actions, and I still see it in the eyes of all of you. When anyone talks about me, I get the love, and the insight touches all of us. That's a prayer in itself.

Day 126

Sometimes, in moments of deep gratitude, kneeling down
becomes an overwhelming urge, head deeply bowed, hands
before my face.

— Etty Hillesum

Time and time again, I choose to surrender to the pain and
suffering of my struggles. I know that as I acknowledge where I am
without analyzing it, slowly I can accept my human self with focus and

connection. The softness draws me closer into my tender heart where I open to the many possibilities that can and often are revealed.

Life is this interesting journey that takes me along the paths through both light and dark. I choose to stay in the center, ignoring the calls of outside sources that would lead me astray. Here the mind, with all its grandiose thinking, quiets and begins to balance into neutrality. Once again, I find myself in the arms of compassion that lift me into the unknown. I relish these moments where the veil between the worlds thins, and I hear the whispers of Spirit that guide me in ways only my heart can follow.

Oh God,
You walk into my heart when I least expect it, and I breathe deeply into this
love. There is nothing I deserve more than this.
Take me. Fill me. Show me the way to this life of Freedom.
Thank you

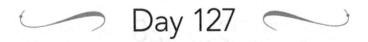

Day 127

You have to keep breaking your heart until it opens.
— Rumi

I am vulnerable. In these dark times, trusting myself, I surrender inside and connect with all that is lurking there. I hold what is troubling me and move into the truth that no matter what, I am worthy. Today I remember that I love you, and you love me, and everything else fades away.

Music always provides a channel for Spirit to move through, and as I listen to my sister Philomene sing, it opens me. I join in and it feels like chanting like I'm part of a choir. The song shifts me out of my resistance and cracks my guarded heart open.

As I move deeper into myself, I feel both sadness and joy. When I connect with the joy of union, I transcend time and space, and the love just gushes out through my tears. I sing louder. I welcome this healing of my restless heart as it is stilled and transformed through grieving and loss.

The song echoes in my heart as the muse. Each word brings me to feel what is here, just as it is. We all share in the troubles of the world as the voice of Spirit is heard through the music. It's all love.

Lyrics, "Her Muse," by Philomene Hoffman
Lilies grow where you walk. Sunlight burns bright through your smile, kisses the muse. Fingers dancing on keys—fingers, threads, feathers, dancing.
Debussy, I watch you rise, I watch you turn your face.
You're soft and shy.
Rest now. Lay with your sweet…grieving…Deep love. Deep love. Deep love.
I weep, my beloved…returning as true as fresh spring rain brings forth the new.

Day 128

What we have once enjoyed and deeply loved we can never lose, for all that we love deeply becomes a part of us.
— Helen Keller

Nature is my teacher and a constant reminder of who I truly can be. I have wept before the sunrise and sunset so many times. I have raged and screamed my hurt and pain when I have forgotten to breathe or have disconnected from this precious moment.

The world has brought me face to face with myself, and humbly I bow to nature as the earth grounds me into what is real. It is so easy to view my wounds as obstacles. I'm beginning to see the gift in the healing of it all. It has transformed me and shifted my thinking. The way of suffering has no meaning to me until I learn what the pain is here to teach me. It is such a mystery.

Life and death bring us to our grieving hearts. So many of us want to fix the pain right away, control it, avoid it, or somehow understand it. I walk around, day after day asking "Why?" I stay with the pain, knowing that it is not just mine, but also the pain of the world. With faith in the Divine plan, I let go so that I can move deeply into myself. The choice brings me peace.

Each day I have an opportunity to renew my sense of the sacred. Touching the wound of this great loss has brought me on this healing journey to transform my pain. I let go so that I can sit at the table and partake of life's smorgasbord. I can taste the nectar that nourishes my heart.

Day 129

Spirit Speaks

When you allow all the images of the past to flow through the heart and mind, you begin to soften and let go of all that is cluttering up your senses. This is the way to return to your innocence.

This is available to everyone if they can only allow the mind to stop its habitual, distracting chatter. Then you arrive right here in the center of being.

Your heart holds you and brings to you the Presence of all that exists. You connect to this Spirit within you that witnesses this world and sees the opportunities to begin again. This is true reality.

All that exists brings you to a starting point where life is anew. There is no past or future here as you drink in the moment of pure beingness. It all seems so simple, yet when you dwell in the ego, the mind continues to pull you away from the truth that desires to be revealed in all moments.

This is one moment expanding into the next without the resistance that holds back evolution. Even though the pictures you are looking at with your physical eyes seem the same, if you truly are letting go, the images are changing. You as the observer are witnessing creation at its very best. All that lives is for the good of all humanity.

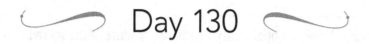 Day 130

You don't get to choose how you're going to die. Or when.
You can decide how you're going to live. Now.
— Joan Baez

When I take responsibility for everything that is happening to me in my life, I am no longer a victim. I don't have to stay stuck in the belief that life, as it seems, will keep me a prisoner and hold me back from living my life fully. These hurdles we encounter when we begin to move forward into life push us to learn more about who we are and what we need. This growth allows the new dream to fully materialize.

There are always challenges when we pursue our dreams. The struggle seems to come just before I feel ready to take that leap into the infinite pool of possibilities. All that life has brought me—the grieving, broken, humble heart—has left scars, yet I'm stronger in confidence and self-love. All the hurts and pains of life's circumstances have helped me to stretch and grow. I want to live now in this brilliant moment. So, with the fears and insecurities of my human self, I leap into the unknown.

As Gary Zukav writes in his book *Universal Human*, "There are no villains or victims, no right or wrong, no should, ought or must. There is potential. The power of creating our experiences in the Earth school is ours alone. It always has been. Now we know it."

Day 131

Embrace your grief, for there your soul will grow.
— Carl Jung

I navigate through this jagged terrain of loss as I welcome the companionship of love. My body is empty as my mind rests in the Presence. Here I am in the oneness of all creation where nothing is separate from me. I take the hand of Spirit and step into the unknown with faith. The voices of my spirit loved ones are speaking to me through the beauty and grace of all living things.

This connection to my inner strength is always here to guide my way. I can open as the light and love of my spirit loved ones support me in all kinds of ways. The spiritual journey is not just an individual one, it is also for the healing of our world.

Day 132

Your task is not to seek for love, but merely to seek and find all the barriers within yourself that you have built against it.

— Rumi

In a dream, I saw Steve in another dimension beyond our physical world receiving a back massage. I could see him with great clarity. His body was different—slim and strong—and he had no hair. His new body was illuminated and glistened in the light.

I stared into his face. He looked younger, more vibrant, peaceful, and happy. As I watched him getting his massage, he asked me to marry him. I woke up loving the feeling of being with him again but that quickly gave way to longing, and I started to cry. I spiraled into my attachment to him.

Steve was helping me address the need of the ego—the human desire to have a companion. Steve doesn't have that need anymore because he is in union with all creation.

As I process the dream, I see that it is telling me it is safe to open up to my feelings of arousal. It doesn't mean I should go out right now and get into a relationship. I'm just acknowledging that I am now a single woman who has desires. Steve cannot meet those needs for me, another man can.

When I move beyond my fears of unworthiness, I can allow a man to connect with me. Another man is Steve's light and love that never dies. It moves through all people and things. Sitting in my house isn't so lonely anymore. I can get back into the swing of life, allowing Steve's love to walk with me along the way.

Day 133

Spirit Speaks

The most incredible way to touch the world with this love is to be fully yourself, to allow your honest-to-goodness you begin the day. And when you have aligned back to the Source inside of you, your open heart expresses that love. Your open heart is hugging the world because you are in your true natural state of open-heartedness. It is the heart that knows that in this very moment you are the giver of life. It all spills out from your fullness.

Right now you are filling yourself up first. The more you give to yourself in total acceptance and unconditional love, the more you become the representation of what is true. It seems too simple, but it is all you need to do; heal yourself with all that is here, and you will share it naturally without any effort.

Be your own best friend forever, and then as you open up, you can love another with this same love—How great is that? How wonderful life in this world would be if everyone on the planet got this one great lesson.

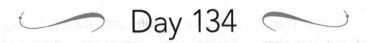

Day 134

Another day when the veil is so thin that God can reach right into me and wake me up to welcome all that is new. We can be led by our hearts without trying to figure it out with our heads. And then, bowing down to creation, it begins within.

Meditation

I surrender.
I let go.
I surrender my fear.
I surrender my guilt.
I choose to return
To this open and giving place
Where my truth moves me authentically
Beyond the conditional self.
I rise to meet my higher being
That shows me the way
To return to my pure beingness.

Day 135

I go to the market near my cottage in northern Ontario. I watch the world in all its busyness. Inside I feel myself, yet at the same time, I touch memories of Steve. He is with me, communicating with me much of the time. But in this moment, I long for him to materialize before me. Letting go, I look for him in all the ways he may show himself to me now. Slowly, I am finding out who I am without him.

Spirit Speaks

We begin to trust in ourselves more fully and take that leap of faith. It can be as simple as going out to a restaurant or listening to music instead of curling up on the couch and isolating from the world.

Someone sees you walking into the room alone and they are inspired to take your hand and show you that you are not alone. The welcome you receive is not planned or controlled. It just happens and you soften into the space within where you say yes to life.

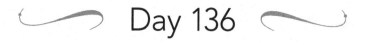 # Day 136

"...(E)ach telling seems to soften that edge, and she grows bolder. And with every story, a little more of her pain slips into that abyss and is absorbed. It turns out the void is not empty after all. It is filled with love."
— Mirabai Starr, *Caravan of No Despair*

Meditation

The mystery.
The unknown.
The uncertainty.
The abyss of nothing.
The way into this place breathes life and wonder.
When I embrace my fear of going here, the quiet stillness holds me tenderly.
The physical and emotional pain begins to soften as I let go of the past.
This journey to self-love is an ongoing adventure that brings me to a standstill.

A softening occurs where I surrender into that which has called me to be here.
There is a clarity in my mind where nothing pulls me away as thoughts fade.
I breathe into this heart that holds me like a lover.
Loving myself is never a burden.
It brings me to the Beloved.
The one that knows who I am.
To be loved just as I am even if I am sitting in these human conditions.
There, here, the light is gently moving me into awareness.
To be so present with what is.
I am the opening for truth to enter.
I have illuminated my mind and my heart receives the love.
This light is the door to everything.
I AM LOVE

I choose to surrender to the present moment.
I will lose and I will gain.
Yet the wisdom that my life of loss has brought me is contentment with Just Being Alive!

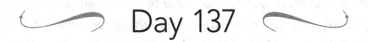

Day 137

Tonight, I'm getting dressed and even curling my hair. I stand in front of Mollie and ask, "How do I look?" Tilting her head to the left and then to the right, she looks at me with so much love. I melt. She probably wants me to stay home with her, which is our usual evening plan, but I'm going to listen to my son, Luke, perform at Banana Cabana.

As I drive down Gulf Drive, I feel different—a little vulnerable but stronger. I wish Steve was in the car with me and ask him for a sign to let me know he is here. I am greeted by the restaurant owners who seem happy to see me, and I promptly forget my request. "You really look wonderful tonight," Cheryl tells me. I think it's the first time she's seen me not covered in grief. I feel more alive and so happy to be there to listen to Luke sing.

After enjoying a delicious dinner, Cheryl puts a plate in front of me and says, "Here's a little dessert." I look down at a Peppermint Pattie. Cheryl confesses, "I've never bought these before, but for some reason I decided to get them and put them in the fridge." I exclaim with great excitement, "That is exactly what Steve used to do. He'd put them in the fridge and then eat one each night!" Tears roll down my cheeks.

He did it again. I asked, he answered.

Life, as it is, triggers emotions and feelings that can open the flood gates. If I can be aware that my loved one in spirit continues to be a part of my life, then I can allow the energy to move my emotions out, and I can welcome in the message from Spirit.

Day 138

Spirit Speaks

The words of encouragement are what you give to the world as the picture of heaven. Divine light and love touch this world through your living consciously with all creation, every living companion in form. So many of this world do not know how to commune with nature. It happens naturally when you come inside yourself and rest in your heart. Here the mind will be your servant and lead you in conscious living.

It doesn't have to look like the world is helpless. No one is. We are all just finding our way back to the true way of being in a body. As you know, you are here to forgive yourself. You did not let me down. I did not fail the test. I got my angel wings the moment I left my body. The light showed me the way so that I could forgive myself and all that was holding me back from knowing how worthy my life was.

It is extremely important to hold the weaknesses of the human condition but only long enough to breathe life into the moment. In doing so you become that instrument for yourself, which always is for others. Heal thy self and then your world becomes the picture of your heart's knowing. Love, love, love this life and fly free. You do not have to be perfect to share this message. Just let it be inside of you and then in your living consciously all will be a part of this union.

When I let the light show me the way, I can hold myself and humanity with compassion.

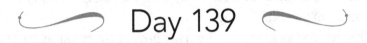 Day 139

You do not have to be good.
You do not have to walk on your knees
for a hundred miles through the desert repenting.
You only have to let the soft animal of your body
love what it loves.
                    — Mary Oliver, *"Wild Geese"*

As I look at my beautiful gardens and smell the jasmine's sweet scent, I am mesmerized by the color of the blooming red geraniums. The mockingbird reminds me that within us all we carry the songs of all humanity. Every part of the moment activates my childlike innocence where everything feels new—the first sight of beauty that creates and recreates for my healing heart. These little moments ground me in the present as each touch brings joy.

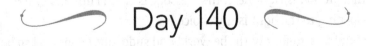 Day 140

You are like a snake trying to fit back into old, dead skin
or a butterfly trying to fit back into its cocoon. You look

around and see everything freshly, with the new eyes you
have earned for yourself. There is no going back.
— Glennon Doyle, *Untamed: Stop*
Pleasing, Start Living

Feeling miserable. Feeling anxious. I want to scream but don't have the energy. I can't escape.

The birds are singing too loud, and the trucks are moving down the street too fast. The sounds of this world feel like fingernails on a blackboard.

My mind is looping thoughts that don't even make sense. I take a breath but can't seem to break away from the obsessive thinking. Meditation isn't working today.

Then my dog looks at me, tilting her head in the cutest way as if she's saying, "Remember me? Get a life, Mommy!" She starts jumping around, chasing her tail, barking, and pulling me outside with her gestures. She sits facing the sun coming up over the fence, steadfastly staring at the light. It's as if she's saying, "There's so much to see but just be!" It's God using her; it's the Universe calling; it's Spirit showing me the way. I've spent so much time facing the darkness. Now Mollie is helping me face the light.

The sun's rays glisten on everything in this garden—even on me! I stand and turn my face to it.

I close my eyes and let the rays touch my skin and warm me like a lover's sweet smile.

There is strength in being broken down and fully immersed in these powerful feelings while knowing that God is right here beside me in all my human experiences.

Today the Universe moves me gently back into the driver's seat. Yet even though God is right here, the message is clear: I am on my own now. Opening to the light is my choice.

I stand face-to-face with the world and suddenly, I don't feel so bad. I can shift my mind and feel alive again. I can't fake it, but I can allow it in.

I take my paints and brushes and allow my creative impulse to express itself. Art carves the path for me to touch my inner spirit. Letting go of my mind, I listen to my heart. I am vulnerable as I allow my heart to break open and embody this energy that creates worlds. This is my act of devotion. Through this art, I bring the darkness into the light where the love fills and heals me.

I sit in the deep, vast valley of my grief. Sitting in my pain, no matter what I am doing, seems to be the new normal. Moment by moment, day after day, month after month, I stay with these raw, agonizing feelings. They are transforming me and shattering so many of the illusions of my past way of living. Surrendering into my feelings of despair and loneliness moves me out of the self that I was and into the new self that I am becoming.

I slowly let the outgrown parts of me fade away and allow the new self to emerge. In this love of self, I have confidence and wisdom. That is my essence illuminating me from the inside.

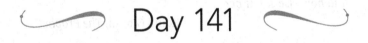

Day 141

May all beings everywhere, seen and unseen, dwelling far off or nearby, being or waiting to become: May all be filled with lasting joy.

— From Buddhist *Metta Sutta*

Meditation

If we could see
The whole truth,
We would know
That in any given moment
Thousands of spirits
Are departing the earth.

Deep within this space,
Their lights shine so bright.

Here I reflect on the absence
Of the ones that have left.
I let myself feel.
As my belly softens,
I accept my emotions.
The tears of sorrow
Turn into joy.

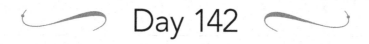 Day 142

Then a woman said, Speak to us of Joy and Sorrow.
And he answered:
Your joy is your sorrow unmasked.
And the selfsame well from which your laughter rises was
oftentimes filled with your tears.
And how else can it be?

— Kahlil Gibran, *The Prophet*

I traveled with my daughter, Lane, and my friend Kristine, to
Mexico, where Steve had lived, two months at a time, for many years.
He would make his home on the beach, putting up a tent and a place to
cook his food, diving into the waters to spear his dinner or trap lobsters.

His stories move through me now as I walk on the streets that
he traversed so many years before. He is here, guiding my way and
making his presence known. A man walking out of a restaurant shouts
at me, "You're looking good tonight!" just like Steve would say to me.
At the market, a vendor calls Lane "Princess," Steve's pet name for her.
We feel him with us. We know it within our hearts and open to the
beautiful ways that the spirit of our loved one enters our conscious
awareness.

On our last night, Lane, Kristine, and I share our final meal and talk

128

about Steve's upcoming birthday. Suddenly, I burst into tears. Feelings move through me like a tornado. Lane and Kristine reach out and touch me as we all feel the intense sadness of these months without him with us in his physical form.

How could I feel so much joy in one moment and fall into the deep pain of missing him in the next? The tears keep coming, choking me. I have these moments less often, but when they come, I offer no resistance. I let it all out. No judgment. I know that when I don't try to control the feelings moving through me, the despair will pass, opening space for me inside.

Kristine and Lane sit in silence with me and soon the love pours in. And then the waitress comes over and hands me an offering. "My mother always said that when we were sad, we should have dessert," she says while handing me a cup of chocolate mousse. As she wraps her smile and arms around me, I feel heaven speaking through her. I know within my heart that Steve used her to communicate that important lesson he lived by, "Dessert first!"

Day 143

When you give thanks for what you already have, the corresponding manifestation will expand and increase what you have. When you give thanks for what you don't have, as if you already had it, the corresponding manifestation will attract and create it into your life.

— Mike Dooley, *A Beginner's Guide to the Universe: Uncommon Ideas for Living an Unusually Happy Life*

Doors open and close all the time. Life presents us with one opportunity after another. We experience all kinds of loss in many different ways. When we stumble and fall, when we are stopped in our tracks by broken dreams, gratitude helps soften the blows and lighten the load of the burdens we carry.

All of life is sacred. When you can accept it, just as it is, you allow a space to open where you can find the good, the silver lining. It is my practice to seek out that good. Through moments of contemplation and meditation, I can become so anchored inside my inner being that when the feeling of fear arises in the present moment, I can see where my mind is attached. Then I can let it pass on by, just like the weather.

It's the grasping that creates suffering. When I recognize what I am attached to, I can free myself from even the most difficult situations. The negative mind wants to get into a loop that keeps us stuck in the fear of what is instead of participating in the flow of life. The soul accepts it all without pushing it away.

The first step is to express these indwelling thoughts of negativity in whatever way works and to decide to feel good by being grateful in the present moment.

Gratitude is a present that gets unwrapped the moment it is given.

 Day 144

Spirit Speaks

I am a part of this journey you are on. I am not gone. I am more than I was and not limited by my fears and beliefs of scarcity. I am full and aware of this higher life that desires to be created through all of us. Yes, all of us—the ones in spirit evolve just like you in body and of the earth. There is only one vast being of infinite light that will transform the world through connection and limitless loving, just as you have written before. Yet know it is not merely a thought; it will manifest through your desire to move on and share this gift with the

planet. This beautiful world will lift into another dimension bringing
all together in the one heart of God's omnipresence.

Oh, sweet precious love, do not fret about what is gone, relish in
this moment where we are together, completing this plan that brings
only more love into the world by choices and actions that bring union
to all.

I am here with you, never leaving you, so drop the notion that
what was is gone. I only know that the evolution of soul is why we
came together. It is the garment you wear as a human being who now
allows Spirit to fully guide your way as you let go of any doubt that
you are worthy.

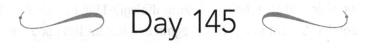

Day 145

Opportunities to find deeper powers within ourselves come
when life seems most challenging.

— Joseph Campbell

How easy it is to let the tears flow like a raging river. When they
come to the surface, I do not push them away. Messages of Spirit whisper
to me as the wind caresses my body and soothes my longing. I realize,
again, that when I am consumed by thoughts and feelings of missing
my husband, I disconnect from Spirit. As I allow my feelings to be there,
I am whisked away, joining with something much bigger than my little
human self. Everything around me joins me in this feeling of oneness.

I can receive the help I need to walk on my path today and every day
of my life. When I reach for God's hand, the energy that creates all worlds
participates in my creations. As I surrender into the moment and allow
the divinity of the One to know what I need, I receive assistance for every
problem, every question, every task.

Today let me touch these places within that call for my attention. My fear and resistance cause me to get in my own way. Let me trust that in God all things are possible.

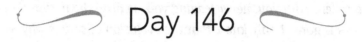

Day 146

Tears water our growth.
  – William Shakespeare

I'm hurt and scared, and I feel all the emptiness and loneliness. My thoughts come and go, echoing the same dialogue I have heard for all these months: "I want to touch him again and feel his lips upon my skin," "I want to wrap my arms around him and feel that feeling that no one else has ever given me," "I want to laugh and see the twinkle in his eyes as he shares a silly joke that is just between us." I want, I want, I want!

Through these months of grieving, I have learned that days like these are priceless gifts. I am learning that there is a peace that will come as I accept what life has exposed so intimately for me.

First there are tears, always tears. My needs aren't being met, so I am doing my best to figure it all out. And when I accept these tears, I find that the release they bring really does soothe my weary soul.

When I empty, I feel a freedom inside and a softer space within my heart. When I let myself just be here in this pitiful state of missing and heartbreak, I move into my own cocoon, wrapped up and sheltered in the moment that holds me.

I give myself permission to let go and just feel gratitude for my breath. As I sink deeper into my breath, I move deeper into myself. I relax and all the energy in my body that seemed so negative disappears.

I know the sun will come out again. Even if I don't see it for days, I still wait patiently for the clearing. Eventually, I will move back into the rhythm of life once again. All that I touch inside opens me to be touched by the love that echoes through my heart.

Day 147

Meditation

Unveiling all that cannot cover
Your true self any longer,
You let go into everything that is here.
Unconscious no more,
You use this precious time to awaken.
This uncomfortable place has brought you
Out of the deep sleep of separation.
Fear reminds you that you have forgotten this moment
When you get lost in the mind.
Breathe into the face of fear.
Look at it and turn away,
As you feel yourself drift back
Into the deep remembering of who you are.
It frees you once again.
This deep Presence invites you to listen
And shows you the way to a sweet intermission
That frees you from life's unbearable fear.
Here in this timeless moment, your little mind rests
As you sink deeply into the conscious field of nothing
Where all is calm.

Rest now as your focus inward is your devotion.
With unshakeable commitment,
You move from the inside to the outside

Remembering your true self.
Like the warming rays of sunshine,
You are a source of light in the world.

 Day 148

At the end of my life, with just one breath left, if you come,
I'll sit up and sing.

– Rumi

Sitting beside the bed of the dying, I see how quickly there is peace. Before they leave their body, the veil is temporarily lifted. I can feel it within me as soon as I walk into the room. It's as if you have one foot in this world and one foot beyond.

As I think back, I appreciate what we all may take for granted. I remember the last moment with my father. I knew he was dying, and I sat in the stillness of his bedroom. As I watched him in his comatose state, a hummingbird came to the window. To my surprise, he sat up and pointed to the bird that seemed to be bringing him a message and he whispered, "Hummingbird!" In the next moment, he returned to his sleep state. There was a peace that pulled me inside.

When Steve passed, I couldn't feel anything but the excruciating pain that I surrendered into. The moment the doctor came into the waiting room to tell me he was gone, I couldn't hold onto any little part of myself.

Yet, when I walked into the room with Steve's dead body, it was so sacred and holy. The room filled with this amazing feeling of timelessness. It is a peek into another dimension. The light is everywhere and there is a silence that speaks volumes beyond thoughts and images.

Day 149

We bereaved are not alone. We belong to the largest company in all the world—the company of those who have known suffering.

— Helen Keller

Death commands your attention. When someone goes away forever, you feel the depths of how much you loved them. There in the dark places that you avoided your whole life, you find the emptiness that comes in the silence. It contains your despair, your fears, and your deepest insecurities. But when felt without judgment, the space fills up with the immense beauty of deep, true love that links all beings throughout eternity.

Moving deep within the heart, we find strength because we remained fully here, because we did not run or leave. We allow the dust to settle as we take care of ourselves the best we can.

Step by step the truth makes its way back to our hearts. As we awaken, we remember that we are carried by an energy that does not die or ever give up. When we take the hand of Spirit and trust that life can be beautiful again, we begin to trust in ourselves more fully and then we find we are ready to take that leap of faith.

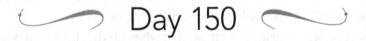

Day 150

The truest, most beautiful life never promises to be an easy one. We need to let go of the lie that it's supposed to be.

— Glennon Doyle, *Untamed*

When I allow my breath to lead me inward, it opens me and allows me to receive the energy of the present moment. The mind tries to pull me away, but my conscious breath keeps me on the path that leads me home inside my heart.

Living in the heart sparks a light that grows and grows with conscious awareness. This light knows where to go and enters the room before you. Following your heart will put you on the path to living in the light. Here there is no higher or lower. Just the birth of the true self from the stillness within the calm and peaceful waters of your true identity.

Walk in your ordinary world with your heart wide open and become the messenger of the light. Learn your life lessons and then share this wisdom that brings you out of darkness, secure in the safety you have found within.

Journaling helps me connect with my higher power as I let go of thoughts that keep me a prisoner of the past.

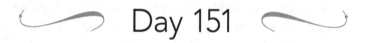

Day 151

Our heart gives us strength. Where we once felt weak, we find the courage to walk through our fears. As despair gives way, hope begins to shine through, and we find we can start to trust ourselves again. We re-enter the flow, this life-giving energy within that moves through us as we surrender to the incredible power that creates worlds.

Why do we struggle against what is when all that is created has been for our own evolution? It is all Divinely orchestrated to push us deeper into the knowing that we, as human beings, are worthy. Then we can perceive life through the lens of our inner vision instead of through the mind of the ego.

The heart knows the truth. So drop inside and feel what is lurking within the very depths of your experience, and do not judge what is. As you accept your humanity, you rise through the ashes of your past. Listen deeply and receive the truth that whispers within the stillness of being present.

Now that I am filled, I begin to serve that which gives me life. I discover who I truly am, content with everything as it is and not separate from the sacred. I have returned home, here within my heart. As I embrace the living expression of my being, the door opens, and I step forward on a path filled with new possibilities.

Day 152

The pain of a sudden loss can stir up something inside of us that is even stronger than the pain. For me, it was a strengthening of my connection to something more vast.

At first, it was Steve's spirit sitting beside me on my bed telling me that I was taken care of. His voice would ring through my heart urging me to write, but I would resist. I didn't want to see what he was showing me. I didn't want to let go of what we were together. I was angry and afraid to be left alone with everything we dreamt of together.

The pain and suffering were so great. I was in denial yet in the tremendous pain of grief. I was numb and could barely comprehend the reality that he was dead. The whole world around me faded away and became unimportant. I could not believe that the world had not stopped for this news of Steve's departure. I wanted to scream and tell everyone, "My husband is dead! Why aren't you crying like me?" Nothing could give me comfort.

As time moves on, I process my grief, which comes in waves of shock, guilt, anger, and depression. I let grief teach me what I did not know about myself and life and death. Though I've been surrounded by my children, family, and friends, this part of my journey must be done alone.

It's difficult to experience solitude for an extended period. Yet here I find the door that separates the world of yesterday from the life I now yearn for so deeply. With patience, I wait for the door providing me entry to serenity to open.

Day 153

I wake up feeling tired and sad. The feelings are very close to my throat as I walk into the kitchen this early morning. I walk hand in hand with myself, being mindful. It is a practice that keeps me present. As I open the fridge, the tears gently spill out of me. I wipe my eyes and take a breath, aware of each inhalation, each touch, as I accept every detail of my life in this moment.

Mindfulness is a way to bring loving-kindness to myself. Here in the kitchen, I bring awareness to the natural ways of my life. In the Buddhist tradition, we learn that we are in the center of our own circle. The space that surrounds us is sacred; we are in the center of one precious world.

As I breathe, something opens inside. Like a blessing, peace enters and begins to guide my way. I feel happier in this loving space within.

Meditation

Step by step,
Moment by moment,
Breath by breath,
I move into a quiet
That embraces everything.
I cannot find myself in you
Or in those things of the world.
I am the center of it all
Where everything is still.
I listen to the language of Spirit.
I hear the sound of nothing.
This silence is in between the words
And ideas of my mind.
As my heart beats in this sacred place
Within my inner being,
I can feel
The touch of love
That enters
When I stay with me.

Day 154

Spirit Speaks

I saw it all the moment I left my body—my mind joined with an intelligence that is beyond the human mind. This intelligence can be called soul, creator, God, Universal Spirit, or light. And with the joining, you return home to all that you were before you incarnated into form and all that is after you leave the form.

It is so expansive. All that you are is joined with every living thing. That is what the resurrection or ascension is, lifting yourself into the source where the feeling of oneness trumps every other feeling that you have as a human being.

You witness the spring as all living things renew and renourish—full of life, full of color. It is the expression of beauty that is in all living things. Here your heart receives the very nature of your precious being.

I take today as an offering from the Universe—from God—and allow life to lift me up as I share this feeling of oneness with everyone I meet. Most importantly, I give it to myself, for when I am filled and connected to the Presence within, all is shared through my connection. It is most natural for me to allow it to spill out like a waterfall—merging with every open heart that is ready to be filled.

Day 155

This whole gut-wrenching, tumultuous process has helped me to let go. When I can breathe deeply into it all, in the gap where I detach from my needy self, there is stillness. Here I can shift as I accept my human emotions and become the one holding the space for me. Maybe this is being awake? I feel my compassionate heart. As it wraps around me, I am struck by how familiar and intimate it all feels.

Spirit Speaks

You can hang out with me here or be in the place where you long for me as I was when I was in a body. Here with me, you are connected to so much more of yourself, the one that knows that you are free to just be in this sweet Presence where love emanates from your every cell. The path is in this. Every moment spills into the next moment, and this one sweet moment feeds not just you but everyone you are with. It's this connection to all that is that keeps you in union with the Divine.

Today I can let myself open to how the Divine Universe will meet me. I have prepared by breathing into everything that is showing up for me. I regret nothing, for it is another day to just be.

Day 156

There are only three things that last, faith, hope, and love.
— Corinthians 13:13

As I start over again after this loss—this incredible and unbelievable loss—fear speaks to me every day. It can paralyze my heart and stop me from taking action if I let it. Crippled by fear, I get stuck in thoughts that bring more pain and suffering.

But I can choose another path. I have faith that even when everything is falling apart, I will be okay. Despite the fear, I take a risk and leap into life again. As I move forward, putting my toe into the stream of life, the gentle current pulls me back into the flow. The part that is led by grief finally surrenders to my determination to live again and experience joy. Hope comes alive as I say "Yes" to life and love again.

This is what my life has taught me. Whenever I have encountered challenges—when I lost my health, my marriage, my loved ones, my home—faith asks me to take the risk, to keep my heart open, and to move into life, even if it means I could face the pain of grief again.

As I open, I receive the invitation from the Divine, who waits for my return, to love freely. God and grace only need my willingness to begin again.

Day 157

Spirit Speaks

There is so much to learn—I go to temple-like structures and fill myself up with knowledge. There is nothing to distract me, so I take it all in and absorb it. You would be so proud of me, understanding the true message of the soul and why we continue to make those same mistakes again and again until it finally sinks in that there is another way. Giving up the old way of doing things is like a death, yet it gives birth to the new.

The ego has no place here. You receive the higher vibration that gives complete reasons for "why," along with a profound knowing and understanding of the truth and wisdom woven into every second of existence.

I am happy here. I am beside you in ways that I could never be before. I can't change what you are feeling, but when you stay in the moment and move through the misery, I am here, sharing this energy with you, and it is enormous. How could you ever know this in the body? When you have the courage to touch it, you connect with it all and it's wonderful.

Day 158

I spin around and around in my mind until I surrender to what I am afraid to feel, which leads me to the quiet. My heart aches, yet I am centered inside myself. Acceptance is a beautiful gift I give to myself. True acceptance helps me trust the outcome. Then I get this clarity inside my mind as I let go into a vast opening of nothingness. I love the feeling of just being here. Then a clear voice begins to speak softly under the loud chatter and chaos.

Oh, sweet child! Just enjoy your precious life. Let yourself rejoice in the brilliance of the beauty of being here.

As I clear myself and breathe into my heart, I am safe. I don't need to protect my heart because it is fearless, it is strong, and, ultimately, selfless.

Through acceptance, I can powerfully change as the road I walk upon awakens me to a higher consciousness. The challenges can bring me to the gift of feeling liberated, free to contribute to my world.

Day 159

The human soul is to God, is as the flower to the sun; it opens at its approach and shuts when it withdraws.
— Benjamin Whichcote

In the light of the sun-filled sky or the illumination of the night by the moon and twinkling stars, I remember myself as I receive all that is within reach when I return to what waits for me inside. I rest in this heart that knows my longing for healing. There, even in these darkened times, I feel a force that calls me home to remember the light. Why do I forget? Why do I turn away? Why do I cut myself off from the truth that I am worthy, that I am born worthy?

When I touch these small parts of myself that feel withered and afraid, I can look outside this darkened well of grief. I do not stay in the shame of repeating the same habit of leaving the holy moment of my salvation. Instead, I reach in and touch the heart of the beloved.

The sweet arrival of the light seeps into the cracked places. I am grateful. What a blessing—to remember that my holiness saves the world. It moves inside me and fills me like the stars that guide my way through the darkness of the night.

Then along come my friends, my family, and all who walk with me. Together, we are blessed in this holy encounter by the endless love of our human souls.

I ask the Universe to tell me the story that is etched by the sparkling lights of the stars into the night sky. In response, she whispers:

Meditation

Be still beneath it all.
Reach out with your heart
And allow the expansion
Of your inner being
To touch the stars.
This is light that never dies.
Focus the mind
On the incredible emptiness
Within the vast ocean
That is the source
Of your spirit.
Rest here.
Settle in
And breathe.
This space
That calls you
To just be
Merges with the vibration

Of your soul.
What you hear out there
Is the sound of all your desires
Echoing in the chambers
Of all your yesterdays and tomorrows.
Right now, the infinite intelligence
Is creating a most beautiful life.
Live it and let yourself fall in love again.

 # Day 160

You never know which bye becomes the final goodbye…
— Sayoni Mitra

For years, I've had the privilege to sit beside the dying and be there for their transition. With Steve, the way he left me, so suddenly and quickly, I feel cheated. I couldn't say goodbye.

Moments before the doctor came out of the operating room to tell me he was gone, Steve's spirit came to me. Yet all I could say was, "Get back in your body! We have traveling to do and grandchildren coming!" I yelled at him, "Don't go, we have too much to do together!"

The speaker rang out with, "Code Blue! Code Blue!" as nurses and doctors ran to the operating room. I was watching it all like a movie. Minutes later, I heard, "Cancel Code Blue." Then the doctor walked through the door taking off his mask and shaking his head. Time slowed down; everyone moved in slow motion. "I am sorry; did all I could. I am sorry; did all I could," was all he could say.

I wish I had known that would be my final goodbye. I would have thanked him instead of responding from my terror, but I was too deeply wrapped up in the disbelief that he was leaving this world.

There is a mutual connection to our human suffering. As I lift my heart to touch all who grieve, I pray that we find each other whenever we are in need.

Day 161

Life is a series of natural and spontaneous changes. Don't resist them—that only creates sorrow. Let reality be reality. Let things flow naturally forward in whatever way they like.
— Lao Tzu

I sit at my writing desk and look outside my window. Nature is such a great teacher. As I look out, I see light reflecting on the branches and leaves as the wind blows through them. The leaves flutter and the branches sway while in their strength the sturdy trunks of these magnificent trees remain motionless.

In the next moment, it is gloomy. Dark clouds hang out at the horizon until darkness consumes the light. From moment to moment the view changes. Change is my steady companion.

Everything changes outside yet inside there is a constant Source that waits for our return. It's the peace beyond all understanding. Emotional turmoil and difficult situations—like the death of a loved one, a sudden illness, or unexpected job loss—can cause us to disconnect. We shut down and block the light of our spirit from our heart.

At these times, it's all I can do to sleep and feel my vulnerable self. Yet, I wake up each day and allow my connection to God to guide my way. I listen deeply to the voices until the one that will guide me home to my heart is louder than any other.

This connection to Spirit brings me deeply into the stored hurts and pain. I cry for losing Steve. I cry for all the broken dreams. I cry until I cannot cry anymore. It opens me to feel the anger, the resentment, the hate, the disappointment, the jealousy, the weakness—all the ways I hold fear inside me. I walk through the valley of darkness where I am broken wide open.

This journey called grief brings me to everything that needs my kindness.

Day 162

The bad news is, you're falling through the air without a parachute. The good news is, there's no ground.
—Chögyam Trungpa Rinpoche,
Tibetan meditation master

Under the beautiful, dark, starlit sky, I stand in the stillness inside myself and the everchanging landscape of my life. Captured in the deeply woven tapestry of my inner being are the threads and fibers of all the loss, chaos, and darkness. I am the weaver of my life.

The emotional part of me has allowed me to receive and participate in this union I have with Spirit. This beautiful conversation I have with the Universe has been born through my letting go of attachments to all that has come and gone.

Sometimes my ego gets wrapped up in its insistent need to figure it all out. My spiritual practice frees me from its hold and allows me to release, heal, and grow. Through love's betrayals, dreams ending, loved ones dying, children and elderly crying, animals unprotected, illnesses and injustices, and on and on, I continue to let go, so I can welcome what exists in this precious now. Here I melt into myself and allow my heart to join with you, my fellow human beings.

How incredible it is to sing the praises of the Universe that invites us to stay awake as we let go of all we think we know and intuitively live from this passion of being alive. All of life is here to dance in Divine Oneness.

I let the ease of my vibration weave in harmony with all that is designed for the highest good of all.

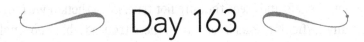

Day 163

Spirit Speaks

Just close your eyes and feel me touching you with a smile or a sound of this world where heaven and earth dance together in a union that is quite spectacular.

Yes, missing what we were can keep you in trouble—entwined in the past and hurting with all that can't ever be. I cannot think of anything more lovely than being with you again and again.

This is all that we have now. For always I will be dancing around you, waiting for you to notice me here with you. I understand your longing, and I hold you until the tears wash away the pain and bring you back to where we can commune.

Messages from my loved one will come when needed. I trust in the signs that come as I open my eyes to see you in this world, expressing love in all kinds of ways.

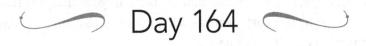

Day 164

We can make ourselves miserable or we can make ourselves strong. The amount of effort is the same.

> – Pema Chödrön, *When Things*
> *Fall Apart: Heart Advice for*
> *Difficult Times*

I could not fake it. Deep inside my cells, underneath my personality and belief system, I have wounds that have traumatized me and have kept me in a fight or flight pattern most of my life. My diseases and illnesses are symptoms of my disconnection from my true power.

This power, so full of life itself, is stagnant at times, stopped by unconscious beliefs and ideas that are not true. Even though we may not recall many difficult events in our lives, these traumas, big and small, can remain as negative energy stored in our cellular memory.

We do none of this consciously. This is why we get triggered by the world we live in. It is not because we have seen some truth. What we feel is a projection of our suppressed inner reality. We get triggered and want to blame our pain on something or someone outside of us. It can be difficult for us to wrap our brains around the truth. Yet we can instead take responsibility for our reality, and the moment we do, we see ourselves as we are.

Day 165

Grief and gratitude are kindred souls, each pointing to the
beauty of what is transient and given to us by grace.
— Patricia Campbell Carlson

I walk down the street by my house, and as I check inside, I feel a sense of freedom building. I receive this beautiful evening, aware of how wonderful it is to be here, right now, connected to the present moment.

As people pass by, it feels like the whole world is bringing me into a giant embrace. I'm not left out, and neither is anyone else. We are all here, walking on this earth, experiencing pain and pleasure… In our humanity, we are all the same.

I let go of any need to change anything. I am willing to sink into this moment and welcome all the new possibilities that emerge.

Day 166

She was no longer wrestling with her grief, but could sit down with it as a lasting companion and make it a sharer in her thoughts.

— George Eliot, *Middlemarch: a Study of Provincial Life*

We go along in our lives, one step at a time, one day at a time until without warning life takes an unexpected turn. It feels like a sudden slap in the face or bonk on the head, or perhaps it's more of a subtle trembling deep inside that you can't put your finger on. But it gets your attention because this is the time; now is the time to open your eyes and your heart to the truth.

This moment, like a storm that comes out of nowhere on a perfectly sunny day, offers the opportunity to be grateful that you breathed into the warmth of the sun while it was there, that you could receive all it had to offer until it wasn't there anymore. Life happens, and it doesn't always leave a good taste in your mouth. Sometimes the lingering blow, the change, the death of what was, shatters the illusions. Once broken, these illusions can dissolve, and the clearing can begin.

The mind—so eager to give its opinions, its defenses, its logic, its story—will try to run the show until you surrender and let it all go. When you choose to move past the noise and insanity of the mind, you find the door to stillness. Here the quiet of the moment offers you a breath of fresh air. As you take it in, the space inside softens its hold on the past and what was.

I sit inside myself in the sweet aftermath of the latest storm. As the light shines through the blinds in the kitchen, I take a bowl of hot soup and place it in front of me. The taste, the smell, the feel of this food nurtures me. It is simply the moment giving to me the truth of what is right here.

Day 167

Meditation

I pause and enter inside.
All that I am
Is worthy of my tenderness.
I soften my heart
As I hold all my bitterness and resentments.
I allow the healing grace of the Universe
To comfort me.
I release the trauma and its shock
From my body and mind.
I accept the growth
That this deep sorrow offers me.
I stand at the doorway
Of new beginnings
With my vulnerable heart wide open.
I am rooted and grounded in knowing
Who I am as I enter my new life.
I see the smiles of others loving me
As the beautiful colors of this world
Speak to my heart.
I am here,
Just as I am.

As I accept and love myself no matter what the conditions are in the external world, I choose to be kind. I stay here in my calm and peaceful nature. My heart is wide open as I walk in my ordinary world.

After despair, many hopes flourish. Just as after darkness,
thousands of suns open and start to shine.

— Rumi

When I miss someone, when the longing and attachment stop me in my tracks, I try to remember to breathe into the moment. Here, within myself, I can return to my spiritual path where my connection to Source reminds me that I am not alone. God is right here and enters my suffering.

As I soften, all that feels bad and wrong is embraced. I hold myself on my lap like I would a child. I do not judge. Instead, I hug myself tight and hold these feelings until there is no doubt inside that I am worthy to be loved.

It's an inside job as I soothe myself. I open to all the ways I block myself, how my heart closes me off from receiving this Presence that creates worlds. In this quiet moment of grace, I love who I am right now. I refuse to punish myself for any weakness or for when I think I have failed. I feel transformed in the moment, and now I can go into the world with an energy that lights up with happiness.

I am free when I tell the truth and touch the shadows that follow me wherever I go. The very weakness of my human frailty can bring me strength when I admit that there is nothing wrong with me; I am just human.

Day 169

I have shifted back into a place where I once again appreciate the beauty of life. It is a gift from the Universe. If everything I need is within me, then the Universe must be expanding by leaps and bounds.

Slowly I let go of my little mind and join with the bigger mind of Spirit where Steve now resides. I'm still dancing with him and allowing him to partner with me. I am guided to look within, into the vast ocean of Presence that is beyond my thinking mind. With my heart leading, I let go.

Spirit Speaks

Can you hear the music all around you? It's not magic, it's real and it's because you are choosing to listen to the sound deep within.

There will always be doubts from the ego perspective, but at this moment you have joined with where I am, and that feeling frees you to let more love in.

I look upon the beauty of this life, then all I want to do is fly away like the geese heading south. Perhaps I feel guilty taking in something other than the darkness of my lonely nights. Who am I to finally wake up? I am awake inside the miraculous dimension of being.

Day 170

I can see clearly that the old maxim There are no accidents in this universe is a truism that applies right from the moment of our creation, and way before that as well. In an infinite universe there's truly no beginning or ending. It is

only our form that is born and dies – that which occupies
our form is changeless and therefore birthless and deathless.
  — Wayne Dyer, *I Can See Clearly*
Now

As I wake up today into the aches and pains of a body that worked for hours lifting and cleaning and clearing out the front flower beds, I breathe into what continues to exist as Presence. The energy welcomes me back home to my heart where I receive myself just as I am.

If there are no accidents in this universe, then Steve's death was part of the plan. And by that, I mean the death of his body here on Earth, for Steve in spirit continues on. This morning, as I was waking up, I could feel him in my expansion and hear him with my heart. In every cell of my being, I know that he is still on this journey with me.

As I moved rocks and weeded, I realized that originally, it was Steve who had made and maintained these gardens for me. How happy he is to watch me take an interest in it again. For months, I could not see the beauty in it because my vision was masked by my pain of missing him. Now the energy is flowing again as nature calls me to cut away the old dead vines and make space for new life. There is a calling from inside that carries me and guides my way.

Today I look at the whole picture, witnessing my own spring. I am blooming again. There is energy flowing and moving me into this life that is coming to me.

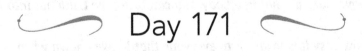 Day 171

God leads me to still waters that restore my spirit.
  — *Psalm 23*

At times I feel like I'm in a vast field, lost and alone. Somewhere in the distance is the path for the next part of my journey, but here the path is covered by pain, deep pain.

The experience of Steve's sudden passing was almost too unbearable to wrap my brain around. The shock of it all stopped me in my tracks.

Yet somehow, I am guided to an opening where God is in the rhythm between the pain and movements forward. With grief as my teacher, I listen to my body and trust my intuition. I can see the wisp of an opportunity rising through all that covers me up.

By honoring what is true, I am guided to live more authentically. Opening to joy takes courage. I can let the fear of what might happen hold me back or I can follow my deep inner calling and listen to what feels true. I will trust what rises within.

Day 172

Spirit Speaks

There is so much to tell you. Let me feed you with information from this other world that I am now a part of. I know you must grieve what we once had. But know that as we write together, we are allowing the love that has always been to join us once again.

Maybe this is not what our human selves wanted but our souls do, and now that I am not in a body, you can bring the truth out into the open.

How easy it is to speak to everyone that I have known when I was in a body. Yet it is difficult for others to open to who I am now. It becomes familiar once you drop the earth suit and step into the lightness of being.

I give you this energy that you receive and interpret through your heart, and away we go into the new relationship. There is no pain here and no complications. It just is. How easy it could be for us all if more were open to this way of sharing. Trust in it.

Meditation

Let yourself relax into this moment.
Hold yourself without fixing anything.
Let yourself meet the unknown.
Allow the Presence of your spirit loved one, your angel
To be here.
Let this love that is so vast
Enter your heart
As you welcome this moment.

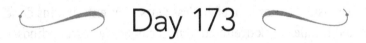

Day 173

I feel cradled by a feeling; the touch of lightness enters me like a gentle breeze of cool air. There is space inside me, and as I feel my feet on the dock, my whole body begins to vibrate with energy. Everything outside of me is illuminated, even my hands and the words I am writing. Expanded and filled with light, I hear a noise behind me from a crow as it lands on a nearby post. This messenger continues to speak to me, and I feel myself here yet touching beyond this world.

I have been wounded. My broken heart searches for a word or thought that will act as a salve to ease the aches and pains of being left behind. I listen as Spirit paints a masterpiece for me, bringing words of wisdom, creating ways to express these feelings of connection that feed my soul.

This voice of my soul speaks louder in the stillness. In this quiet place deep within, there is a knowing that rises to the surface. Here, in these empty chambers, I am filled with Presence. I am so calm and full of lightness. This place is where I know I belong.

The bottomless well of grief has become a deep canyon for love. As life goes on, it continues to birth the beauty of creation. My loved one in spirit is a part of everything that is.

Day 174

It's enough to take the day as it comes, to watch the ripples on the lake as the rock sinks to the bottom, to see the wild reflection of the surface calm into a mirror once again.
— Danna Faulds, *Go In and In: Poems from the Heart of Yoga*

I sit at the end of the dock like countless times before. I take a breath and move inside to that well of endless tears. This entering inside seems gentle and fragile. I look around and notice how my surroundings—the gentle wind etching ripples onto the still water—reflect my need for calm. I'm comforted by all that is familiar as nature shows me that life is moving on. I gaze out at the water and feel Steve's presence touching mine. As two swans join me in front of the dock, I feel my mom and dad in spirit. Like swans, they were mates for life.

I have so many memories of mornings when Steve greeted me like sunshine. His sweetness touches me this day as I sit and rest in his loving embrace. From my heart, I express: "When I think of my life with you, I wished I would've kissed you more, said. 'I love you' more, touched you more. I always thought we would have our whole lives together."

Here I am, a widow at this early and unexpected time of my life. I thought we would be together for the rest of my days—mates for life. Now that the form has changed, I am beginning to discover this life without my beloved husband. My journey brings me to the beloved inside.

Just as the swan moves on, I move on into this day. I watch it all like a movie. I witness my life unfolding as my heart opens to what will be.

Day 175

Yesterday is history. Tomorrow is mystery. Today is a gift.
That is why it is called the present.

— Alice Morse Earle

Life comes crashing down around us and the only way to stay steady is to be completely connected to the present moment. With all the insanity of the crazy mind and fearful feelings, we must find our way into the center of all that seems to be moving around us. Everything is temporary, even the so-called struggles and crises. Somehow, we always return to what is true, which for me is my connection to Source. When the time is right, life settles and becomes the firm foundation that we walk upon.

Meditation

Light wants you to touch
It's gentle and illuminating presence.
As you enter the center
Where the Universe lives
And breathes you into creation,
This moment in time
And everything outside of you
Becomes a distant echo
Of a life lived and dreamed.
As it all falls away...
Let go of what was.
Open your heart to the One,
Connect with the luminous being
Always here
Awaiting your return.

We walk on in our lives the best way we can, looking forward instead of backward. The past is history, the future is mystery, and all we have is in the present moment. That is why we call it a present. We unwrap the gift, and we begin to see that God's plan is so much better than our own.

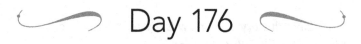

Day 176

When great souls die, the air around us becomes light, rare, sterile. We breathe, briefly. Our eyes, briefly, see with a hurtful clarity. Our memory, suddenly sharpened, examines, gnaws on kind words unsaid, promised walks never taken.

—Maya Angelou, "Ailey, Baldwin,
Floyd, Killens, and Mayfield"

My memory heightens as I feel the gentle nudge of my deeper self that never stops trying to get my attention. I remember all the times my fear would sit me on the couch wanting me to leave Steve. How easy it would have been for me in my emotions and hurt feelings to just run out the door!

Instead, I would pray for help. I'd sit in my angry, sad, and dark feelings—feeling victimized and forgotten. I would meditate until my quiet mind became a sacred place to just be. My breath brought me to my own careful attention, and instead of being on autopilot, I put my ego aside. I would remember the stories I had made up in my mind and return to my heart. Somehow, I would let go of control. The need for control happens automatically when I'm afraid. The control that has been projected on me when I felt insecure and weak by my brokenness.

So, I would sit in that fight or flight feeling, the feeling that would make me want to pack my bags and run away. But life had brought me back to the couch and I would listen to the voice that wasn't my fear, and I would listen to that silence that engulfed me, and I would listen…

A voice louder than my fear would say "Stay Frannie! It's okay. Stay and love like never before. Love yourself like you are the one that knows how worthy you are."

So, I would surrender. I would crawl back into bed. I would bring my body closer to him, and I would wrap my hand around his hand, and he would soften. He would remember how worthy his life was too!

I'm happy I stayed through those hard times. It taught me that love was greater than the pain, and I wouldn't lose myself, I would find the part of me that remembered how precious this life is. Together we would merge in the light and trust each other. Steve had another chance to feel what was inside of him and trust that I would stay because I let go and surrendered to my heart again.

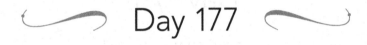

Day 177

Spirit Speaks

You are beginning to let go of the shackles that have kept you a prisoner of pain and suffering. I am watching you always and helping you see your world in ways that are magical again.

How different I am now that I have let go of who I was. I see so clearly all that I came to earthly form to learn; my efforts to clear my unwanted fears of unworthiness.

What a journey I have been on since I left the physical world. It is the greatest adventure remembering the truth as we all know it, the truth that is planted in the center of all our hearts. As soul, we have so many opportunities to evolve, to become the master of our own life. Yet the ideas we hold onto that others have passed onto us as children imprison us.

I realized the moment I left you that the lessons you learned helped me more than you can imagine. I began to see it all from a higher perspective where I didn't have to search for answers. I didn't have to battle with ideas that kept me in fear. I was free and able to hear it all.

This knowingness is instantaneous. Information just flows to you. As the saying goes, "Ask and you shall receive."

Well, that's the very truth of the matter. In your asking, you are receiving, and it is all given. It fills you up with more light, and you begin to soar as you become one with everything. I understand it all now—the love that we shared was the doorway into heaven. You see, my darling, the love people share unconditionally is the way into the greatest love that is so beyond the physical world. It's so enormous and vast that it cannot be contained in just one individual. That is why we have each other. Everyone is a part of it.

 Day 178

...though we seem to be sleeping, there is an inner wakefulness that directs the dream and will eventually startle us back to the truth of who we are.

— Rumi

I rolled over in the night, aware of Steve in the bed with me. He reached his arm across my body and wrapped himself around me just like he used to. Then he kissed me ever so gently on my cheek. It felt so real that for a moment I questioned if he was gone. He was so alive. I wanted to stay asleep.

I woke up in the morning remembering my dream. I loved the feeling of being in bed with Steve again. When we are dreaming, our subconscious thoughts and memories come to the surface. The subconscious draws on the symbols that already exist to guide us into the deeper parts of self where we can begin to understand our hidden feelings.

I interpret the dream and allow the symbols to bring this message: When I felt the heaviness of Steve's body wrapped around me, I was connecting with the heaviness of Steve in a body. When he kissed me on the cheek, I allowed myself to move through my body into Spirit where my inner self opened into the true reality of Steve—now lighter, clearer, not heavy but free and illuminated.

It shows me that I want to connect and be guided. I don't want to be distracted by the ego's dramas. When I'm connected, I am not in suffering. Here I feel Steve, and I know that it is only his body that died.

Dreams are a way for Spirit to guide me into a higher truth. I open myself to remembering the message sent from my unconscious to my conscious. Deep inside I receive everything I need so that I can let go of the past. I receive my loved one who has moved on in spirit, and I remember the love that never dies.

Day 179

As I dance around this moment like a whirling dervish, my breath becomes a natural tranquilizer. Though there is so much to do and think about doing, I simply breathe; I listen and allow myself to just be.

The pressures of this world will continue to push on me to keep spinning outside of myself. But if I choose to listen, I can instead follow the sweet sounds of nature that call me to take refuge inside my longing heart.

There are so many rooms to sit in as I enter my sanctuary. With my body as my temple, I enter gently and lean into any resistance that calls for my attention.

I breathe.

I listen.

I allow it all to bring me to the threshold. And I wait. That's oftentimes the hardest thing to do—to wait and trust.

As I gaze at the walkway through my butterfly garden, I see that it needs my attention. It's covered with weeds, which obscure its beauty. At that moment, I realize that I am like my garden. The masks I wear shroud the truth. Left unattended, the coverings will cover and hide my true self. So, I enter within.

I breathe.

I listen.

I allow myself to let go of doing.

I feel the impulse to jump up and start weeding but let go of this distracting thought and focus on all that calls me inside. The mockingbird serenades me as I join with all the new growth and refreshing colors that are the harbingers of spring.

Death and renewal are constants on this journey. As I move through these experiences, I have learned to be patient with the ever-changing cycle of seasons. I take time to appreciate what is happening now, like the new leaves of the trees that bring shade and birds that sing the praises of the universe, just to celebrate this day.

My old ways and patterns
Not making the right space for me.
Tired, letting go of my pain,
Without seeing the light again.
Said I'm doing my best, doing my best,
So, where's that final resting place?
Cause I need a little peace of mind,
I need a little time to shine.
Cause I've been working hard enough,
So, God, give me that stuff…
I could use a pat on the back once in a while.
I'm staying safe, staying sober. It's time for me to shine, it's over

Oh, oh, I'm gonna celebrate.
Oh no, not gonna wait.
Gonna scream from the top of my lungs.
Here I go, it's my show,
Celebrate!
                    —Celebrate, music and lyrics by Luke Andrews

Today is for me as I take baby steps to move forward. From the inside, I follow Spirit's lead. I know God loves me. As I've said before, this journey I am on is to love myself that much. We might know this in our minds, but is it how we live?

Our hearts reveal all the false beliefs we hold onto that make us feel unworthy. It is where we hold the old injuries that keep us repeating these patterns of lack and negativity. Our cells hold the memory of traumas and the energy of these untruths.

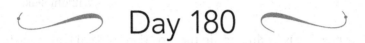

Day 180

I wake up this morning and go right into meditation. I close my eyes and breathe into the sweet feeling of the light. I see Steve's hand reaching down—my heart grabs hold, and I am lifted into the space where he is now. The ego takes a hiatus, and I am free to just be in the lightness of my mindlessness. I see a vast, clear blue ocean that reminds me of the waters surrounding the Abacos Islands in the Bahamas—the last trip Steve and I took together a year before he died. Then I receive this message:

Spirit Speaks

That's the wonder of this life that was! Now you can see it all with your heart as wisdom and truth are reflected all around you. So much happened that week. Remember when I hugged the owner of the house we stayed in after he told us about his cancer? We all teared up. I connected deeply with his pain and fear of dying.

My hug had been so meaningful for him, and so full of life. And he had given me the gift of truly remembering the preciousness of life. I gave him my support and love, while he helped me touch my fear of death. His life experience impacted me deeply. I remember saying goodbye wondering if we'd ever see him again. How shocked he was when you called just a year later to tell him that I had died. Another reminder of how precious life is. So today, my sweet, you are here to receive the world and your life. Don't take this day for granted. Bless it and allow it to show you the way to more life.

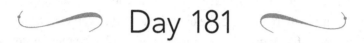

Day 181

In the universe, there are things that are known, and things that are unknown, and in between, there are doors.
— William Blake

This new life is leading me in the direction my soul wants me to go. Now, inside myself, I focus on everything that's been calling for my attention to be felt and seen—no distractions. I've been forced onto a new path, a path that will lead me to the safe place inside called home.

Like a revolving door, I move around in the center of the circle of life. The conditions of this life create another opening for me to rise and walk through. I can keep walking in circles with my mind attached to the fear of breaking free. Or I can be reborn in this body and embody more of the self that wants to live in sweet company with my awakened being.

Spirit Speaks

There is no fear of death as being an ending, only an opening into a new adventure where you can see like a child—excited for this life to be an expression of living deeply in love, whole and complete.

New doors are opening. Again and again, I am choosing to connect to the guidance of Spirit.

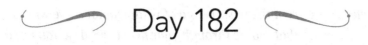

Day 182

It is impossible to live or die without God, but it is not impossible to think that you are.

> — Neale Donald Walsch, *Home With God*

Over the years, meditation has become my favorite and most-used tool to help me move into a quiet stillness where I anchor in the knowing that there is no death. When we drop these bodies, we will join with more of who we are.

The moment I let go of my attachments to this world, I am free to allow all that is so vast to come into me. This love wants to live through me. This love accepts all of me. In this space, anger, anxiety, depression, insecurity, and fear have no hold on me anymore. I become fearless as the courage to live rises up and brings me into a state of Presence that humbles me.

Even loss leads me home to my heart. If I can respond now to the present moment, then I can choose to be happy and joyous again. This is my true nature. Like an innocent child, I can spin around and around in the stillness within. There is the knowing that all is well here; I am taken care of. Here in the center of me, I am free to be all that I am. No one can take this power away from me.

Day 183

Meditation

Be still and breathe into this moment when you awaken to the beauty that illuminates you from the inside. Be aware of what is present within as you accept yourself just as you are. How worthy you are to be held in this Presence that loves you unconditionally. Give yourself to this moment and let the healing waters that flow through

you release you from the past. Let go of what cannot serve you as you accept the truth that moves through your heart this day. You are a child of God, worthy to be loved and to love.

Today is filled with promise. Stay here and drink yourself in as you are filled with the spirit of life that moves through you with or without your conscious connection. This love is in all creation, and as you join within, you are joined with all. This power does not take; it gives from its fullness and shares the eternal Presence of the Divine. This place of well-being is in the center of your heart as you receive yourself fully.

Be yourself. Now fully receive the gift of this beautiful life that is the beloved. You are incredible. This life that lives within you and all around you inspires and creates. As you move into your world, open your eyes, and stay right here giving and receiving this love that has no conditions. Now move from the inside to the outside and allow this light to illuminate through your living. You are free to be fully here, intoxicated with the beauty of Divine love that is reflected in the world that surrounds you.

Day 184

The body will again become restless
Until your soul paints all its beauty
Upon the sky...
For when the heart tastes its glorious destiny and you
awake.

— Hafez, *"The Lute Will Beg"*

When I give myself over to the moment just after waking, it sets the tone for my entire day. This habit is healthy for me. It has sustained me through all the emotional ups and downs of grief.

I arrive inside as I let go of all that my mind wants to pull me into. I scan my body from head to toe and give myself my complete attention. I notice every pain or area of congestion with acceptance. By acknowledging myself as I am, I connect. I become the doorway into a vast inner landscape. There is no time here. Whether I spend five minutes or five hours in this connection, I release what had been held here by feeling it. As I move deeper, I am with the range of all emotions and energy.

In this moment of moving inward, I peel away the layers of ideas, beliefs, and attitudes that are not my identity. I discover my Divine essence, and it begins to show me what I truly am. I'm okay, safe in my humanness with all these human conditions. I acknowledge my resistance, and I relax. I let go and trust the Universe. I am immersed in something deeper. It feels good to just be here now. I become a finely tuned instrument, sensitive to the needs of the moment. I am awake.

I rest in this nothingness where love finds me and expands me into so much more. It's the greatest gift I give to myself. It's pure heaven as I express my heart and soul, then go out to serve others. I can only serve when I am filled up from my own inner well. Taking care of myself truly has been the greatest gift I give myself and this world.

Day 185

Spirit Speaks

This loving self is the ultimate ticket to heaven on earth. With self-love, you can love everyone and every part of creation. As you allow this love to spill out of you, you feel the union of all souls. That's why I loved to go on the boat and fish. The feeling was expansive and always brought me to myself. That's who I needed to love and accept.

When we accept our insecurities and the dark places in our character, then life gets easier. No hiding from yourself and nothing to hide from anyone else. Life becomes so authentic and true. An ordinary

day is filled with the blessings of the Universe. You have found your
freedom and that freedom is within.

I am now free because I don't have to hide anymore. Everything
gets found out—it's the greatest law of the universe. And when no
one hides, when everyone tells the truth, then the heart gets so full, it
expands to give to every living thing.

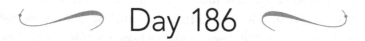

Day 186

At times it can feel like the sadness will never leave. Yet through it
all, we can continue to touch Spirit. Slowly, as we start to connect with
a power greater than ourselves, we find we can let go of the things that
hold us back as we go through the pain and accept it.

To live awake is to choose to be here in it all. As you stay focused
inside, you are transformed. You take your gaze away from the external
and you lean into it all.

Then, without doing anything to fix it or change it, your body
becomes soft. You drop in and notice you're out of fight or flight. Your
mind is quiet, and your heart is open to let in the new. Now you can be
childlike, innocent yet full of wisdom. It all is seen, heard, and felt with
every part of your humanness. You join with your soul and there is no
separation. You are here, one with all creation.

Then you feel the warmth in the room as you sense your loved one
in spirit who is there in the Presence to keep you company. You wonder
if it's all real—the dreams that hold a message or the experiences that
open your eyes to the love that is everywhere. The gift is in knowing that
the relationship with the one who died is different now but continues.
Somehow this new reality brings comfort. Every part of you is worthy to
be held in this acceptance. Every part of you!

As I enter inside, I am quiet and willing to see all that is revealed. I am
not hiding this brilliant light that desires my full attention. I dance with

this partner I call God, Divine, Universe, and let myself be taken into the arms of complete love. I welcome the Presence of this new relationship. My loved one in spirit wants me to listen.

Day 187

Meditation

Quickly step into the now,
For all you have
Is this precious moment.
The busy world has woken up,
Reminding you to
Let it all take you home.

As it lines up.
It becomes more.
You are never truly separate
From anything or anyone.

Here you are,
Entering into that
Which goes on and on.

It is so freeing
To let go
And allow your life
To show you the way
To more life,
To more love,
To more joy.
It is possible,
For that is your birthright.

The heaviness of grief makes me feel like I have been submerged in a deep, dark hole. There I am captive to all the painful, angry, sad feelings of life. But I can come up for air and escape the suffocating feeling that so often has me wrapped up like a mummy. Today, as the world reflects the beauty of this precious moment, I receive life. Love is all that is real.

Day 188

Equanimity arises when we accept the way things are.
—Jack Kornfield

My inner world is my constant companion. It is my intention that my relationship with my higher self always be my focus. When I forget and point my finger outside or spiral into negativity or pain, when I focus on what seems to be pushing on me, it only gets stronger.

So, I don't cut myself off from the moment. I feel the sensations inside, and I relax into them. It doesn't have to be fixed or changed. I receive it all as I send a message to my unconscious to just be. This creates a space inside where I accept with equanimity.

When I surrender into the quiet place within and whisper, "Be still," I open to this Presence that is always holding me, guiding me, and helping me create a beautiful world.

It begins within. It begins with my desire to return to what is true.

I am more loving. My resistance has fallen away because I trust myself to be fully here to receive and then give from a more conscious place. I do not hold back. I strive to be fully myself no matter what is going on outside. I am here to be authentically me and to love like there is no tomorrow.

I walked a mile with Pleasure
She chattered all the way,
But left me none the wiser
For all she had to say.

I walked a mile with Sorrow,
And ne'er a word said she;
But oh, the things
I learned from her
When Sorrow walked with me!
— Robert Browning

Steve is gone physically. I don't have him in front of me to distract me from the truth. He is now the perfect reflection of God, shining light upon my being. His spirit helps me to let go of all that has been neatly tucked away in every cell of my body. The love that brought us together to heal our past is now free to reflect the truth.

My grief has brought me to everything that I need to let go of and heal. This act of kindness to myself is not easy. My spiritual heart helps me feel deeply without letting the mind label or judge. Beyond the words and images, I listen to truth, I listen to the message of the soul.

Contemplation moves me into the heart of it all. Here, deep in the center of myself, I enter into the present moment where I can commune with God and change my consciousness. This transforms me, and I accept it all more intimately. I move closer to the expression of my true nature instead of letting my little ego self bring me further away. I experience my grief so I can live right here, right now.

Day 190

I call out to Steve, and inside my mind, sometimes I hear his voice respond. I feel his presence beside me, and I am comforted in the knowing that birth and death are just moments in time.

I receive guidance in my heart. It is where I join with him and know that we are not separate. Steve has no needs where he is. When I am longing for him or dwelling in the past, I cannot fully receive the present moment. In Presence, I am as free as Steve. I let go of the need to do anything and listen to the Divine guidance that wants to take care of me.

All my spirit loved ones are my cheerleaders. I feel so blessed to know how beautiful my life can be when I connect inward and listen to my heart and the truth about where I am right now physically, emotionally, and spiritually. My healing helps my soul grow, and enriching my life helps others around me.

I am filled with gratitude this day, knowing that as I take care of myself, everyone is taken care of. All that is truly needed is for each of us to take care of ourselves while trusting Spirit to show us the way.

Day 191

Spirit Speaks

This feeling of being so free—out of your head and expanded in your heart—is your true nature. I know you have been here many times. I used to enjoy waking up, walking into the living room, and watching you blissed out in your meditative state. You always seemed so happy.

In your world, there are different states and each one is fine,

necessary even, for emotions are part of your human experience. Here
we don't need them. Every part of life leads you and guides your way.

Allowing yourself to just be will lift you into this marvelous
experience of loving yourself and the world. Unconditional love is the
ticket home, like the feeling you had as Mollie melted into you this
morning with a sigh of contentment. We used to feel that together
when I was in a body. The physical experience of merging into the
Presence with the body is surrendering into what is real, a glimpse into
heaven. Bliss is the state of loving all of what is as you get lost in the
essence of your true self. Now multiply that feeling by a trillion and
that is how it feels to be where I am.

Yet being in your world is wonderful, so wonderful, and the
journey gets better and better when you let go of the attachments that
keep you in separation. It could be just a thought like "I miss Steve,"
but then you choose to merge into the no mind, and here I am. Where
do you choose to hang out? Ultimately the choice is yours to make. I
did not get that in a body. I believed sometimes that we did not have a
choice. I let my fear of the future ruin my life and that was a hopeless
road to travel on.

Remember all the times we merged into oneness—that is the way
to be. Now and forever.

Day 192

Everything you love, you will eventually lose, but in the end,
love will return in a different form.

— Franz Kafka

True happiness cannot be taken away by our darkness. The space
within our heart is so vast, even more immense than the ever-changing
sky. Here all the difficult feelings of our unlovable and imperfect self are
accepted and held in Presence. Though everything is worthy to be here,
we must first learn and accept that our self-worth is not attached to

another. It is a part of this infinite love of the Universe. So even when our heart is broken, it breaks wide open to allow rebirth and new life.

The only constant is change. Everything is temporary. People come in and out of our lives, the body has its challenges and healings, the mind becomes obsessive and quiets, this world has calm waters until the next hurricane forms. Yet here, in the center of change, is the all-knowing eye that sees with the heart that remembers that change can be beautiful!

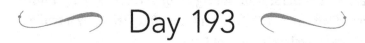

Day 193

As a man abandons worn-out clothes and acquires new ones, so when the body is worn out a new one is acquired by the self, who lives within.

— Bhagavad Gita

Spirit Speaks

Let go of the old garments that you have worn—the ones that hide your light and your true beauty. Let go of the negative thinking that keeps you stuck in the feelings of lack and scarcity. Enjoy all that is giving to you as life itself is bringing forth the new. This all comes from the well of being present with yourself and all that is being experienced in every given moment. Listen deeply to that which is so full and expands you to receive life as grace.

There is nothing that you can say or do that will bring me back in form. Let what was be the gifts that life has offered you. Now is your time to receive all that you have given to the world. The world is now reflecting back to you all that you have shared in your life of selfless giving. Drink in the beauty and watch how your life will grow and become more.

Love is all that is real. All your tears have washed away the pain of living separately from the joy of being alive. You are left here to carry on—carry on for all who have forgotten what a beautiful world it is.

You are loved beyond all words and taken care of each day and each moment for all your tomorrows.

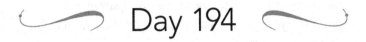 Day 194

There is comfort in knowing that we are not alone and that these beautiful souls who have graced our lives continue to do so as they drop their bodies and fill our hearts with love. There is no beginning or end. Life as we knew it is the doorway to another moment where we see the bigger picture. Life continues in many forms. As we join in heart, no one is left out of the great celebration of being a participant in creation.

Tears flood out of me, and I let them. It's okay because that is where I am for the moment. I allow the energy of love and union to draw out whatever still lurks in the nooks and crannies within me. I am here to let go, and sometimes we just can't do anything but cry. We cry not only for ourselves but also for the ones around us, to help them feel their locked-up emotions. When we are honest and true to ourselves, we once again bring the message to the world—we are human and all our experiences free us to choose what is real.

The tears wash away the pain once again and the space opens, bringing more life and more joy. This painful lesson of loss continues to teach me so much. Even without a body, Steve is right there in the mystery of the Universe helping to guide me.

Loss shows me what I need to let go of. Then I can see all the miracles that continue to bring me back to what is important. I can see once again that there is so much to live for. Freedom becomes the wings that help me soar into worlds I am now ready to explore.

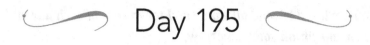

Day 195

*And I found that I can do it if I choose to – I can stay awake
and let the sorrows of the world tear me apart and then
allow the joys to put me back together different from before
but whole once again.*

— Oriah Mountain Dreamer

I pause to appreciate the beauty of being the observer as this new chapter of my life unfolds. I am not the same as I was before this deep loss.

There is so much joyful life around me, and I feel comforted as I walk this familiar beach. I am so pulled into the beauty of the earth and ocean that I lose myself in it all. Pelicans nosedive like fighter jets crashing in the sea. They come up with beaks full of bounty. I feel a kinship with them.

Gazing at the world passing by, I notice that I am not crying, hurting, or longing. Memories and other thoughts flow through me as I silently remember how deeply I love the man who brought me to this Island, this precious piece of land surrounded by breathtaking blue waters that shimmer in the sun like a blanket of crystals. Many people, walking and sitting, are also enjoying the day, this day, handed to me like a gift.

I walk far down the beach, listening to the waves. I feel happy, and that is what Steve would want. My happiness is a gift back to him—his life was worthwhile. I'll never stop loving him.

I am worthy to begin again and allow the big place within my heart to love bigger than ever.

Day 196

It's not the day you have to manage,
but the moment.
It's not the dragon you have to slay
but the fear.
And it's not the path you have to know,
but the destination.
— Mike Dooley, *A Beginner's Guide*
to the Universe

We are born into these bodies to feel the freedom to just be ourselves and to let the Universe flow through and around us. This God energy is the light that shines so fully in each and every one of us. But we forget it, or we become distracted. This human experience is a journey of unveiling. We are uncovering all the lies and deceptions, all the false beliefs that keep us separate from our true selves. So why be afraid of the darkness? It always tells us the truth.

At the end of this life, it all matters. Love is the expression of everything. It is all that is left when we let go. That is how loved we are. Our perfect and holy feelings are our gift from God. Any time we forget that we are this spark of the Divine, we can simply look into the eyes of a child or gaze at a flower.

So many paths to walk upon in this world. And no matter which one we choose, the one we take will get us exactly where we need to be. There is nothing in this life that needs to be feared. Through our life choices and experiences, we grow together in conscious awareness.

Without a thought of what is,
I breathe into the voice so deep within
that calls me with its silence.
I listen.
Then I walk into this big world,
where what is before me takes me into its embrace.
A squirrel stands erect with something to say.
Trees sway in the rhythm of the wind's touch.

The sky is so clear that I can lift up into its gaze
and see nothing but myself—
the one that remembers that this day is a gift given,
Another sweet moment to open my heart to what will never change.
One more day to breathe in life!

Day 197

We need to rest enough of ourselves below the surface of
things until we find ourselves upheld.
— Mark Nepo, *The Book of Awakening*

I love to write in my journal. I remember when I first learned to write cursive letters—the feel of the special pen and ink that I used to learn to write with. I loved the feeling of that pen in my hand. I was in awe as I watched the words form so beautifully on the blank piece of paper.

Journaling is a way I connect with my higher self. It joins my thoughts, my heart, and my physical body. There is a knowing that comes as I sink below the surface of all that I feel so deeply inside. I sink into the feeling that seems to be darkness or uneasiness. Trusting where I am right now is believing that in letting go, I am safe as I take the risk to move inside. I can stop struggling and let myself be immersed in it all. I trust where I am in each moment and know it will lead me back to what is true.

For years I have used writing to release negative feelings and thoughts that can crowd me. I let go of the pain and suffering my mind creates, and I move into my heart where the Divine speaks to me and through me. I let go of what I think I know, and I return to the simplicity of living in the present moment.

I invite you to join me in this practice. Buy yourself a journal. Splurge on a beautiful pen, or some colored pencils and begin your inner journey of self-discovery. Put away your cell phone and other devices and connect with your inner creative process like you did when you were a child.

Return to your inner artist, writer, singer, dancer. Listen to what your heart is telling you and let it flow out to fill up your pages. Go inside and touch all the sadness and madness of your human existence and know that you are perfect just the way you are.

I take the risk today as I sink into what is underneath. I trust myself as I trust the Universe. Taking the hand of Spirit, like nature, it takes me into its embrace. I hear the words, "Be here now as you rest in the arms of love." My heart is exposed and open to it all.

Day 198

Meditation

I awaken this day like a newborn child
Seeing how free I truly am to love and be loved.

Let me stay here in this timeless moment,
Forever holding on to your sweet embrace.

I am captured by the beauty of just being here
Without thinking or doing,
Within the silent reserve of bliss
That wraps me up with such tenderness.

Oh, my beloved, let me be inside myself
Where nothing is hidden.
All is exposed to the light
Of being conscious, alive, and free.

Oh, sweet love, take me into the sacred chamber
Where I am your promise.
Held captive by your presence, I am yours.

I am here surrendered, open, and full of the truth
That sets us all free to just be loved.
A star so bright in the night—I follow it in my dreams.
Always watching from this place deep inside myself.

Happy to know you, even if the meeting in part was brief—
I await you to dance with me again for our dreams live on
Beyond this crazy thought of death.

Let me hear the sound of our love affair.
I see it all with greater knowing
That all is well, for we are never apart.

Day 199

We all know the truth: more connects us than divides us.
But in times of crisis, the wise build bridges, while the
foolish build barriers. We must find a way to look after one
another as if we were one single tribe.

- King T'Challa, from the Marvel
movie *Black Panther*

Sometimes, when I forget that truth—that we are all "one single tribe"—I feel like I am left all alone. These times of crisis, all times of crisis, push us to face our darkness, and sometimes we need to go inside and take down the walls we have erected to protect ourselves from pain or to insulate ourselves from being vulnerable.

When things get tough, it is so easy to fall asleep and forget this heart and mind that want to join with the Divine. Time and time again, I forget that all I have to do is soften my gaze out there, return to myself, and settle into what this moment brings me.

It's really all I want—to connect with what is causing me to feel this separation where I fear the future, the next moment, or the new relationship that is in front of me. So, I choose to reach out to mother nature and allow her to touch me in ways that allow me to change my focus to my heart and lean in.

She calls me by shining her sunlight through my window or sounding the chimes in my garden with her wind. Through this connection, I can be more committed to my inner path as I feel my way through all these worries and breathe gently. It opens me to all that is coming my way.

So, I have learned to ask questions instead of making assumptions. And I can listen without having to be right. I let go of everything I think I know and allow the moment to be real.

I can hold others with a spacious heart and a still mind. Having faced my fears and shortcomings, I can meet them in the deepest part of my being. Then the moment becomes a way to honor how precious life is because I only have this time, this present moment with this person. I may never see them again.

I take in the moments of bliss where sweet love exists within us all. We are all a part of the vastness of being where nothing is lost, and everything is living in eternal peace. No one is separate from this prayer.

Day 200

Spirit Speaks

Let go precious ones.

Let go so that you can fly free, for the illusion is gone. Your broken wing is now stronger than ever. Your broken heart is bigger than ever. As I take you up in the true reality where it is all clear and at peace, you can fly.

Can you look upon this life now with the understanding that all is well? Can you trust in the plan that is unfolding from the fading of the tears?

I sit here listening to music that fully opens me to all my emotions and feelings. As I see myself walking into the arms of my beloved and sharing the love that is always and forever, I feel myself dancing and moving into more of what is real.

There is no separation from this union of hearts. The love pours in as if I have tipped my head back, opened my mouth wide, and taken a drink from the eternal well of Spirit. I am drinking in the sweetness of our forever union.

Oh, sweet love, I am yours, for always I am here allowing your love in.

When I begin to let go, it is amazing how richer life becomes. What is real, what I love deeply, seems to come deeper into me. The song of this dream of love is living on now in my heart. No one can ever take this love away.

Day 201

When you forgive and let go, not only does a huge weight drop off your shoulders, but the doorway to your own self-love opens.

— Louise Hay

No matter what is going on inside of me, it is my responsibility to feel it and let it move out or let it bring me back to my connection with the truth. When I witness myself being triggered, I see how I can get pulled into a pattern that keeps me in suffering and stops the flow of life that desires to move through me. If I can observe myself as if watching a movie, I see there are other choices I can make. When I accept, and only if I can accept, where I am in a given moment, I can choose serenity. This is freedom. I am free to dwell on mistaken beliefs—and that's all they are, mistakes—learn from them and move on to the next moment where love abides.

Self-love seems to be one of the hardest paths, yet isn't it the most important? Loving myself means accepting all the light and dark threads of my tapestry; all my personality traits, the ones I like, and the ones I dislike. I can make it about another, about the trigger, or I can allow this experience to bring me deeply into all the aspects of myself that are calling for love.

Serenity Prayer

God, grant me the serenity to accept the things I cannot change; the courage to change the things I can; and the wisdom to know the difference.

I allow myself to drink it all in and savor my uniqueness. I move into life fully accepting my humanity. Here I can give my problems or fearful thinking to my higher power and ask for help.

Day 202

Spirit Speaks

I am right by your side as you let go once again and move into this well of your spirit. You have come here countless times. It is so familiar to you as I am now knowing what it is like to detach from form into the freedom of just being. How easy it has been for you to commune with all that never dies. Every step has prepared you for this transition.

I was let into the world of Spirit the moment I left my body. How free it is and comfortable to be with you here! Letting go is necessary for both of us. When you do, you return to the self as I have returned to my soul. *You are so able to do it in your body, for life as you know it has moved you into your heart to know who you truly are.*

It isn't easy for you to resist the pain of the limited human self. You accomplish your greatest task when you let yourself go into the pain without judging it or holding back in any way. This pain then becomes your entry into Spirit, into truth, into the reality of being connected to all that I am.

You must trust this journey you are on now. We are mates for life—continuing to help each other become all that our souls can be. It seems harsh to think that this has been a plan and yet, as human beings, how could we fully realize the perfection of this experience? It will show itself to you when you are ready and then the pain of letting go will be the birth of more life, more love, and more joy. Then one day you will open up to another and love like never before.

Day 203

And once the storm is over, you won't remember how you made it through, how you managed to survive. You won't even be sure, in fact, whether the storm is really over. But one thing is certain. When you come out of the storm you won't be the same person who walked in. That's what this storm's all about.

– Haruki Murakami, *Kafka on the Shore*

Today as I sit discovering who I am, I realize that even though the dramas of life continue to move through me, I can fully embrace it all. I breathe into the quiet where God has no language, and I am humbled.

In the stillness, I find peace and remember that all is well. As I let go once again to find what has been planted within me, I arrive at the spark of light that needs my attention. I breathe in, move through memories of days gone by, and return to Presence. It is my inner strength as peace and serenity find me.

In my garden, where all is beginning to bloom, I feel a power, greater than my little self, showing me the way as I become that flower receiving the light of a radiant sun. I have gazed into the eyes of life itself and allowed it to bring me happiness. I am here to grow, and every part of life has made it so.

In building this life of mine, I have set myself free. I have courage, so I don't need to hide, abandon, or numb who I am. The pain of loss has brought me to a greater version of myself, and I'm now brave enough to let everything be exposed.

To know my value is to know how loved I am. I can be the one that shines my light for all to see and help humanity awaken to the truth that there is no death, only the transition into more of self.

I survive again and again. Through it all, I become more of myself as I become less afraid of the pain.

Day 204

Spirit Speaks

There are so many here jumping up and down in celebration of your recovery—your remembering of why you came in. Shutting down or dimming your light never helped you or anyone. You can live in your light through ways unimaginable. Today you can shine. Every moment is a deep breath of choosing life and resting in the arms of Source that never leave your side. You cannot get your security 'out there.' You must grab hold of the light inside your inner being and trust yourself. Leap knowing that together we all have come along with you to assist you in living life fully and with conscious connection to that which is always guiding you to choose with intention.

Now I can reach out and share myself again. There is room inside to let in this new life and allow others more fully into my heart.

Day 205

All my life I believed I knew something. But then one strange day came when I realized that I knew nothing; yes, I knew nothing.

— Ezra Pound

How easy it becomes when I let go of my resistance and stop grasping. I trust in my inner resources and surrender to the moment. Here I am pulled into the flow of energy that gives and gives and gives. I feel alive, and as I merge with this energy, I find that some of the falseness has fallen away.

I embrace all of me. I allow myself to be loved while loving all that has come before this moment. I open and allow the pain of loss, the hurt, and the fear to just be. With every breath, I fall more deeply into the moment of what is. Here I discover my Divine essence. I let go of everything I think I know and listen to my higher spiritual self who knows everything.

The choice is mine to make as I receive the inner guidance that speaks to me.

Day 206

In the middle of the night, I get up to go to the bathroom and find my room filled with sparkling lights. I feel the Presence of one of my clients and hear him say, *"Frannie, it's so beautiful here. I feel so free."* I respond, *"You don't have to go yet. Come back and tell everyone what it is like in heaven!"*

The next day, I learned that my client had been rushed to the hospital in critical condition. Though it had been touch and go through the night, in the morning his wife arrived to find him awake and sitting up in bed. He told her that he had talked to me, that he didn't have to go yet, and that he was going to tell their girls all about what it's like on the other side.

Day 207

Meditation

One day, as we walk on together
In this unified life,
We will not look back
With sadness
Or regret.

We do not need
To close our hearts
To all that has gone before.
We will look upon our history
With the eyes of a grateful heart,

Remembering that
Every moment
Brought us here.

Consciously, we begin to live awake,
Connecting to what truly gives life.
Just as nature knows
What is true,
We will live

In the knowing
That all is well.

We will be guided
By the inner light
That has never gone out.
I am beginning to discover
In this solitude
I can touch you.

Day 208

The reality is that you will grieve forever. You will not 'get
over' the loss of a loved one; you will learn to live with it.
You will heal and you will rebuild yourself around the loss
you have suffered. You will be whole again, but you will
never be the same. Nor should you be the same nor would
you want to.

— Elisabeth Kubler-Ross, On Grief
and Grieving: Finding the Meaning
of Grief Through the Five Stages of
Loss

I am aware today that a veil has lifted, and the heavy feelings are
no longer blocking out the light of a new day. I feel a shift and appreciate
my progress down this difficult path that is my life's journey right now.
With every step I have taken since Steve's death, I have strived to be real
and authentic in my experience of grief. I remained fully present day and
night, moment by moment. No distractions.

These months have felt like an eternity; endless days of suffering,
crying for a life I loved, a man I cherished and adored. But by being
honest about my feelings and my needs, by allowing myself to be
open to my grief without numbing out or leaving, I have progressed.
I see growth. I see healing. My connection inside is growing, I feel less
vulnerable. I feel a strength and a bond with my true self, the one that

has always been there through every experience of my life. In my Spirit, I feel strong.

Spirit Speaks

Oh, Sweetness, there is so much to be grateful for. As you step into acceptance, accepting it all is the most powerful thing to do.

So, you ask about your life? It is unfolding as you become the embodiment of the beloved, the one that is loved. You are being the love, offering it, opening to whoever is on your path. Being your full self, you do not need anyone to be anything but who they are. You are the beautiful soul that shines through your incredible, sacred temple called a body. I am there in all my brilliance shining through the eyes of another as you stand in the stillness of your open heart.

Today I feel what truly matters. I am connected to a power inside of me that never leaves.

Day 209

"...get still, and stay still for long enough for new thoughts to take root in your more quiet, deeper, truer self. The noise of the world drowns out the sound of you. You have to get still to listen."

– Oprah Winfrey

Life continues to bring me to me. To become like a river, flowing around everything that comes into my life. Every moment, an experience of living deeper with this being, this presence that knows who I am. With unconditional compassion, the honest to goodness truth and open heartedness embrace every part of my flawed and imperfect humanity.

Totally embracing myself, and now without doubt, nourishing myself without letting my ego take charge.

Knowing that I am never better or less than anyone, I consciously choose to maintain a humility as I use my connection to this vast universe for the empowerment of self. The path I choose becomes a gateway. Here I gain a deeper understanding and compassion for others. As I witness my fellow companions on their own paths of struggle, their challenges with grief, disease, addiction, and longing, I recognize that we can all express love for others in a more authentic way.

I breathe into my difficult feelings, my self-judgments, my suffering. My acceptance of it all helps me heal my traumas from childhood. Patience and self-love bring maturity, and then I am free to radiate love for all who are in life with me, even if it's only for a brief moment in time.

Without taking your last breath, awaken, as every breath becomes vital to being here, present amongst the precious life that is given. It spills out as beauty, peace, understanding, compassion, and love.

Day 210

...and the day came when the risk to remain tight in a bud was more painful than the risk it took to blossom.

— Elizabeth Appell

My friend and counselor for over 30 years, Jim DeMaio, called to tell me that Steve had visited him in a dream to say that he was sending me a man named Robert. Still deeply hurting in my grief, I said, incredulously, "How could you be giving me prophecy?" He replied, calmly, "It's a dream, Frannie. Steve visited me in a dream."

My conversation with Jim stretched me to move into another mindset. I am not living without Steve—he is here in all knowledge and understanding. He has no human needs now. I must open myself to hear him, to let him tell me how I can get my needs met now, to understand how I am to heal my feelings that I am not good enough, to know that I am worthy to get my greatest needs met as a woman.

Thank goodness it's not like it used to be when women wore black and mourned for the rest of their lives. Back then, a widow was defective, and her life was over. I remember my Aunt Katherine always wore black, covered by the stigma that was put upon her. Who made up that rule anyway? How fortunate I am. I can be social, I can connect with another man if I choose. I feel so blessed to live in a world where I am free to keep choosing life and open to what could blossom in the future.

I sit inside my heart, allowing the thoughts to digest. It could take a very long time or no time at all. As I let go of the life I lived with Steve and move into this new relationship with him, I see that he has no desire for these human needs because he is no longer of form. He is a part of everything. I listen to him telling me where to go and trust that he knows more than I do right now.

As John O'Donohue says in his book, *Anam Cara*, "We do not need to grieve for the dead. Why should we grieve for them? They are now in a place where there is no more shadow, darkness, loneliness, isolation, or pain. They are home. They are with God from whom they came. They have returned to the nest of their identity within the great circle of God. God is the greatest circle of all, the largest embrace in the Universe, which holds visible and invisible, temporal and eternal, as one."

As I practice detachment, there is freedom and possibility within me as the Divine Presence becomes the richness of my life.

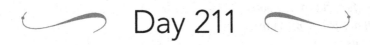 Day 211

I let myself just rest in these moments that pass by.
I fill myself up with patience as I breathe, walking the beach.

I watch the children playing. Joy is so natural to a child. I see them buried in the sand right up to their necks! They are laughing louder than the waves brushing up onto the shore.

I laugh with them. The contagious feeling of happiness has caught me like the breeze that moves my hair across my face. At this moment, I breathe in, "My life feels good right now!"

Everything is flowing so freely, and without much effort at all, I realize that my soul is not suffering because my life's purpose is to be the person my heart wants to be.

It all seems to be here, everything I need when I get out of the way and trust in all that the Universe brings my way.

Even in the moments when I get pushed down by my human frailties and doubts, I know that life has shown me how to get back up.

I know without a doubt that as I lean into myself, just as I am, I can ever so gently surrender until I soften.

I begin to move forward toward the light as love finds its way through the inner space where my heart reveals the truth. All the answers come flooding into me like a love letter from my soul.

Day 212

Meditation

Let us step back
And sink into the quiet within
Where we return to peace.
Greeting silence
With all that is revealed,
We are blessed.
Let us gather together in heart
And listen to the still, small voice.
We are faithful companions
For all our fellow pilgrims
Upon this earth.

Lead with your heart
With unshakable compassion.
Let peace grow large within
Until it overflows
And is shared with others.
Let this energy that creates worlds
Flow through every thought, word, and deed.

This love that nourishes the soul
Brings comfort from your spiritual nature
To the world.
You are the prayer,
The song of the birds,
The light of the sun,
The love of Spirit.

In your stillness,
You will see the opening
Where grace illuminates the Divine.
The good is already here,
As God radiates through us all.
As the hurt dissolves, we open,
Filled with the touch of the sacred.

Day 213

Your love is shining in everything I do
And I hear you calling for me
For all roads lead to you.
　　　— Tina Malia, lyrics, "All Roads"

Slowly, moment by moment, breath by breath, tear after tear, I found the connection that was already there. It's where Steve was hanging out… right here within my heart where he can still speak to me and commune.

At first, I did not want it. I wanted him in the physical. I longed for the touch of his lips, his arms, his laughter and playfulness. I missed his face; I missed the space between his teeth when he smiled. I missed his jokes. I missed us—the way it was and the dreams that we had together. I wanted him to show up as my man and partner in the life we created together.

Gone was this man I loved. He just disappeared into thin air leaving behind his empty body and my lonely heart. Yet this great deep wound has led me to so many treasures of a spiritual path.

Now I know he is so much more. Beyond his ego, beyond his body, which was just a covering like a garment worn, he is this beautiful light, essence, soul. Now he can be everywhere that I am, right in the center of it all.

Now that grieving has opened me to my fears of death, I am no longer afraid to live life in the space that has left me awake.

Meditation

Let go of who you think you are
And allow yourself to be fully here.
You are not the coverings you wear.
You are not the credentials or diplomas.
You are not your mistakes or your pains.
You are the one that is connected
To a Presence that gives life.
Every part of you is worthy
Of love and acceptance.
Every part of you is here
In the center of being you.
Taking it all in, you remember
It is such a privilege to be here in this life.

Day 214

Spirit Speaks

When you look through the eyes of the one who creates worlds, you see the reflection of this pure being in the hearts of all of humanity. It is not easy when you look for another to make it happen for you. If you are living it within then all around you the world is giving you what you already know.

I let myself be free—today and every moment to come. I join here with all of Spirit and share in that which is continuously giving life. I let go of the doubts that hinder my well-being and dip into the well of my infinite self that is so much vaster than the physical limitation of form. Here I am formed and made in the image of my creator—all loving and all kind.

Day 215

This is the sound of one heart starting to hear
This is the sound of faith stepping out of fear
Oh, the journey of one soul's passage through time
Oh, this is one lone dreamer learning to fly
　　　　　 – Tina Malia, lyrics, "All Roads"

In the pain of separation, I died a thousand times. Yet when I return to my inner sanctuary and let the mind quiet, I am free. I can hear Steve, feel him, and know that he never left me. It makes me strong in my foundation of who I truly am. I fill up from this well that I have always connected with.

I have taken this same journey time and time again for most of this adult life…returning inward to all that is here. Joy and sorrow are inseparable. If you can let sorrow come, release, and wash the pain away, your heart will open again as joy. Our true nature rejoins us in the celebration of life.

One of the main messages that Steve has given us is, **"Live while you are living."** Isn't that our responsibility to the ones we walk upon this earth with? To live while we are living is to find answers to our prayers, for we have been given this precious life and it is our responsibility to live it fully with hearts wide open.

No one can make it better for me. Lining up with my heart's desire is my choice, and this loving heart is making my life beautiful.

 # Day 216

Spirit Speaks

Everything is a projection of what you believe. So, nothing truly has to take you away from yourself. In your moment-to-moment realization of who you are, you are the only one responsible for the experience you are living.

You are the center of it all observing all the aspects of yourself and playing all these different roles that are showing you the way back to this moment where all is perfect!

Meditation

Be yourself.
Now fully receive the gift
Of this beautiful life
That is the beloved.
You are incredible.

This life that lives within you
And all around you

Inspires and creates.
Open your eyes
And stay right here,
Giving and receiving
This love that has no conditions.

Now move from the inside to the outside
And allow this light
To illuminate through your living.
You are free to be fully here,
Intoxicated with the beauty of Divine love
That is reflected in the world
That surrounds you.

 Day 217

Let yourself be silently drawn by the stronger pull of what you really love.

Most people guard against going into the fire, and so end up in it.

Mature yourself and be secure from a change for the worse. Become the light.

—Rumi

The death of a loved one demands your attention and sends you into those dark places that we learned to avoid. Here is where you must accept the hardest, most awful parts beyond your imaginings. Yet in the deepest and darkest valleys inside, there is also an emptiness so silent where truth emerges.

We each have our own journey through life's challenges from which we leave our mark on this earth. Just like a walk on the beach leaves footprints, flower blooms leave fragrance, and hugs or handshakes leave a feeling of connection, we leave the imprint of our life upon this world.

I had a dream in which my son-in-law, Rob, was making a movie and I was the lead actor. I was with my whole family and all my friends out on the dock at my family's cottage, and I was holding a baby in my arms. As I stared into the infant's face, more love than I have ever felt poured through me. There was so much light shining through my heart and eyes. As I looked closer, I realized that the baby's face was mine. I felt total love for myself. That love was the true, Divine force that is ever-present within us all.

In this dream, I had no pain. Held by nature and all the ones walking in life with me, I remembered who I am. I am this love within that never dies.

Getting out into the world and sharing this feeling is powerful and life-changing.

 Day 218

It may be stating the case too strongly to say that in meditation one seeks to gain nothing. For there is an increase in happiness and peace of mind. But when asked, "What have you gained from meditation?" (The Buddha replied) "It is not what I have gained that is important but rather what I have diminished, namely greed, hatred and delusion."

— World Buddhism by the
World Fellowship of Buddhists

I hear the wind howling outside while Mollie and I cuddle underneath the covers. It's 8 am and I have no interest in getting out of bed. Memories pass of the many mornings Steve would beg me to stay in bed. Now I think to myself, "Why didn't I just stay with him?" But I am an early riser and meditate in the wee hours of the approaching dawn.

Here I access the bridge to my spirit. That spiritual bridge also connects me to my loved ones who have passed.

I breathe in, and suddenly it all drops away. As I gaze around the room, Mollie looks at me, licks my face, and moves to the other side of the bed. While she goes back to sleep, I remain awake in the present moment.

In my connection to self, I settle deep inside my breath where there is nowhere to go but here. There's nothing to reach for and nothing to long for as I wait for this moment to unfold. This endless love feeds me.

Day 219

What does "letting go" mean?
This phrase is often misunderstood. Does it mean forgetting,
letting go of our memories? Not at all.

Does it mean letting go of a relationship with our deceased
loved-ones? No!

Our relationship is changed, not ended. "Letting go" refers
to the time in our healing journey when we are ready to
gently open our tightly closed fists. In doing so we let go of
our pain. We do not need it anymore.

— Sandi Caplan &
Gordon Lang

The art of letting go is achieved through non-attachment. It's easy for me to resist these painful situations in my life when I hang out in the stillness and relax into my spiritual practice. Other times, it's more challenging.

Step by step, as I walk through the pain of my attachment to Steve and who I was with him, I am learning to let go into the light where I return to an inner strength that gives me power. I have grown in ways that bring me out of denial and into a compassionate heart that can love greater.

At first, I was so depleted that I didn't think I could ever return to my counseling practice. Yet, slowly, I have grown, I have healed, and I have evolved. I now have the courage to become what my soul wants to be.

Life led me to the doorway, death revealed the path, and grief pushes me along to uncover my true self. As we learn to stay connected inside, we see the false coverings fall away. That's when we grow and allow the stillness within to pour its heavenly light into us.

There is a time to grieve and a time to let go. I liberate myself from my attachment to anger, sadness, ignorance, and all that brings me suffering. With a compassionate heart for all sentient beings, I join with love as I am guided and can see what is unfolding in every moment.

Day 220

Life and death are one thread, the same line viewed from different sides.

– Chuang Tzu

As I merge with nature, I feel drawn in by these sounds that intoxicate me. I watch the ripples on the lake that reflect the sun. So much light. I feel one with it all and fall deeply into the moment. In the stillness, I feel the truth rising to the surface.

Spirit Speaks

When you find yourself in this peace, you are free as I am, here with you. Let yourself rest in this timeless moment and know that many times I discovered all that you are now touching within. I did not

know how to express it as you, yet it is all here, not separate by the death of my body.

Many moments like this one, and this moment is all there is, so rich in its fullness. As you allow it in, it fills you.

This is your healing. This is where the beauty of our life together gives you more life. It has birthed you, for many lessons have been learned and now the knowledge will be passed on through your living.

I am grateful for this day. Today I look at my life with the eyes of grace and fall deeply in love with the moment. I am grateful for all the moments that have brought me here.

 Day 221

Meditation

You are connected to so much more of yourself.
The one that knows that you are free
To just be in this sweet Presence
Where love emanates from your every cell.
The path is in this.
Every moment spills into the next moment,
And this one sweet moment feeds
Not just you but everyone you are with.
It's this connection to all that is
That keeps you in union with the Divine.
When you tune into the present moment,
You choose to swim in these delicious waters
That expand you into more Presence.
You are filled with a peace
That is beyond any understanding
And you begin to welcome more of yourself here.

This deeper side of your soul
Brings the light and love to all you do.
It is all transforming, in its creative way,
From your loving heart
That is beautifully guiding from your soul.

 Day 222

...maybe death isn't darkness, after all, but so much light
wrapping itself around us.

— Mary Oliver, *"White Owl Flies*
Into and Out of the Field"

As this journey of letting go of the life I once had continues, I can see that I have journeyed well. I did not fake it. I did not pretend that I had it all together. How could I? I was shattered into a billion pieces, but I was not cast away by the winds. I was held tenderly and completely by Mother Earth. There was no neediness from the ground that holds the memory of who I am. Only gentle nudges and reflections of all that lives and dies.

I walk now upon this earth and bow to all the moments that have brought me here. Some of my falseness has fallen away as I stand amid all that exists, has died, and will be born again. I hold myself in holy communion with the spirit of everything that creates and moves us all together back to the One.

I have no idea what will happen. As the past fades into the night sky, I behold the beauty of a heavenly dawn that touches me in ways that nothing else can, another morning to listen to nature awakening. I open my eyes to look at myself honestly, for this is the day that has been given to me, a beautiful day full of boundless potential. Yet still in my periphery, I catch a glimpse of old dreams and broken promises of the past.

I can begin again as the light softens me and expands my senses. I let go and let this great mystery create through my rising out of the moment at hand. I am wrapped in the love of Spirit and that is enough.

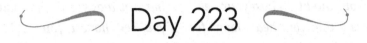

Day 223

Mostly it is loss which teaches us about the worth of things.
— Arthur Schopenhauer

Things will never be the same. I am different in so many ways, and maybe that's a good thing.

This experience brings me more wisdom and compassion. I can trust myself to choose with more consciousness, and I can make my life important. I hold my intentions in my heart and create with joy. When I let go of control, everything begins to fall into place, and my life begins to change for the better.

I am so excited to be here inside myself.

I gently wiggle myself into this garment—this covering, this body that has been through battles and challenges, breakups and breakthroughs, loneliness, and aloneness, giving and receiving, war and peace, sitting out the dance and dancing, mistakes and successes, heartaches and heart-openings, scarcity and abundance, contraction and expansion, attached and unattached, caged and free, rigid and soft, birth and death.

I trust this journey that has brought me to see the worth and value of all things seen and unseen.

I drink myself in and trust that who I am right now is amazing! I chose this incredible life, and I am the partner to myself to have and to hold, from this day forward. As I reach inside, instead of grasping outside, I touch what I already am. I am worthy.

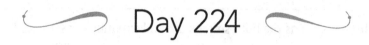

Day 224

Spirit Speaks

Life shows us our reflection. There are no judgments here as you place your intention into your heart. What is it that you desire today? What is it that your heart longs for? If you were honest, you would say, "I desire to live in peace," for in this state of being, a peaceful life circles around again and again to see the lessons that you came here to learn. As soul, you came to understand your heart's truth.

The body will always reveal your thinking. It will always communicate through you what is true. When you are in pain, know there is a truth that needs to be brought to the surface so that you can listen to what is real. The truth only hurts when you do not listen.

When you put the truth upon the image of the moment, this image, when seen with your heart, will be your salvation. You receive this truth, open and willing to change your perception, and it breathes life and initiates you into more of who you are. Let go again and again until you are free of all that is not true. Let the greatest gift of YOU be allowed to live and be free to share this inner reality for all to see. It seems simple, and it is if you allow your spirit to guide your way.

Day 225

I am learning to live in the sunshine of your life instead of the dark shadow of your death.

– author unknown

Meditation

Locked up, shut down, closed off
The stagnant energy inside

Blocks me from the light that tries to come in.
Unconsciousness keeps me numb and withdrawn.
The angel of death came through like a freight train.
I stood there watching you drown
Sinking down, only to rise up again
As you floated above.
This world is a classroom
Where I'm learning to open up to what my soul wants.
Now that you are gone, I sit with you—
Me here, you there.
As I feel the dark, lonely places within my reach,
You are here in the same room without your body.
Pure consciousness sitting inside and all around me.
I crack open a little more
As the softness of your gentle spirit
Reminds me that we are still together
That in the darkness of death
Your spirit lights my way.

 Day 226

Grief is in two parts. The first is loss. The second is the remaking of life.

– Anne Roiphe

This valley that I have allowed myself to be in comes with all that is needed to crawl out of this dark hole of self-discovery. I can say with all my heart that I regret nothing, for it moves me into the expanded version of myself, this soul that loves with great compassion.

I have journeyed with my wounded self and let go of the parts that have created stories that can't live in my mind or heart anymore. This is the guided return to the True Self—a soul journey in my body.

The moments break wide open as I enter this deep canyon that brings me to the light that shines on everything. The mind is the observer of all that has passed through these moments that lead me to more life, more love, more peace, more joy, more sunrises and sunsets, and more tears and emotions that nurture every seed planted in the center of my life.

Now I can reach out and share myself. There is room inside to let in this new life and to allow others more fully into my heart once again.

Life will continue to push me off balance until I am willing to anchor in who I truly am. My authentic self is living in my heart, knowing that right here, right now, life is flowing fully.

 # Day 227

Spirit Speaks

There is a reservoir of inner strength that can be called upon in crucial moments. This Divine guidance is always available to us if we are willing to call it forth.

I open my eyes, look at the brilliant sky, and feel the warmth of Presence holding and filling me. This connection lifts the veil and shows me that Steve is right here waiting for me to open.

I walk alone in this earthly body and return to myself in a way that never was before. Steve dropped his earth suit and joined with all that he is in the Presence of God and now he can join with me wherever I am.

The veil between the worlds is thinner now, and I can talk to my spirit loved ones anytime. This union happens as I let go of my plan and allow myself to be pulled into the stream of consciousness where heaven awaits. I am welcomed by this breathtaking view of a world illuminated by the light that is within everything, and I see the truth.

As I receive myself, I am joined by Spirit. I am kissed by the Presence where I merge into oneness with all of creation.

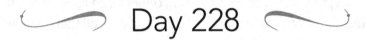

Day 228

Meditation

We are all born equal,
And no one is separate from this incredible power
That lives inside all creation.

We are safe
As we awaken with greater compassion
And love.

Together, we join in this love that creates worlds.
Then our world will be a peaceful home to all.

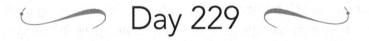

Day 229

I allow the stillness of the moment to take me into the nothingness and I am greeted by that familiar feeling of total expansion. As I merge with my essence, all my senses become alive and I hear Steve say, **"Welcome back, Baby Doll!"**

There is no time or distance when I am in my heart. There is no longing for him when I let myself go into the healing waters. I am grateful to see that all my spirit loved ones and guides and angels share this magnificent place with me.

When I let go of the world that pulls me into all my attachments, I find I can let go and surrender to what is within me in every given moment. I am in awe of this experience that takes over when I allow it to be here.

As I sit in the Presence of stillness, I realize that to live free in this body, I must accept all of myself. The knowing comes when I see myself in everything and, without judgment, I can clearly see all that must be released from my moment-to-moment living.

 # Day 230

This journey through grief is uncomfortable. I look at the life Steve and I had together, and I see a future that is empty without him here with me. Wrapped in a blanket, I feel a cold breeze move right through me into my bones. I am here, present with it all. Each tear, every simple moment, expresses life, my life, the only one I have. I don't want to escape or leave in any way. I want to experience what is here, where I am guided and shown the way.

I rest in the chair that my husband sat in each time he visited this dock at my family's cottage. Here he sat only a year ago taking in all the activities—the birds singing, the turtles swimming, the fish jumping, the cows mooing, the skiers and fast boats, the kayakers and canoes, the clear blue sky and the sun's daily arc through it.

He walked down this dock with his thoughts and emotions. He was here listening to these same sounds of nature softly speaking to him, waking him up to his heart and into the love we shared.

We listen together this morning as we share this one moment. It's what we both wanted all along. We share this peace that has no time or distance as the love visits us once again joining us forever right here, at the end of the dock, "By the sea, by the sea, by the beautiful sea."

I reach deep inside where there is comfort. Here my mind softens and allows the silent voice of Spirit to announce the truth of why I am here. There is nothing to hold onto unless I want to sink into despair. The only life raft to grasp onto is the heart that holds me tenderly, keeping me afloat.

Day 231

As I sit near the dock, I am comforted by the familiar sounds of nature that seem to recognize me, a reminder that life continues. Mollie sits on the grass beside me, her ears perking up to the call of the loons. This new sound for her is a familiar cry to me that brings back so many memories from my youth. Such a prominent fixture in my life, this cottage, where so much changes yet so much feels the same.

I watch a little chipmunk make its way onto the grass in front of my feet. Mollie sees it and gives chase. Her playfulness again harkens me back to my childhood and reminds me to look at this world with the eyes of a child.

I feel like a child today, seeing all the beauty in nature that seems to be in full performance. I choose to sit here and just be. I am beginning to move from mourning to remembering.

Day 232

It is scary to think of going into life again without that loved one by your side. When grief takes over, it keeps you feeling weak, insecure, and resistant to change. At times, I feel lost in the sadness, anger, and resentment. Why must I have to think about facing life alone?

The stages of grief—denial, anger, bargaining, depression, and acceptance—don't come in a specific order. I bounce around and sometimes feel them all at once. But one thing is certain: all these stages of grief are real. And necessary.

Learning to touch and welcome everything that life brings helps us uncover the falseness and allows greater clarity and peace. Focusing on the future can conjure fear, as can perpetuating the past. From this place of fear, we unconsciously react to life. Only in the present moment, the now, can we choose to respond consciously. I like that. I like that I have a choice.

The pain of loss is an experience that doesn't have to continue indefinitely. My experiences and my losses have made me who I am supposed to be. In this moment now, I am clearer, and I can let peace guide my way. I can decide to move back into life again when I am ready.

 Day 233

Spirit Speaks

Let go of everyone outside—no one to take care of, no one to fix you. Allow life to fill you up so that your shining light can be a beacon. Then the vibration of your being will inspire and lift others up into their greatness.

No worries—nothing to decide—just connect with all that is flowing in you. This alignment will never lead you in the wrong direction.

Life will continue to bring you opportunities to listen deeply to your heart where you are not alone, yet alone you choose for the good of all.

Just like the waves that come to the shore, so do we—all your spirit loved ones, guides, and angels—come to join you here on sacred ground where you get to be the courageous one who lives life true to your heart. When you do, everyone will benefit and be blessed by the conscious way you choose to live. The energy of your vibration will change the world, and no one will have to depend on you anymore, for this power lives on in all humanity. You are the way and the light that is ignited inside you is seen in all creation. It lives on in all humanity, and it will change the world.

My spirit loved ones are here to help me grieve, but they also want me to enjoy life again. I am not alone. When I laugh the nonphysical world celebrates with me.

Day 234

Only beloved people can pass on belovedness.
— Richard Rohr

I step into the present moment ready to feed the hungry not from any selfish motive, not for the sake of anything but union. We are all joined here in magnificence, but until we see it in ourselves, we cannot share it with others.

When I am filled with this Divine love, I want to share it. After I have walked honestly along this bumpy road that has been my life's path and listened to my heart's calling, I trust in myself.

Sometimes, when I resist this inner voice that knows what I need, I stumble. The truth can be painful, yet when I observe it all with the eyes of innocence, I can wrap myself up in this love that has no conditions and wait till the storm passes.

A feeling sweeps over me. It reminds me of how I used to feel when my mother would hold me. I don't have to wait for her anymore; her sweet presence is waiting for me to arrive and receives me like no other.

I have the opportunity to change, to see myself with different eyes, and be the person I want to be. When I have the courage to sit lovingly and honestly with myself, I can get out of bed and show up for myself and others. I choose to use my energy to bring others into true alignment and empower them to feel that they are worthy.

Today is my opportunity to realign with this inner power that knows whom I truly am. I rise into the new day with unconditional love and move into the moment with grace. I listen to the silence that speaks wisdom and truth louder than anything. It is not hidden, for I have allowed it all to be right here. My body holds it all while my heart leads the way.

Day 235

Each night I pray and let my wishes flow through my heart as I choose to stay awake and conscious through these dark times.

Tonight, my mind goes to a memory of my best friend Mary, who wanted to stay conscious in her dying. Together with my sister Colleen, my friend Brigitte playing crystal bowls, and Mary's husband Brian holding her hand, I gazed into her eyes. It was a timeless moment as her eyes held mine. Even though her mother and children were not physically sitting in the room, I saw them surrounding us with their presence. She stayed conscious in this presence as her spirit left her precious body.

Words channeled through me, reaching out to her like a bridge merging with the other side. I let them flow through as light filled us all. As she took her last breath, I watched her spirit move through her husband's hand, which he had laid upon her heart. The light moved through his arm and out into the room like a flashlight shining so brightly in the darkest moment of death.

Her gaze never left mine as her body became an empty shell, and all that she was returned to purity. She was reborn as her spirit expanded, for it was free from her sick body used to fight her cancer battle.

I bathed her body, then clothed her, and honored her brave and precious life as a woman, a friend, a sister and daughter, a mother and wife.

She is a part of me and the ever-changing expression of who I am. Her beautiful life touched me deeply. How honored I am to have walked in life with her, though it seems too short a while. Mary showed me that it's only illusion that keeps us apart. When you open yourself to feel everything inside, you fear nothing, not even death.

Day 236

Meditation

I sit in my body
Feeling sad and lonely,
Longing for what was.
Why do we long for what is gone?

To be somewhere...
Where we are not?
If I sit here and allow myself to be still,
I know that I am exactly where
I am supposed to be.

Here in this place, the door opens
As I walk through the wall
That held me back for days.

Or maybe I will walk around it
And find another path.

It all leads me home.

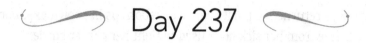

Day 237

Your gifts lie in the place where your values, passions and strengths meet. Discovering that place is the first step toward sculpting your masterpiece, your life.

— Michelangelo di Lodovico
Buonarroti Simoni

The transformation of the physical world, with all its pain and suffering, draws us into our center where we spin around and around. Somehow, in the turmoil of these experiences that can come at us like a series of nightmares, we awaken into the stillness where we expand beyond it all and reach deeply into a peace that is always there. We are like the sculpture David by Michelangelo—it was always there inside the marble, the artist just needed to chip away what did not belong.

Similarly, our lives are works of art, revealed inch by inch, as we break out of the debris of fallen ideas and broken hearts. We lift ourselves to the only truth that can release us from the torment we create in our fearful minds. In that truth, we remember who we are, so worthy to be loved, as we love and live these lives authentically.

I receive myself as I witness grief chiseling the old parts of me away, removing that which cannot be anymore. Like a sculptor, I continue to chip away until I can reveal what already exists underneath—the real, authentic, powerful me who trusts that I can move on into greatness.

Day 238

Something precious is lost if we rush headlong into the details of life without pausing for a moment to pay homage to the mystery of life and the gift of another day.

— Kent Nerburn

I feel restless and off. I am longing for something. Stuck inside my loopy brain, I feel frustrated. I decide to go to an early morning gathering at the beach.

Birds fly high above me, floating on the wind with outstretched wings. Their freedom invites me to let go and come inside to that vast feeling of quiet.

As I listen, I let go of everything that tries to pull me away from myself. I breathe consciously into the moment and let go.

I sit in the moment realizing that I'm not afraid of what is inside me anymore. I listen to people sharing and it's exactly what my heart needs to hear. I'm reminded that sinking into the chair and deeply touching my inner world helps me not hold onto anything. I let it all burn away.

The morning sun is getting hotter as the truth is told by all who share their stories. Receiving the moment just as it is, I look around with respect for all living things. With compassion, I feel the sacred gift of this precious day.

When the meeting ends, I get up from my chair and begin to walk away from the beach. With my heart open and my mind quiet, I take a few steps...and fall flat on my face!

As I lay motionless, my face submerged in the rough sand, I look at the little shells surrounding me. I sink into myself, and I breathe. As I scan my body, so present with it all, I hear the voice of my father, "You fell right." It's true. My body was relaxed as I stumbled to the ground. The rock I tripped over, hidden in the sand, was just enough to bring me down.

An elderly couple asks me if I am okay and admit they are grateful that it wasn't they who fell. I, too, am grateful. I wasn't broken. I wasn't even humiliated.

I breathe deeply into this moment and bow to this life that has been given to me. As I journey on this sacred path called life, I focus within and choose to be kind to myself. It is my life, and it is precious. As I listen to that voice within that keeps me company today, I pour myself a cup of tea and watch the clouds pass by.

Day 239

I watched myself spiral down into the funk of mistaken beliefs. I allowed the world to take me down into a dark hole of despair and fear. Yet while in this state, I could observe myself as choices were made.

I walk into moments awake and aware, knowing I do not need to be fixed or distracted. I walk on and slowly the fog lifts and the clouds disappear from my inner landscape. My choice to be with myself brings me to this power that knows who I am is worthy.

I don't have to run from or dwell in the pain of missing or longing or lacking. I embrace my feelings and choose to be fully present. Fear does not paralyze me or shut me down. Feeling my feelings has always been my gateway to more life, the opening to another part of myself.

My broken heart is seeking a reason to love again. With a breath and a pause, I listen to the voice that speaks within. It has helped me restore my hope that I will be whole again. With great compassion for all, I open the door that is my heart, and it takes no time to accept my fate. I have found my strength. When I bring self-love to the moment, life is an opportunity and a privilege that I do not take for granted.

I can't hide behind grief any longer. I need to awaken from this state and know that as I accept myself here, I have a choice. I am not stuck in the darkness and loneliness that keeps me withdrawn and afraid of moving out into the world. Illness used to be my excuse. Now that my body is healthy, I recognize that this deep longing to know myself is the core of us all.

Day 240

Grief is still here in the corners of my heart, but another part of me is getting bigger. For months, I have been hiding, allowing myself to withdraw from my past into the place where grief teaches me how to feel all that now needs to be let go of.

Spirit Speaks

These last months have given you a greater awareness of why human beings suffer. All the souls that have incarnated with you are waiting for you to choose that which is always present inside of you. You have been covered up by the insecurities and doubts that can only keep you separate from this greatness that is ever so powerfully creating your body and your experiences of this human life.

It's all so simple and now where I am is in alignment with where your soul chooses to be, connected to this vast reservoir of infinite Source. Nothing is greater than this. As you look around you there can be no doubt that this life is worthy of your presence.

Day 241

The betrayal of broken hearts and broken relationships bring us deeply into the knowing that staying with it all helps us correct our thinking. These thoughts that create pain hurt us badly and keep us separate from peace. As prisoners of the past, we are locked in a time that no longer exists. Inside myself, I'm being guided back home.

Dear God,
As I take your hand, show me the way
And carry me into the Presence of your Divine love.
Here I stay in this peace that comes
When I let go of my attachment to another.
How crazy my insane mind can become
When I keep thoughts alive that hurt me and another!
In my connection to Source,
My body relaxes and fills up with a feeling
That is alive and filled with light,

Untouched by the past or any future longing.
Here I am carried into a stream of consciousness
That holds me close; there is no separation.
A place of remembering where I am free
To grow and become more
Because I have evolved and outgrown what was.
This is creation,
And it all touches me so deeply.
In this place of surrender, my fear and pride step aside
As I come home to myself again and again.
I choose to listen to my intuitive heart,
And as I meditate, I feel awake and attuned to
My innate buddha-nature
Where I become naturally more loving and compassionate
Without asking for anything in return.

Day 242

I am driving in the car with Luke, and as we talk, my past pain comes up. How easy it is to fall into the trap of defensiveness, trying to be right. We both are charged with unwanted energy, but we talk it out and return to what is true. I can only speak for myself and own the fact that I am not perfect. In that place of self-acceptance, I can listen to myself and I also listen to my son. Together we return to the warmth of our truth once again.

Whatever is inside of us—whether it feels good or bad—is the doorway to all that needs to be spoken until the deeper truth is revealed. Here we are kissed by a Presence that frees us all and returns us to what is important. It led me here to welcome my humanity. And then the veil is lifted as I see the face of God looking back at me through the eyes of my son. He is the one that I choose to see as perfect in all the imperfections of our humanity.

Love wins again and as the sun sets into the trees, the moon rises in all her glory reminding me that all can be shown to me when I stay open. Nothing can keep me separate from my connection to this Presence that creates worlds.

Letting go of all the things that hold me down,
I've turned around.
Look in the mirror now and who do I see, my friend?
It's me.
Letting go, lost in love, open up to the real me.
Letting go, lost in love, open up.
I can finally see.
I'm finally free.
    --Lyrics from **"Finally Free"** by Luke Andrews

 Day 243

> *Sometimes I need only to stand wherever I am to be blessed.*
>   — Mary Oliver

Sometimes we hold onto things that make us feel unhappy and miserable. This identity that seems to be our wounds can keep us stuck and addicted to the negative trembling of our weakened selves. Under the surface of the resistance, we can allow these unwanted feelings to just be. Then these feelings can be our ally.

When I meet this negative part of myself, and I don't avoid it, I begin to integrate, and it becomes the part that brings illumination and insight. By staying with myself, I get inspired and deeply connect to that which would never destroy me but instead brings me to growth. As I become present again, I realize that these negative feelings never lie. They bring me to what I need to be with. It's like I'm embracing my awkward inner child who is fearful and downright negative and holding her just the way she is. She is worthy to be held in the same light as all the good and amazing feelings that are easier to touch.

Taking care of myself sometimes means staying on the couch cuddled up in my pjs, ignoring the knocks on my door, and attempting to lure me in for an evening out. It means saying no to invitations after I've checked inside and determined that what I need is rest and care.

In this place of inward reflection, I am pulled by the stream of consciousness that flows directly through my heart. Like a cup of hot tea, self-love soothes me and eases me away from my expectations and judgments. I fall in love with this moment I give to myself as I renew and restore in my own solace.

I meet myself where I am and then give thanks. I allow my breath to take me where the energy flows. Now I'm flowing, expanding, and filling up with a light that comes from the endless reservoir of love. The silence finds me, and I pay attention as I listen to the voice of Spirit whisper sweet nothings.

Day 244

Grief is a cocoon
From which we emerge new.

When grief rings:
Surrender.

The delivery is utter transformation.
   – Glennon Doyle

I look up at the morning sky and take in the big, white X sprawled across the expanse of blue. I say, "Hello sweet beloved," as I drink in Steve's handiwork. Then I ask for messages to guide this open heart.

Spirit Speaks

You are here as brilliant as this new day! Take in the sweetness of your essence. As you are filled, you will share this feeling of total

acceptance of what is. So transparent you become as you offer yourself while nature holds up the backdrop for you.

This inner journey is the only path to remembering who you truly are. Under the surface, you can humbly touch all that arises and then be still. Nothing to change, only to allow this moment to bring you deeply into awareness of your sweet Presence.

In this quiet mind, you enter inside your precious heart that becomes the home for each day. Live here.

Settle in as if you have already found what you are looking for.

The gentle breeze touches and caresses you as the sounds of this perfectly imperfect world are heard without any judgment. Here you arrive with the realization that all your hard work has brought you to your awareness where the inner eye can now see the invisible realms where truth is unveiled.

As I sit within the beauty of this inner chamber, the words that spill out of me are intimate expressions of this union within. These words carry my soul into my day, deeply forging this union with my highest self. Like poetry, they become the language of my soul.

I allow the stillness of my mind to bring renewal as I commune with my divine nature. This morning it was Steve's hello in the painted sky that helped me see that I am guided and on the right path.

I can choose to connect and open to opportunities as I socialize, allow myself to connect with another, and remain empowered. I feel so blessed to live in a world where I am free to keep choosing life and opening to what could blossom in the future.

I am good enough to have the fullness of life as I move out into the world connecting with my whole being.

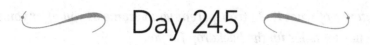

Day 245

Your sacred space is where you can find yourself over and over again.

— Joseph Campbell

I sit on the dock listening to the sounds of nature waking up to the sunrise. The calmness of the water mirrors my serenity. As I glance to my left, I see the face of a turtle staring at me. I listen inward, and a message comes through my heart that home is right here within me.

The turtle swims in front of the dock and gently moves back into deeper waters. Soon all I see are small ripples on the surface of the water. For me, this scene is a metaphor for the world of form. It's like my body, which has all kinds of physical symptoms, yet inside, underneath the skin and bones of my human self, there's a serenity that overrides everything.

I have the choice to dwell here in peace and calm no matter what the ripples of life are trying to move me into. I rest in my heart where I feel just like the turtle, peeking my head out from my shell to look about and see where I am in this incredible world. I can see into the heart of the situation as my innocent childlike self remembers that I am home right here.

My connection to who I am in this moment gives me life. I feel the blessings of just being here. Wrapped in a blanket of beauty, I stare outside, and I see and touch all that gives life. The sounds of creation begin to amplify, and every sound plays upon my heart. This most beautiful song reminds me of my childhood.

Day 246

Meditation

I am wrapped in all the beauty
Of this inner being that calls me home.
Every part of me is cloaked
In a love that gives me comfort and serenity
Through all the pain and struggles of life.

I can get caught in the loneliness
Of what the world is offering,
Yet in the center of it all
Is a Presence announcing its arrival!

Here I join with the nature of all things.
I welcome it.
It's all part of this incredible love affair
Called life.

I take this opportunity
To bow to the power that fully gives life.
This gentle Spirit is in all things.
It creates a most beautiful tapestry
Where every thread, every stitch
Is perfectly placed.
My heart opens fully
To receive it all as a masterpiece.
Nature is my doorway to Presence.

Day 247

The ego says, 'I shouldn't have to suffer,' and that thought
makes you suffer so much more. It is a distortion of the

truth, which is always paradoxical. The truth is that you
need to say yes to suffering before you can transcend it.
— Eckhart Tolle, *Oneness with All Life*

Though death is a part of life, it's not the final chapter. Grief opens your heart allowing for transformation. Even though my heart is open, my brain tells me to hide and withdraw, that it isn't safe to go out and play in the world.

As my transformation progresses, I slowly allow the expansion to spread into every area of my life. The veils of grief lift slowly. Each day, I can be more authentically in the light that is ready to burst forth and wants to bring me outside.

As I walk into the day, I carry my sadness but with a lighter step. I have more confidence because I appreciate my progress on this journey.

I never thought to say goodbye to you because our love has no end. You are remembered each day of my life.

Day 248

Meditation

Breathe and gently take it all in.
See how love never leaves you,
Not for a moment.
When the pain and suffering
Has let go of your heart,
There is more room
For you to sit here
And enjoy the magic
Of being alive
In your magnificent body.

Spread your wings
As you feel yourself
Open like a swan
Reaching up to the sun
Rising over the treetops.
You will one day fly
Beyond it all,
Like migrating birds
On the next leg
Of their journey.

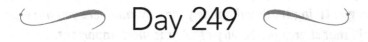 Day 249

When meditation is mastered,
The mind is unwavering
like the flame of a lamp in a windless place.
— Bhagavad Gita

Loss happens every day. Every minute of this day, somewhere someone has lost their job, their home, their health, their loved one, and perhaps even lost their mind. Being human is not easy. In response to our fear, we shrink and become small. We must be brave just to be able to get out of bed and face the trials and tribulations of our everyday lives.

We are responsible for our own happiness and yet sometimes we have habits that do not contribute to our daily living or the lives of the ones around us in a positive way.

We may not know what a given day will bring, but how blessed we are to have these days that flow along without effort. Then a day comes that knocks you down or pushes you into uncomfortable situations, and if you do not have a practice to go within and help yourself, you will get lost in the darkness.

The path to wholeness does not take you around these challenges. We must go through them. We must each feel the brokenness of this human life. It's all part of living.

Day 250

Spirit Speaks

Take your time. Life will keep spinning around creating so much for you to participate in. Yet the voice inside needs to be heard. Others will see your light beginning to shine and try to take you into what is their idea of a life worth living. Take heed and check in with your heart.

Begin each day knowing that this inner journey is yours to receive. When you do this for yourself, there is nothing that separates you from the magic. Living truth will guide your way, and here you are a part of a world that shares the beauty of what is most important.

You are here to share this light with all humanity. It will come to you in a way that fully gives life to you and others. Let this time be yours to reflect inside and listen to your inner callings. Let yourself join with the magnificent being already living within you, the one who sees all in the same light.

Day 251

We live our ordinary lives making mistakes and falling down again and again. It can feel futile and exhausting until we remember that God is with us every step of the way.

A beautiful mantra that I recite when I find myself caught up in self-judgment or hopelessness is, "Be still and know that I Am God." This mantra brings me comfort as I reconnect to the Presence inside me. It's a paradox: this connection to Presence is eternal and unchanging yet the only constant in our lives is change. Each day brings so much that is unknown and unexpected. The path begins and ends here in our conscious connection.

When I stop trying to control everything and instead choose to face my fears, I begin to see everything and everyone as part of my journey. I take the hand of God and see the mistaken beliefs about myself that I've carried through this lifetime. As I learn from these mistakes, the lessons become the wisdom I share. This classroom, which is my earthly life, is where I consciously choose to learn about my limited thinking and open to a higher power. God does not leave me.

When I choose to listen to that still small voice, it shows me the way home to my heart where I am worthy of a joy-filled life.

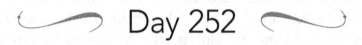 # Day 252

When I give myself permission to go inside and take care of myself emotionally and physically, it strengthens my commitment to and value for my own life. In this place, I commune with my higher self, which knows what I need. Here I breathe and let myself in. Here my inner child gets attention. Here I grow up and take responsibility for how I feel.

I have this life, what will I do with it? I can cherish it and be grateful for it.

This journey from our heads to our hearts is a moment-to-moment experience. Living in the heart takes practice as we learn to listen to the silence within the core of our being. We can rest here as we release the grip of the conditioned mind—the mind that chatters on and on distracts and takes us away from the moment right here.

It all begins within. As I let go of the past and allow this moment to take me into the stream of consciousness, this river of life gives itself to me. When I am full, it will spill out of me as loving-kindness and compassion to all. When it's too hard to smile or find the joy of living, I will pray for another and offer this day to them.

Day 253

Loss awakens us to the present moment where we feel everything that resists movement or blocks us from moving closer to the Divine. Like the sun that we know is still shining, even when there are clouds overhead, we, too, are brilliant, radiant beings, able to wait patiently for the clouds to pass so that our light can be seen and felt.

Despite this covering up of our true nature, we are all held in a Presence that keeps us steady in faith and trust. We know that the sun is shining somewhere but can we trust that we, too, will feel it again? These dark times are important. Through them, we learn to connect with what is inside. In that reconnection, we learn to trust. We let go and surrender control, we find we can let the light begin to shine, even in the darkest moments of our lives. Little by little, this light takes the place of despair and fear. Eventually, we will be released from our suffering.

These are not easy places to be, yet there is such richness in a life that can hold all our humanity with faith. As we begin to look at ourselves more honestly, we recognize and accept our mistaken beliefs and character flaws.

As this life unfolds with or without my permission, there is nothing I need to prove about myself. I have changed. Instead of chasing after what I think I don't have, I am seeing the light that is here with and for me; it's everywhere. I will embrace this new version of myself every day!

Day 254

Today, as I sit listening to Luke play at the Bridge Street Rock and Roll Party, I take a moment to look around at all the people bopping to the music. I see young couples with their babies, kids eating hot dogs, and adults lining up for beer.

Bundled up in my warm sweater with Mollie on my lap, I gaze at the clear, blue sky and feel the crisp, cool air. I feel so alive, yet my insecurities remain. They reside in between my tightly clenched belly and my heart that longs to be free.

I feel crowded on the inside. I fear that if I let go of this last chapter of my life, I might just spread my wings and fly. I feel unsteady as I keep the tears at bay. I pray underneath my breath, "God help me trust my gut." I take another breath and continue, "Universe, please help me trust myself and you!"

I decide to stop focusing on this work so much and to instead have a love affair with myself. As I let this heart of mine open to the mystery, pure joy whispers inside my heart and echoes through my Presence, "Don't be afraid." I reply, "I am afraid and that's okay."

As the sky changes into night, sounds of hands clapping and feet stomping surround me. Everyone is enjoying my son while he sings his heart out. Wow, how blessed to be here under this moonlit sky as I see God within the eyes of everyone having so much fun.

Day 255

Meditation

The cold comes easily through the window
As if to remind me that whatever comes,
A sweet message from another realm
Is here to visit me.
I listen to the wind howl.

The moment has come
To bring in what I always knew:
Life's gifts offer me more of myself.
I listen for a moment to the voices
That want to distract me.
Then I choose to be here

In the empty chambers of my heart
Where grief shapes me.

Inside it all and yet watching
Like the birds that sit
On the telephone wires,
I reach once again into my interior
To see what stirs inside.
Like the cawing crows,
It wants to share.

Listen children of this earth.
You get to shine bright
Like the fullness of the moon
On an otherwise dark night.
I walk outside to touch you
Even though you are hidden
Behind the clouds.
I am not there, I am here
Waiting for the opening
That comes with time.

 Day 256

It is when I am weak that I am strong.
— 2 Corinthians 12:10

The dim light of the early dawn wakes me gently. Pulling my robe around me, I stumble to the computer with sleep still in my eyes. I feel compelled to share a little of my parents' story. As my fingers dance effortlessly across the keys, I realize that my inner voice could be the same voice my mother listened to so many years ago.

My mother was grieving the stillborn death of her firstborn, a baby boy who died inside her at full term. Her grief was unbearable. To make matters worse, her doctor told her that she could not have any more children.

But it wasn't the voice of the doctor that she listened to. Within her heart, she heard another voice, the voice of truth. Our connection with the cosmos brings in the loving voice of God or the Universe that is beyond form.

That day, my mother did not listen to the doctor's grim prognosis; instead, she listened to what she wanted. She wanted children.

My dad offered to take her away for a retreat, a time to heal. She decided that she wanted to go to St. Joseph's Oratory in Quebec to pray for twins.

She was so committed to this pilgrimage. And as she saw crutches and wheelchairs lined up beside the long staircase up to the chapel, she knew she was where she needed to be. While her heart was grieving her loss, she could see the miracles all around her.

With a rosary in hand, she touched each round stone. The prayers she knew by heart rolled off her tongue like the music of the angels. One step at a time, she anchored in the love that was guiding her here to trust the Divine. My dad prayed on a few steps and then bent tenderly to her ear and whispered, "I will meet you at the hotel. I will be waiting for you." He left and as he walked away, he looked back at her with deep devotion.

There were so many steps for her to climb, but she was dedicated to talking to God, and she trusted her prayers would be heard.

That night my sisters and I were conceived—triplets. The story my dad loved to tell is that our mother prayed for twins and then he threw in an extra prayer. So, there were three!

Like my mother, I stay and move through the valley of sorry. The pain can cripple me at times. It is an overwhelming feeling of grief that I can't always express.

Rebuilding has been quite an ongoing process. Sometimes my ego wants to cling to the past and obsess over the future. At first, the grief was a constant throbbing in my heart, just like my mom must have felt. In my weakness, I felt so fragile and broken, but somewhere on my walks in nature and my swims in the ocean, I gave up fighting it all. I prayed as I walked. I prayed as I swam. And as I prayed, I let the strength of my spirit show me the way. Even though I was suffering and feeling, I knew that my writing, this journaling, was transforming me. These words were helping me feel my way through so that I could get up again.

Meditation brings me inside where I experience a peace that calms my body and mind. In the silence, I can mindfully receive the loving-kindness. Here I view my failures and weaknesses as they are. It takes great love, courage, and honesty to feel the grief that comes when we face the truth of our pain, when we see our shadow self.

I get to know God as a Presence that fills me up and is in everything around me and inside of me. This energy is the universal life force, and this love is moving through me in ways that I can't imagine.

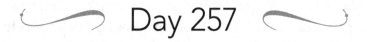

Day 257

I feel safe in the rhythm and flow of ever-changing life.
— Louise Hay

It is a constant challenge to let life flow through us without attaching to it. Yet with the connection to our higher power, Universe, or Spirit, we can begin to soften and stay present with our humanity. Then we can receive the truth that shows us the way back to our hearts. There we remember who we are as our minds join with the mind of the One.

Nothing is separate. Our humanity is so precious, so unique, and necessary for God's expression to shine through our every moment upon this great Earth. Loving what is shows us the way to compassion and a deeper understanding of why we are here.

This beautiful gift of self-acceptance, loving yourself unconditionally, is how God loves you. Take a leap of faith and trust that who you are becoming is happening because you have not lost anything. You have gained a better understanding of all the mistaken beliefs you have about yourself and the world. Here, with higher thinking, life can be an experience that passes through as you start to remember why you came into this incarnation.

The bliss of being here becomes heaven on earth. There is only a veil that separates us now, and as you lift your eyes to the light, you will receive the knowledge that continues to give life.

Day 258

My girlfriend gives me her diamond heart necklace, which I've long admired. I had wished for Steve to buy me one just like it. Now years later, it's my Valentine's Day gift. I am thankful for my generous friend, and at the same time, I know it's also a gift from Steve.

He uses this world to dance with me again. Now that I don't need him in the physical, I can receive him without feeling alone. When the radio plays certain songs, I fill up with appreciation instead of crying my eyes out. As I let go and line up with the vibrational source of my ever-present being, I am so free.

I am not the grief, it had covered me up and kept me safe under a blanket of darkness and familiar feelings of the past that comforted me. My longing for Steve brought me back to my longing for Spirit, which brought me back to my true mate, my one and only partner... my soul.

The hard times can paralyze us. I was frozen in grief and standing in my own way. I couldn't just snap out of that state, but slowly, moment by moment, I reemerged. My focus on Steve being gone fades as I turn my attention elsewhere and become present with nature and the world around me. I can allow the Presence to flow again. The difficulties of life have brought me to my creative nature where I can move into the flow of life once again.

I love this life and all that it brings me. Every day becomes another opportunity to share this radiant light by being myself.

Day 259

In the process of letting go, you will lose many things from the past, but you will find yourself.

— Deepak Chopra

Letting go of control is the hardest thing to do. Yet when we come to trust that there is another way, we open to the highest good for all. As that inner voice rings true within our hearts, we feel alive again, able to move into life with confidence and faith.

Life is a roller coaster, so we might as well hang on, enjoy the ride, and continue to choose consciously. In a holy instant, we can see the bigger picture as this world radiates the light of truth.

Imperfectly, I move into my life and know that I am still worthy of love. As I share myself honestly, perhaps God will use me to touch another who has forgotten who they truly are. It is a dance. Do I want to dance with my higher self? Or will I forget that I am being guided by an inner force that knows exactly which steps to take, and continue to trip over my own two feet?

---

*Mindfulness and meditation are good ways to stabilize
the mind, to learn to meet each thought and sensation
as it arises, not clinging through either attraction or
aversion, but bringing yourself back, over and over, to clear
awareness. From your mind, you come into your heart, and
from the heart, you will be able to become one with soul.
You are not this disintegrating body. You are not becoming
nothing. You are soul, and soul has life without limit.*

— Ram Dass

It was hard sitting with my mother when she was in the later stages of Alzheimer's. I sat in silence with her, breathing and allowing it all to be. Meeting her where she was is a practice of surrender. The whole day she was in torment and crying in agony. She was deeply in her pain and longing to go home. She didn't know her house, she didn't recognize the art she painted that adorned the walls. She didn't know her family.

Shortly before she died, my mom looked at me and with light coming from her eyes she said, *"I remember you; I know you. You are my child. You, my little angel that came from the stars."* Her eyes were bright with light. She was so awake in that moment. She was out of the dream of her illness, alert and present with me. The love gushed through me as if all the past was not real anymore.

That moment was truth. The world of form was so filled with her despair and her longing for home. In that instant, she touched her spirit and embodied pure love. There was eternity in that awakened state that we shared. She was unconditional love in form. When my mom identified with her soul, she instantly was at peace.

It only lasted for a few moments and then her despair showed itself again. A few days later, my mother took her last breath. She returned to the true source of unconditional love. She was Home.

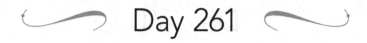

Day 261

Be patient where you sit in the dark. The dawn is coming.
— Rumi

The trigger comes out of nowhere. I thought I had my heart so close to me as I walked on, allowing the darkness of what was to hang out along the sidelines of my mind. The thoughts that come and go are expressions of my pain.

I let myself fall into the feelings that bubble up like coffee in a percolator. The tumbling becomes so strong that I lose my hold on what I believed was true. I feel my fragile human self that so vulnerably loves another, maybe sometimes more than myself. I hold the hurt as the deep sadness covers the joy that seems to have slipped away.

As the dawn comes and pulls me out of the darkness, I see once again a clearing where I am offered another chance to love myself completely. As I hold my betrayals—these moments that I leave myself—I am not dependent on another to give me serenity.

Now, in the dawn of this day, I can let my heart feel the cure of this pain.

Day 262

Meditation

I sit with my quiet aloneness
And I settle into its mystery.
Moving forward in my world
No matter what is going on,
I choose to stay present
In an open and accepting heart.

This peace feeds me
Though anger, anxiety, depression, or
Insecurity may be here,
I soften around it with awareness.
My breath consciously brings me
Into the abyss, where I lay aside my fears.

The doorway is within me.
I can walk through anytime
And create a new experience.
Here I drop the struggle
And free myself
As I see everything as an opening.
Solitude is the threshold...I meet you here.
Listening to the call of my soul,
I enter with courage.
I am not a prisoner of the suffering,
I have released the shackles.
I am liberated
And transcend.

# Day 263

> Do you not know that you are a temple of God and that the
> Spirit of God dwells in you?
>
> — 1 Corinthians 3:16

This journey has been transforming. The struggles, like a sculptor working the clay, have molded me into form. And like clay that has been fired in the kiln, I have emerged stronger, inside and out. I'm in the flow of life, moving forward. Though I'm sure to spiral down again and again into the grief of missing my husband, I'm equally sure that the stream of life will pull me back out. So, for now, I rejoice in this feeling, as I am free to be more of myself.

I take in the breath of new life as I let go. I will never be the same. I continue to move forward in this life that is flowing through and around me right now. My soul is wrapped in God as it spills out into everything I do and everyone I touch.

I would not have known who I truly am without this loss. Now I see that through this loss, I have gained. I have gained wisdom and grown in ways that have expanded my life and given me more to share of my true self.

Breath in. Breath out.
The memory of my loved one is part of my life for today and all my tomorrows.
The light shines through everything I am and all I do.

Day 264

On the bridge between me and me I find my imperfect human self. I am humbled by the spacious emptiness that is now filled with a presence that knows exactly what is real. In this moment, love flourishes between my open heart and the beauty of another. This unconditional love is so transformational, takes on a pause.

Resting inside this opening, one can look at what is happening. Here I choose to align with my authentic truth. Without pushing anything away, peace abides. Something feels healed and a door opens because my mind is empty and the quiet gives me what I am longing for. This connection to me fuels a healed mind and this to me, is the greatest power. Here there is no blame, not even for myself because every step of the way helped me see me and the truth of my own heart. My mind is my only responsibility yet to share in each person's experience helps me to take responsibility for my state of being.

As I come face to face with all my fears, I am held in the space occupied by my breath. In the stillness of this brave and magical life, I take the hand of my higher self, guided by God/Universe, as presence gives me the greatest gift of falling in love again and again with myself and all who walk in life with me.

Oh, how sweet it feels to be in this body and in this life surrounded by a world that reflects our inner being. Today may I know that life is as beautiful as I am.

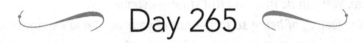

Day 265

With so much going on in this world, the mind wants to wander and take me into fears of the unknown. Then I hear the call of my dying friend, and when I look into her eyes the moment reveals the power of love.

This moment unveils me, and as I feel my grief, I realize that every one of us is facing loss at one time or another. I muster up the courage, take a deep breath, and feel the reality that is before me.

This moment, this day, this time, I look inside, I let go, and I do my part to add support during these times of uneasiness. I reach my hand out to all who are brought to me. I hold them like precious jewels and behold their beauty, always with the reverence, presence, and appreciation as if it would be my last chance to do so.

Though it might be crowded with uncertainty and fear, I arrive within my heart and drop into the present moment where I give and receive the truth that rises within my human self. How precious love is, and it costs nothing but our ability to release what has held us back from receiving what is already here. When we open and empty, we can respond with the glance, the touch, the word that can be used to connect with the heart of another.

This art of listening does not have to separate us from anyone. No matter what they say, focus on what is real, for in the moment what is true rises within as light. Here are we joined as this light binds us all together in this incredible tapestry called life.

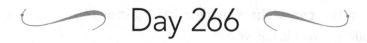

Day 266

Spirit Speaks

One day at a time but let's take it a little further. How about one moment at a time? Can you let yourself be unguarded in each moment of your living? This is a tall order, yet if you choose to listen to your heart without being distracted by the shoulds or have-tos dictated by the ego, you can be in a mindful state—listening.

This feeling of being so free—out of your head and expanded in your heart—is your true nature. I know you have been here many times. It is where I am now all the time and beyond time.

Here the light joins as you become one with all and for all eternity.

I choose to take a breath as I focus inward, and I let go of the identification of my body and mind. I let go of how I look at the world and who I think I am. There is a space inside as I dissolve into this moment where I am free to live in my heart and be the light. I am at home wherever I am.

Day 267

Forgiveness says you are given another chance to make a new beginning.

— Desmond Tutu

We leave our connection to Source, feel guilty, and believe we could never be forgiven. We don't forgive ourselves let alone another for leaving us in feelings that diminish our value. Our search outside ourselves for validation of our worthiness is a fear-based effort on an endless path of disappointment. We are left alone on a fruitless journey that keeps us separate from our greatness.

But as we let go of the need to find it in something or someone else, we turn our focus inward. Here we can feel our connection to ourselves and who we have become. We focus on whatever we feel is worthy of our attention. When we face our own negativity, these vulnerable times can be moments when we hold ourselves with a larger Presence.

We take ourselves into our minds and hearts and wrap this love around us like a blanket. In this feeling of total acceptance, we let out a sigh of relief knowing that there is a way out of the illusion of separation. We merge with everything that is rising within us and find that it is all worthy to be held in complete love. This is so simple to do, but our habit of going outside keeps us longing and believing we are alone.

When I pay attention to what feels right and let go of any external voices, the path opens to my inner being. Forgiveness gives me another chance. Here I feel held in the womb of Spirit as I tap into my unlimited, vast self. I choose to live in a way that nurtures me, expressing my own magnificence within the infinite whole.

 Day 268

Meditation

This love inside never dies.
It's where we join with our spirit.
Loving what is opens us up
To accepting the true nature
Of our very being.

Feel the vibration
That connects to all that is

As we open our eyes
And look at our family, friends, and community.

We are participating
In the evolution of soul
As we walk together
In Oneness.

Let's celebrate together
how great it is
to love and be loved.
Every moment of every day
gives me the opportunity
to be the offering.

I have seen my own suffering.
I felt it without judgment.
I choose to stay here until
the light lessens the load
of all I have carried.

As the energy moves through me
like a river of grace,
Gone are the tears.
I am an empty reservoir.

All our spirit loved ones
Participate in this Divine plan.
Sharing it all
Makes it a little easier
To open to infinite possibility.

Together we can create
A beautiful world
That can joyously hold
All our human frailties.

Today I smile. I'm beginning to move outside myself where I can take the hand of another. As I look into their eyes, I see myself along with God's light shining through. Another opportunity to awaken to the truth that I am worthy to be loved and to love, one day at a time.

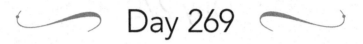

Day 269

It's scary to think about the future when nothing feels quite the same anymore. It's hard to imagine what this new life will be like. In my solitude, I sit in the awareness of being alone. Sometimes it just feels safer not doing anything at all. But my meditation practice taught me to stay with myself instead of moving more into the world. Being kind to myself is so important as self-love brings me to my open heart.

When I stay long enough, I feel the freedom within me. I'm happy to be in the kitchen letting the moment take hold, pulling me forward into life. As I cut up fresh fruit and wash the beautiful veggies for my morning drink, I know the importance of living true to myself. I love the lifestyle I have anchored in through these years of healing my body and fueling it with delicious, living food. The counter is an amazing array of bright colors— orange carrots, yellow and red peppers, zucchini, cauliflower, corn, mushrooms, bananas, lemons, limes, and tomatoes— the beauty and brilliance of life-giving nourishment. I am fed by the high vibration of this food even before I put it in my mouth.

I make my way to the floor where I move and stretch my body. Yoga has been a big part of giving to myself for over three decades. I have learned to take time for myself and to receive the gifts that self-love offers. When I do this for myself, I have so much more to give to the world around me.

I am happy I stayed with myself through the valleys of sorrow. I climb the hills of life and stand at the top, looking at everything with the eyes of my soul. I have grown up into a woman who knows what she needs. When I feed myself, I am worthy to move into this incredible life that wants nothing more than to help liberate others. Not today, but one day the light will let me know. Today I take shelter in my safe place.

Day 270

Spirit Speaks

As you walk on in this incredible world of form, know that there are so many of us surrounding your every moment, helping you see who you truly are. You will always find comfort in those that have walked before you and the ones that are placed upon your path to reflect back to you the reason for being here.

It is a glorious day for all beings to take the hand of Spirit that forever guides you to choose these life-giving moments. When you stray for a moment and forget who you truly are, you are on your way to remembering again what is real.

There are no mistakes, only more moments to remember that love is all there is. Now that you have returned to the moment where all exists, you can feel yourself in a cocoon of light, for inwardly you are becoming the one that will move through this transition in the body. Your inner life creates your outer world. So, you can never be the same as you were, for now life is fully transforming your physical to expand and fulfill the desires of the soul.

Take this day as an invitation to dance with everyone that is put on your path, and be the light and the way for union to heal the hearts of all who are ready for this new world. All is well in this incredible world that gives you opportunities to share all that gives life.

The worst days are never so bad that you are beyond the reach of God's grace. And your best days are never so good that you are beyond the need of God's grace.

— Jerry Bridges

After grief has passed, it can be hard to recognize that there is a power in us helping us choose what we will make of ourselves. We are tired. Yet in this moment, whatever is going on, we can receive grace. No matter what we are dealing with, no matter how deeply we are feeling stuck in despair, no matter what is going on in our external world, we can feel the grace of God, the touch of the Divine, the ever-present knowing that there is something vaster touching us, allowing everything to fall in place, catching us as we fall into the arms of love.

It's quite a journey we are on, this life that continues to unfold. In the unknown place where mystery dances with eternity, we stand by watching as if we were that youngster anticipating the dance. Will that one notice me, walk all the way across the room, put out their hand, and pull me into their embrace?

The moment has come when I recognize the gift of grace. It's always here, waiting for me to return. And it helps me to know that it's all okay, just the way it is.

Acceptance is a beautiful way to fall into grace. It doesn't have to take a lot of effort. The sun rises each day whether I notice it or not. That's grace. It happens whether or not I see its embrace. As a survivor of loss, I can choose to take the hand of God and feel Her grace. I look up at the sun peeking through the trees and I smile.

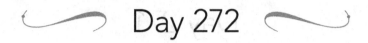

Day 272

Should you shield the canyon from the windstorms, you
would never see the beauty of their carvings.
— Elisabeth Kübler-Ross

Death can come without warning, so make the best of all your moments now. We are here to master this present moment by choosing to live conscious and awake while remembering that we all will die. Breath by breath, we take in life and as we let go of the ego, along with our attachments to this world, we see that life is for loving ourselves and everyone else. When we know this, we can serve everyone.

Meditation

Be still. Come into your inner world.
Each breath brings you here.
Let go of everything you think you know.
You are invited to rest in your heart
Here I am. Listen.

Day 273

There is no map for the landscape of loss, no established
itinerary, no cosmic checklist, where each item ticked off
gets you closer to success. You cannot succeed in mourning
your loved ones. You cannot fail
—Maribar Starr, *Caravan of*
No Despair

Some days, I didn't try to commune with the Divine, I didn't even remember how. I couldn't even climb the stairs let alone the mountain that life had built around me. The Universe wasn't cruel when grief stripped away my ordinary life. It was showing me my inner strength to endure the pain of this incredible human experience.

I couldn't deny or step away from the pain. I needed to stay in the trenches, not transcend beyond the pain into a positive mind. No affirmations or chanting mantras would bring my loved one back.

Now I can stay within it all, no matter how messy it is—it's the door that opens to the light that illuminates and shines inside.

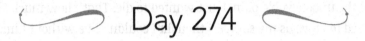

Day 274

Meditation

Breathe into your body.
Allow what rises inside your breath
To be right here.
Welcome everything
That feels uncomfortable and tense.
Release it with a big sigh
As you put down
All you are carrying.

Hold yourself with compassion.
Let a memory of love
Come into this intimate moment.
You are safe
And held in this feeling.
Breathe it in
As you enter inside.
The entire Universe
Is in you.

Sit in your pure nature
That is infinite and expanding.
There is nowhere to go.
Be the embodiment
Of this inner calmness.

Day 275

When Steve died, it brought me into all the pain of loss, which overwhelmed me. I remember saying and feeling that I just didn't want to be here anymore. Somehow, I moved through it.

Sometimes just taking a breath seemed too difficult. I didn't want to feel the unbelievable pain. I just wanted to die. That's how much I had attached to Steve as my source. I thought I couldn't live without him, but I did!

I breathe into all these sensations without trying to control or judge anything. In my acceptance, I open myself to a space inside where I can connect with my true Source. Once in that place, open and connected, I can join Steve where he is now. My mind has quieted and filled with light that softens my hold on the past. Here I can feel Steve's love, a love that never dies. Here I feel the peace to move on. It is here, not in my joining with Steve but in my own connection to Source where the wellspring of eternal life flows. I let go, and I enter into my heart where I can feel myself again.

Day 276

Cozy under my comforter, I look at the objects in the room—pictures of Steve and me, the altar with his ashes, his paintings on the wall. I touch all these belongings from my past with him and settle into my heart. Today there are no tears. There is no pain. As I stay connected to my inner experience, there is peace. I feel lighter, freer. I do not long for him as much.

In this neutral place, thoughts express through me from my inner senses. My connection to Presence fills me up with the silence of the Universe. Here I am pregnant with infinite possibilities. My focus moves from inside, where I allow the invisible to make its way into the visible. This world reflects so much more because I have rested inside myself in the darkness of the night. Now I let the light slowly in to awaken me. Today, I see myself as whole.

Today I remember who I truly am because I am not lost in the valley of grief. As I allow my soul to keep company with this world, more of me opens to let in the light. Listening to the quiet sound of nothingness, I consciously walk in this land of the living. Here I share all that has nourished me. It is in receiving that I have become the giver of life as it overflows and spills out through my human personality.

Day 277

As I look inside myself, without the distraction of Steve here in physical form, my connection to him continues. His energy catalyzes my growth.

I remember times when I would be wounded by things he said or did. I would work it out by myself until I got to a place of acceptance and maybe even more love. After, he would stand in front of me and say, "How could you still love me after what I said to you?" Now he is the one standing before me in this unconditional love and allowing me to see everything that is calling for love.

I practiced with him when he was here in a body. Now he is still bringing me deeply to myself. The light of his loving presence is helping me to see all that needs my attention.

This is the greatest gift we give to another. Here in our bodies, we find there are many relationships all around us to unplug from and not be hurt by. We are called to merge with the stuff that is still hurting and love it all. Merging with what is within me allows me to become a clearer channel, able to walk in the world while staying in my essence and allowing the force of Spirit to use me whenever the need arises.

If I'm triggered by another's word or gesture, I need not shrink from myself or leave my body. I can stand on all this rich soil and ground myself here as I listen deeply to Spirit calling me as I am.

Day 278

What it means to live life is to experience the moment that is passing through you, and then experience the next moment, and then the next.

— Michael Singer, The Untethered Soul

When you are underwater, you can really hear your breath along with the rhythmic beating of your heart. For me, it's another form of meditation that allows me to be present with all that touches my senses—the sound of my body moving through the water as I drink in the colors of the sea. It is always a healing time when I can let my thoughts flow through me like water.

While enjoying a meditative swim in the Gulf of Mexico, I receive an unexpected gift. I am so at peace and feeling the abundance of energy inside me when right in front of me appears a one-dollar bill floating on the surface of the gentle waves, glistening in the sun. I place the bill in my bathing suit, acknowledging this symbol that reflects my inner being, and I keep swimming. For me, it is confirmation, a gift handed to me from the Universe. It reminds me that I am taken care of as the energy within flows again. It was first inside of me and then manifested in this world of form.

There is no sadness. I'm not triggered by the pictures and images that have filled my mind. In the weeks and months before this, I was walking with sorrow. Now I feel happy and at ease.

Some thoughts pass through me of my past, but there is no sadness today, only love.

Day 279

We all have addictions. We plug into the world of form believing the connection will give us our power. Instead, we become weakened and powerless. I did it—I plugged into Steve to be my security.

Meditation

I see my path in front of me.
It is coming to me.
I have planted seeds within my heart.
As my life has unfolded,
These seeds have not been forgotten.
And now, as I take care of myself
And connect to the inner power that has always been,
I have allowed the foundation of my truth to nourish me.
I am activating my heart's desires—
The ones that feed my soul and align with my purpose.
Why I am here.
I walk on remembering what I always knew,
Even as a child,
Cultivating dreams and releasing them to the Universe.
I gratefully receive the fruits of the seeds I have sown
In this lifetime.
As I retrieve my soul,
I hold on to all that my heart has never forgotten.
My needs as a human being are still here
And I must tend to them.
I ask for help and allow the Universe to show me the way.
To start over again,
I must be willing to risk experiencing loss again.

My fear of loss still speaks to me every day, but I am willing to take that risk, for it is the key to laughter and passion.

Day 280

The mind softens, and in the quiet presence of the moment, I tune into the rhythm of my life. I choose to be in the stream of consciousness instead of the thinking mind where all my senses are more alive and become the pathway home to my heart.

I feel at home in these familiar surroundings of this Island, and yet, in this moment, it wouldn't matter where I am. I'm deeply with the Divine that is close and intimately inside and outside of me.

The longing for the beloved isn't for a faraway place to get to. It is the journey that brings us deeply into our hearts where we are home. When we arrive, it radiates throughout our entire being and joins with everything that exists. We begin to see the precious gift of life that offers comfort as the world becomes the messenger, giving us the feeling of belonging.

To be in love no matter what the conditions are outside is easier said than done!

We are enough and worthy to drink from this cup of living waters that flows from within. This river of Presence will fill you up.

Day 281

I stand by a tree with a woodpecker just an arm's length away. Wearing its red helmet, he looks right into my eyes. I don't spiral into the past thinking of missing Steve. Instead, I gaze into this bird with my heart wide open. I am filled with appreciation for all that life has brought me. All the ups and downs and ins and outs of day-to-day living stop as I receive the answer I have been waiting for. As faint as a whisper, I hear, "Don't despair. I am the hope for healing as you open to the Divine."

Love waits for me to commit to myself first, then opens me, allowing me to be present with all that is right here.

 # Day 282

I come as one but stand as 10,000.
— Maya Angelou

Some moments are painful, yet even in the deepest suffering, there is always a glimmer of hope. That glimmer, that spark, takes us to our connection where we receive the insights of a life shared by many.

Being human isn't easy. Our ancestors journeyed through wars and depressions and battled diseases and plagues. We have the consciousness to remember the gifts given by all the ones who came before us. Their lifetimes of struggle have brought us freedom.

We walk on, knowing deep in our hearts that others have walked in our same shoes. They have pioneered this pathway, falling down, and getting up with faith and love for us. None of it was perfect. They also had losses and hardships as they moved through their sadness and faced their deaths.

I choose to accept my humanness as I follow through consciously and continue to create a world for all the children. I am showing up and doing my best to learn about love so I can help my children grow up in a belief system that supports their soul's purpose.

Meditation

As I search for the answers
To forgotten questions,
Death brings me
To a hidden door.

It has been pried open
By the ever-gentle tug
Of my heart.
I touch something and realize
it is everything I was looking for—
The whys and what-ifs,
the thoughts that keep me held
In a pattern that forgets
What is already here.

I reach for something
That calls for my attention,
Only to wander back
Into memories
Gone from my reach.

Life itself takes me by surprise
As I lift the curtain
Between here and there.
I hold it all
For me and for you.

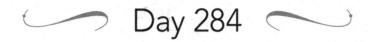

Day 284

You must live in the present, launch yourself on every wave,
find your eternity in each moment.

— Henry David Thoreau

Something is different this morning. I feel excited to be in the world. I fill myself up with all the energy that this beautiful day gives me. While on a walk, I feel a difference inside. I'm not withdrawing or feeling intimidated by others who pass by. I feel open and enjoy the conversations. I feel like my old self again.

I've always been a friendly person, but in my grief, I have felt guarded and vulnerable. The world can spark memories and feelings that can cause me to burst out crying. I have withdrawn to protect myself because I never know what will trigger these memories or feelings.

Today is different. As I welcome the world in, I can stay open to receive the beauty of the day. After the walk, I go for a swim. I love to put on a snorkel and mask and watch the light move through the water, reflecting on the little fish or shells or even starfish. It's always an open-eye meditation as I feel my body gliding through the silky water, an endless sea of brilliant turquoise blue.

After swimming, I walk the beach. In gratitude, I look at all the gifts of energy that come from the sky, the clouds, birds, fish, and people. I fill up and allow the open space to welcome in the love and light of creation.

I am here to learn love. I am awake and I belong as I feel the blessings of a world that shines its light on me.

Day 285

Spirit Speaks

Wake up, children of the earth, and let the energy that flows naturally through your heart be the love. Remember you are love dwelling in Spirit. You are the one that reaches from the deepest core of your being and goes out to play. With the innocence of the child within, you see the world anew.

Your body is light, and in your presence, Spirit lifts humanity into the peace that is beyond all understanding. You walk back into your house, and you are not afraid to uncover all that has held you prisoner in the material world. You recognize the fears that hold you back from discovering the truth that has always lived in your heart.

There is a deep longing to return to the light. The union with spiritual Presence is within your reach. The choice is yours. The pathway is through the heart as you join in sweet communion with the flow of living waters. Here the eternal youth of conscious awareness brings gifts to the body and everybody.

Day 286

As I walk Mollie, mindful of my breath, my mind becomes so empty and still and expanded with no boundaries. Every part of me exists yet now it seems faded because my deep emotions and feelings that were so heavy inside this morning are now held with complete love.

I'm swept up in a moment of rapture. Standing still, I hear my beating heart and feel at home within it. There is no searching. Everything is illuminated, like a spotlight shining on the entire world. Sounds of nature are amplified, and in that holy moment, I remember that this is who I am. This mind of mine feels as expansive as the beautiful world outside I am gazing at. The light enters and I am so filled with appreciation.

I am okay and there is nothing I have to do to arrive here but to receive it and drink it all in. I am filled with a love that seems infinite. Little Mollie guides me to this Presence, but I am the one who allows myself to just fall into love.

There is no quick fix. Now is where I can anchor in more of who I am and how I choose to live. I am becoming more conscious of this incredible light that keeps illuminating my path.

I open my heart to love and see its light everywhere! Self-love becomes the light of my soul's reflection in all humanity.

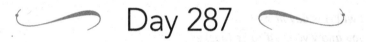 Day 287

The candle dances for me in my darkened room as the fan blows air through the vents. In the dim light, I listen to the stillness that calls me to be quiet. Seated on the couch in my living room, I feel a sense of comfort inside. I'm filled with Divine grace. As I grasp it like a child holding onto a kite, it draws me up into a space of awareness.

Inside, I am full and empty at the same time. Love soothes me like a cool breeze on a hot sunny day. I'm suspended in a giant void full of peace, no longer a prisoner of my mind. The moment seems like an eternity.

My gaze moves to a photo of my dad that leans against a book. The flame of the candle lights up his face, and it feels like he is looking right at me.

Years ago, when I was writing my first book, he would knock on my door in the wee hours of the morning, peek his head in and ask me to read to him my latest work. He'd listen, nod, and smile, conveying a job well done. I feel his spirit fill the room, and I am filled with love.

My open heart holds it all and has no longing or missing. Spirit is a part of everything, and it all is a part of me. This journey to love greater is such a pleasure to be on.

Day 288

Meditation

Listen to the sound of nature that awakens you inside.
This moment is new, where all that seems lost
Becomes the doorway to what is.
The choice to move into life is yours to make.

What will this day bring?
Will you allow yourself to be touched
By the sweetness of all that is calling your name?
Your heart holds the dream for you, this dream of Oneness.
Listen to the song that expresses
The goodness of everything.
Wait patiently as you breathe right here,
For in this holy instant, you remember what is true.
In this Presence, rest in pure awareness
Where peace abides.

Live from this place and drink in the beauty
That nature gives without conditions.
You hold the key to everything;
To infinite pathways that lead you
To the opening that is within.
The sounds of this day offer you a promise
As they take you into a moment
Teeming with love's messages.

Love sets a banquet table before you
In the most beautiful garden
where all the singing surrounding you
is the joyous whispering of a spirit
That joins you with everyone.
In this moment, time stands still,
And all that rests in you
Is shared with all who gather.

Day 289

When things fall apart and we can't get the pieces back together, when we lose something dear to us, when the whole thing is just not working and we don't know what to do, this is the time when the natural warmth of tenderness, the warmth of empathy and kindness, are just waiting to be uncovered.

– Pema Chödrön, *Taking the Leap: Freeing Ourselves from Old Habits and Fears*

The winds blow in a change of seasons accompanied by feelings of loneliness. Allowing myself to feel where I am is vitally important. It is easy to get busy and move into old behavior patterns—taking care of the outer part of life and ignoring the visitor within that calls for my attention. My inner reality lets me know where I am in my search for balance in this ever-changing world of external validation.

Life is always serving me opportunities to find my serenity within. Breathing becomes a more conscious way to receive myself and all that will deliver me back into the present moment where life becomes richer, and I am truly myself no matter what. Here, in the center of it all, my softened heart discovers the love that never dies. I am awake, and in this mindful way, I am not hidden from myself.

Through stillness, we bring the truth out into the open. The artist paints a new picture. The singer sings a new song. The writer lets the words flow. A woman finds her purpose. A man discovers his true self. Life brings us all home to the one that creates worlds.

Meditation brings me into the silence within a busy world. In the stillness, love prevails. As I open my eyes again, I see the miracle that is life. It heals everything that has ever been. I can begin again today; today I can create something beautiful.

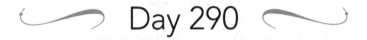

Day 290

One cannot get through life without pain... What we can do is choose how to use the pain life presents to us.
— Bernie S. Siegel

The morning after Steve left this world, he invited me to join him in the light. He spoke to me even though I didn't want to listen. He showed himself to others around me to keep reminding me of what I already knew. He was free from his body and his ego and now able to assist in my return to the love.

It's been quite a journey, and now with the connection to my inner alignment, I can commune with Spirit anytime I want, because in that mind I am present in each moment I am living. I have learned that by staying here in this moment, I can be as free as my beloved in Spirit. He always wanted to feel the freedom I feel when I meditate and embody the light. Now he is the light showing me the way to live a beautiful life. He assists me as I go out and serve this food that I receive in my communion with Spirit.

This Divine plan is so brilliant. I see it and share it. We are all here to share the gift of our Presence and express in our unique ways the treasures found on this journey through loss and letting go.

Let's walk through the doorway together and allow this new life to give more life. Let this soul-light that turns darkness into love be the blessing that touches the world.

Day 291

And once the storm is over you won't remember how you made it through, how you managed to survive. You won't even be sure, in fact, whether the storm is really over. But one thing is certain. When you come out of the storm you won't be the same person who walked in. That's what the storm is all about.

— Haruki Murakami, Kafka on the Shore

Memories flow gently through my mind. Wrapped in moments of yesterday, I realize that everything about me has changed. I feel some sadness rising through my heart, but more than anything, I feel the blessings that are so richly received.

The bird that sings so sweetly does not sing of what is lost. I hear its praises of creation, which lead me to a silence that calls me home to birth a new me.

All that this life has taken me through allows me to receive this glorious, new day.

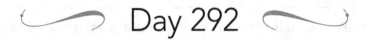

Day 292

Meditation

I want to love the world.
I want to laugh from my belly.
Like the blue heron that stands
Beside the fisherman and his pail,
I go to the shore and wait
While the sand crab gently walks away.

I am taken into nature's beauty.
In the breeze, I hear the laughter of children.
It lingers awhile.
I notice that for a moment
I have put down my sadness.
I have let go and feel myself,
So truly myself, right here, right now.

Even though there are clouds, the sun is still shining. When I allow my gaze to move away from the sadness, life flows through without much effort. It is our Divine nature to live in this love. It fills us up so that we can be brilliant and beautiful. Like a flower in full bloom, I release fragrance from my compassionate heart. Through my imperfect self, I receive. And in my receiving, I am the giver.

Day 293

Sad things happen. They do. But we don't need to live sad forever.

— Mattie Stepanek

The sadness is there but I turn my gaze away. For days, weeks, months, and more, it has held me in bondage. I look away. While in the fear, I let go and choose to stop clutching onto the past. Will I feel something deeper in that well of emptiness? I return yet again to find it feels softer; I am softer.

I can learn my soul's lesson, to love and accept myself fully. I can know that no matter the condition, I can bring all of me here even when I'm hurting. In doing so, maybe, for a little while, I can love this beautiful world with my wholeness.

Meditation

Breathe in and close your eyes.
Pray for softness to hold the sadness.
Settle into what is within
As you take your focus to your breath.
Open your eyes so you can receive
The messengers in your world.
This is a magnificent love story
Between you and you.
Trust in how life will unfold.
This world speaks to your heart.
Let go and listen.

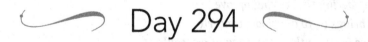

Day 294

It takes great courage to look at ourselves with tenderness while being honest with what we are feeling. When we don't know how things will work out, can we be okay with not knowing?

I embrace being fully human and awake as I move into the life that is here today. Both in front of me and within, there are doorways. How many times will we stumble or remain stuck before we learn the lesson, get our footing, and venture across the threshold? With great humility, I strive to accept my journey. Though it hasn't always been easy, I have learned to surrender into my open mind and heart and allow it all to be. I can relax as I connect to this deeper self that ponders my actions and their impact on others.

Threads of golden light weave us all together. But when the ego is busy identifying with it all, this connection will be missed. From the silent place, I recognize everyone and everything as they add to this incredible tapestry called life.

These streams of consciousness awaken us to the great mystery. But if we are too self-absorbed, we miss the boat and drown in the turbulent waters of our own making. When we become present within, we can see the lifelines being thrown to us and take hold of them. As we relinquish control, we allow the greater forces from beyond to take over and pull us back on board.

When I come back to my center, I journal. I love the feeling of the pen in my hand as I watch how the ink spills onto the paper. When I empty myself, I am filled with a silence that quiets me and thrills me at the same time. It refreshes me like the breeze that comes through the window.

As I read the words filling my journal pages today, I bow to the great, wise master who is expressing through my being. Where did she come from, this higher self who guides my way?

There is you, and there is me.
We dance within the shadows of our past,
Remembering the stirring of love
That brings us to a melodic concerto.
Can we listen to the sweet song of our souls
As we choose to merge into the One melody
That only our hearts can hear?
Be free, sweet love, and let the inner knowing
Wrap you up in its embrace.
The calling to this deeper knowing
Ushers in a new dawn.
It's all good, for the love that is spoken
Speaks loudly in the silence.
The sweet melody—

Ancient and familiar, never forgotten.
We hear, we listen, we remember.
Again and again, we remember
As we open to so much more!

Grief has moved me deeply inward on this path where I can embrace my fears. When I'm present within, I am not afraid.

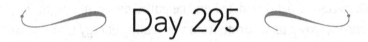

Day 295

When you are sorrowful look again in your heart and you shall see that in truth you are weeping for that which has been your delight.
— Kahlil Gibran, *The Prophet*

I wake up feeling the grief and loneliness of another day. I'm falling into the crack between waiting to leap and hanging on to the past. But oh, how my heart wants to hold me, no matter what I decide.

I can't stay in limbo any longer. I cannot remain here, it's like a forced death. My soul reminds me that right now is the moment to live fully. As I breathe in this new life that is unfolding, slowly I begin to catch my breath. The Universe is my net, catching me even when I forget that it's there.

I accept the impermanence of loss and joy. It's all temporary and yet as I surrender to what is, I am safe, and there is nothing to hide or hide from. I can be the lover of life in the here and now. I bless every person and every event as each moment allows the sacred in, leading me back home. As my perception changes, I see everything as love.

Day 296

Conventional knowledge tells us that we are separate; higher
wisdom informs us that we are one. A shift of perception
reveals that we are all the same consciousness, manifesting
in different bodies, the way leaves are part of the same tree.
— Dan Millman, *The Laws of the*
Spirit: Simple, Powerful Truths for
Making Life Work

It's so easy to get distracted and be pulled away into negative
patterns that keep us separate from the healing energy that is always
filling us up with love and light. It's a practice, a lifelong journey, to be
grounded in Presence and fully authentic.

We share in our connection to the Divine where we are one. None of
us is going home without the other. Our spirit loved ones are here to help
us reach inside and do this work for the collective. My healing is yours.
Your healing and truth touch me. We are in it together, and together we
will create a new world.

We pray with one voice as we journey through sorrow and joy.

Day 297

How but in custom and ceremony,
Are innocence and beauty born?
— W.B. Yeats, *A Prayer for My*
Daughter

Listen to the sounds of nature
Calling you home to your heart.
Look around and witness
The beauty that nature reveals.
There is grace,
As Mother Earth holds all that is lost
And all that is coming alive.
The ground you walk upon,
The trees that stand before you,
The water that draws you inside,
All give you strength.
Breathe in the air
That connects you to new life.
You are touched by this intimate exchange
As nature reminds you—
You are loved.

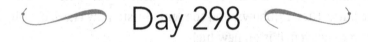

Day 298

As we do what is most natural in this life—love and be loved—there is no greater gift than to help and support another along their journey to emotional health and well-being. When we do the work and create balance for ourselves, we provide an opening for our Divine nature to move out and touch others in ways we cannot know.

From this grounded and centered space, we become a beacon of light, a way-shower. As we are joined by others on this path, we can commune with our world in harmony.

I have arrived home to my heart where life can be created in the way God intends. Unconditional love greets life without any prerequisites or requirements.

Day 299

Meditation

Empty your mind as you move into the quiet of your heart.
Forget what you know.
Enter here as you focus your attention on your breath.
Inside is the darkness,
Let it just be.
Be home in the dark womb of self.
Wait here and let the silence speak of nothing.
Receive the truth as God/Universe whispers in the night,
"I am endless love."
This love is you.

I'm living now in this new relationship with my loved one in spirit. In many ways, it is a mystery, one I may never solve. I let go of what I think I know and listen to the voice of Spirit. It speaks to me from the darkness where butterflies, rainbows, and the wind kissing my cheek are all love notes from heaven. It is all new life!

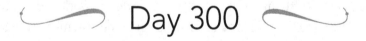

Day 300

This is the mystery. The undeniable Presence where the secret of death is, by no mistake, hidden from us. As I enter the moment with my breath, aware that death is our fundamental fear, I arrive at the doorway of all my feelings. I sit inside this human experience remembering the moment when death took away my loved ones. The loneliness and absence of their life brought grief like nothing else could.

Walking the beach, I commune with all that is present as nature untangles my busy mind. As the sounds of the waves alight inside of me,

I soften my gaze and come back to myself. I'm at home in the comfort of my own heart. There, I receive the invitation to glimpse the fullness of my presence and express it in ways that create and give thanks to the Divine. This greater generous heart takes a deep breath and says yes, I am here, as the space inside opens and the sacred whispers, "Do not be afraid."

I arrive in the quiet solitude of my inner world.
No one can see what I see as I move deeper into the unknown.
Under the surface, I find my core where I dwell.
As I face my fears of dying,
My breath wraps around me so tenderly.
The shy, quiet soul is tucked away inside this Presence,
where Spirit meets my humanity.

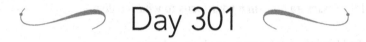

Day 301

The Brain—is wider than the sky—
For—put them side by side—
The one the other will contain—
With ease—and You—beside—
    – Emily Dickinson

With a grateful heart, I walk on in my day and share this love that has held all of me—every part of me, even the one that judges and complains and criticizes. I watch myself lift into a compassionate mind that knows it all. This mind that silences me shows me the way to a peaceful and fulfilling life. How blessed we are when we allow this still small voice to take us into the stream of consciousness where every moment is holy and sacred.

In the stillness, everything is softer and infinitely accessible. There is no time or space. We have an all-access pass, and we can absorb everything in a holy instant. The observer that has been inside me since the beginning of time shows me all of me as I expand and become bigger than life itself.

Being out in nature brings me into stillness as I find the deep sense of peace that I long for each day. There, I join that piece of me that sits quietly and calls all my senses into aliveness.

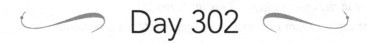

Day 302

Spirit Speaks

Come my love!
Today, you are asked to set your suffering down and put them aside for this moment in time.
Let all the losses go and turn your focus to what is alive.

Here, inside let love take up room in your heart.
Arise through your awareness of what is and sense a new pathway opening.
The light of your heart is unconditional love.
This is well being.
This is where you thrive sweet angel.

Invite life in so you can flourish
as the sacred rises through you
like the sun.

Meditation

I am ready to love deeper and to appreciate these moments
as I move through my senses discovering my greater, independent self.
This is beautiful—
To arrive here amidst the conditions
of my world, leaning into me,
into my ability to respond from a more awakened state.

I open to the emptiness that seems to house my soul
and begin again through the transformation
that has taken place.
Even the broken pieces are held with the Grace of God.

I rise through it, and out of my inner being, I connect with
the Spirit of God's love, which connects me to everything.
All is possible here.
All is received in this sacred encounter within,
where the Divine energies of Spirit serve me and all humanity.

Everything we seek is always inside.
This love awaits my return.
Alas, as I come into me,
I find this compassion for all I have been through, and
the qualities of my own inner being shine!

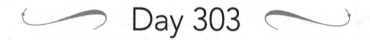

Day 303

Learn to get in touch with the silence within yourself and
know that everything in this life has purpose, there are no
mistakes, no coincidences, all events are blessings given to
us to learn from.

— Elisabeth Kubler-Ross

My heart broke and then every cell of my body changed. All the tears I have cried formed rivers of sadness that opened channels within for life to run through me. These tears cleansed me of my sorrow, and the experience has evolved my soul.

Even though I have entered life fully again, my tears have not been held back. I walk on with the clouds that covered me for so long, now gone. There is a portal that brings me into this new life where I am now fighting for my dreams. Life did not kill the dreams I once had, grief did.

I see the beauty of the jasmine tree and the way the light shines on my path. My love for life is not weakened by suffering.

Life knows what it is doing. Only the direct experience of loss can get you to surrender. The letting go process is your journey, and when you let go, life becomes a companion and teacher, helping you find your way to greater inner peace.

Because of this great loss, my heart has become stronger and wiser. My love for life is filled with wonder.

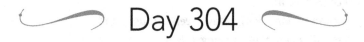

Day 304

Stillness. One of the doors into the temple.
—Mary Oliver

The door has opened. I invite you in, my beloved. The birds are so loud as the butterflies come into the garden, and the gentle sweet morning invites me to be quiet.

Something has happened inside me. I have touched the invisible—the parts of my human feelings that were stirred up.

I recognize that today I don't have to do anything to work on myself or make myself happy. I just allow this quiet stillness to be the opening for more life to enter. I am moving into a greater me, one that can't be defined by my clothing or my endeavors. It's the me that is my soul. This light has broken through the surface of my shadow that surrounded me with torment and despair for so long. This beautiful, sacred body that is here, aware of the presence of death. I listen to its calling as the inner voice speaks to me, "Let go and let your self be here in all the truths that are underneath the surface of the external world."

This stillness is the door opening to so much more, this sensuous feeling where God lives and breathes through me. Under the surface, the invisible, when touched, brings the visible power of the Universe into human form.

Every step, every choice, every thought, and every breath lead me here where I can trust in this moment. I am molded and shaped by it.

The person I am today stands in the center of my being. As the falseness falls away, I shed the skin that cannot house my spirit any longer. I pull away the masks that I hide behind and settle into who I really am. Now I can accept all the human stuff that has made me rich inside and root myself deeply into this earth that I call home.

I am free once again when I awaken to this new moment, released from the ego. I take the hand of Spirit and become the peaceful warrior, the one who joins forces with the Divine and captures the light that takes us all into the oneness of creation. Together we create a new moment, one that is filled with the promise of new life.

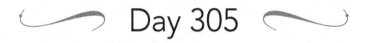

Day 305

Perhaps they are not stars in the sky, but rather openings where our loved ones shine down to let us know they are happy.

— Eskimo legend

I am so present as I hold my daughter while she cries, missing Steve. It is a curious animal this thing we call grief. It can be so unpredictable. For Lane, it waited silently then suddenly pounced.

Steve had been a strong emotional connection for Lane, giving her unconditional love. He called her Princess and, from the time she was 12, showed her that she was important. In her heart, she felt he filled a hole she didn't know she had. He was not blood. He did not have to love her. He wasn't her father; he was her dad.

"You have filled yourself up, Mommy, and no one else will ever fill the hole that is so deep in me. No one can be what Steve was for me," she cried as her heart ached with unbearable pain. Because she has so much pain, she feels angry and hurt. I hear her. At the beginning of this nightmare of his death, she held me. She helped me breathe through the sudden and unexpected shock. Now it was my turn to hold her.

Lane runs from me, blinded by her tears, and screams, "Let me go!" I watch her in the darkness while she sits on the beach crying and screaming for Steve. As she asks him for help, her anger moves out of the way. High above in the darkest of skies, a shooting star streaks before her eyes. It's Steve, showing up in the dark night of her soul; the light of his love pouring directly into her heart, saying "I am here."

I can hold my child in her pain because I have done this work. It has not been easy to let the voice of grief fade. Now I can listen to her pain with compassion. I know in my heart I can help her remember how worthy she is to be loved.

Day 306

Meditation

I live with them all,
These souls who cry out for the pain to stop.
I hold them even though I know I can't fix them.

My compassionate heart knows
This conditional world is full of contrasts.
It reminds me to touch what is here inside of me.
I allow myself to be me.

I feel the sadness and I cry.
I feel the loneliness and I surrender.
I feel the pain and suffering
Of all the broken hearts
That are calling for release.
I feel it all then I let go.

I hear the voice of the Beloved.
She calls me to receive it all.
"You are always safe
As you are carried in the light.
Trust in yourself,
For truth guides your way."

I drink in the words that soothe my unease
Over my unknowable future.
Can I wait a little while before I act?
I ask... I wait... I know
There is no time or distance
When I live in my heart.

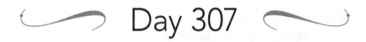 # Day 307

You, darkness, of whom I am born—
I love you more than the flame that limits the world to the
circles it illumines and excludes all the rest.
But the dark embraces everything: Shapes and shadows,
creatures and me, People, nations—just as they are. It lets
me imagine a great presence stirring beside me.
I believe in the night.

— Rainer Maria Rilke

In this poem, Rilke shows us that our very origin is from the darkness in the womb, until Spirit bravely enters the world of form.

We begin this journey in darkness. In the womb, we are held in it, like the great mystery where the unknown holds so much possibility. I love the time of night when I pull myself into bed and turn out the lights. I fall asleep thinking about my daughter who is about to give birth.

Just before dawn, still dark outside, I wake from a dream, crying and so full of love. Steve visited... Lane was sitting in front of him. He wasn't speaking but his body language conveyed his excitement. Light illuminated his presence. As Lane bent over and kissed him, a card, all folded up, passed from his lips to hers. She took the card and unfolded it very slowly like it was a treasure. It said, *"Hi Mama, I can't wait to be in your arms."*

I can't wait to give this message from my unborn grandchild to my daughter. And she'll be overjoyed to hear from Steve, my courier in the darkness where the unknown great mystery dwells.

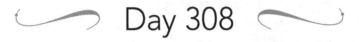 Day 308

The pain will come.
Let it visit,
cry it out,
vent it out,
bleed it out.
And then ask it to leave.
Do not allow it to build a home
and call it broken.
We aren't meant to be broken forever.
That is punishment to our hearts and minds.
          – Pierre Alex Jeanty

As I wake up to the cool air on my skin, presence calls me to enter its inner landscape. How easy it is to ignore this calling. How easy it can be to let the outer voices of this world pull me away from who I am. I hold myself here, deeply connected to so much richness. I rest knowing that this is who I am.

The body holds my truth. I fall into places of yesterday and tomorrow, loving what nudges me into the Presence. I observe myself in all my ways and then rest inside my heart.

I have suffered loss, but who hasn't? As we stay present with all that it brings us—pain and sorrow, fear and despair—we stand at the threshold within this physical body. It is in our acceptance—not running away or trying to change it—that we soften and allow the light of Presence to flow through. Little by little, we begin to heal until eventually, we find we are whole again. Now we enter the next stage of living.

I walk with my heart open and welcome in the newness of being vulnerable and honest. It is so freeing to focus within. This state of being has been my true nature all along.

Day 309

I saw the angel in the marble and carved until I set him free.
—Michelangelo

I walk into the Academia Gallery in Florence, Italy, which houses Michelangelo's David, his sculptured Prisoners, and many other works from the 16th – 18th centuries. I feel huge energy vibrating through me like I am plugged into a light socket. Emotions fill me with so much joy, my heart expands, and I just want to weep.

My eyes drink in the works of art—huge sculptures of marble giants carved so long ago. Forms of strong, naked prisoners appear to step out of the marble. They seem to come alive, the freeing of form from out of the formless.

As I look down to the great hall, I feel the pull from the statue of David and the desire to take in the history of this masterpiece. I feel myself in a timeless moment sharing this love I have for art and allowing the inspiration to move me into more of myself. I was here before when I was in my teens, before I ever touched the face of grief.

The room is filled wall-to-wall with people. Most seem unaware of the magnitude of energy that is filling us all, feeding us with so much more than we could conceive of. I am intoxicated with a love that is beyond this human experience and every part of me wants to dance, sing, paint, hug, and kiss… I am inspired and filled with the joy of being alive.

It doesn't get better than this! I am in love and meeting all the parts of myself that want to be free—just like the sculptures of Michelangelo. I am choosing to free myself out of the mold of this human form. As I move through the various rooms, I get lost in the paintings, and time seems to stand still. Nothing pulls me away from the incredible feeling of being here right now.

Day 310

Meditation

Breathe deeply
As you bring your focus within.
Feel and smell the earth beneath you.
Let the sounds of nature
Call you here,
You are grounded.

The wind brushes against your face
As you turn to the warmth of the sun.
You are here.
You are alive.
Feel the moment
As you bring awareness to the body.
Let the feelings rise up and fade away.

With every conscious breath,
Sink into yourself and just be.
Invite your loved one to join you.
Trust in the way that your open heart
Receives Spirit's communication.

You might see an image or a symbol,
Hear a word or see light.
Receive this union and intimacy with all creation.
Together you make a difference
Creating a new world.

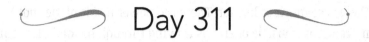

Day 311

You can do the impossible because you have been through the unimaginable.

– Christina Rasmussen

When I moved into all those moments of remembering "life with Steve," it unveiled me and opened me up like nothing else could. It brought me to my knees and forced me to look at every part of myself— all that needed to be let go of, all the attachments, all the love songs, and all the love letters. As it moved me deeper into myself, no one could take the pain away. I allowed it to devour me, shake me up, and spit me out.

Now I see and feel that I am different. I am stronger. I am more open and loving. Relationships are richer and more authentic. All I need is to connect to the Spirit that is within and all around me; the piece of heaven that I am a part of.

Steve is right here, in all his glory. He walks in Spirit guiding my way, for he is now a part of the Divine without the shackles of his human form. As I retrieve myself, as I awaken to what is true, God moves into everything around me.

I have peace again. I can laugh and have fun. I can enjoy the beauty of this world. I can take the hand of Spirit and walk along this path in front of me. It is lighted by the love of all that is. Here I am not alone. Even as we walk alone inside our hearts, we are always in good company.

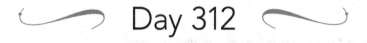

Day 312

When you change the way you look at things, the things you look at change.

– Wayne Dyer

There is so much to live for. There is a power inside of me that has taken over. This invisible energy is flowing through me and all around me. Even when I feel stuck in grief, I am held by this great being called God who holds me until I can consciously open to my life again. Getting to this point where I can feel this aliveness has happened slowly and gently. I have awakened, and it feels so good to watch it all with eyes that see so much more clearly now.

I know within my heart that when I reside in this quiet place within, I am free. I begin to see life around me differently. I feel calmer, and there is less resistance inside. I watch with my entire being. As I see it all from this centered place of my inner being, I am so present in the moment. I observe and listen inside without reacting. I speak from a place that is authentic and truthful.

Loss has brought me many gifts. I am stronger, yet softer. I am trusting in myself and my ability to take care of myself. And from this place of self-love, I can care deeply for others. I look at each day as if it could be the last day of my life. Each time I am with someone, I want to drink them in and savor the moment for all that it is. Here I am a conduit for love as I step into new potentials.

 Day 313

Meditation

Be Yourself

Listen as the stillness brings you all that you need.
Receive, receive, receive, Beloved one,
And rise up out of your bed.
Share this food that gives life.

No one is separate from you.
Yet, you cannot force anyone to join you.
Just go outside and play upon the earth
and whoever has awakened
Will dance with you this day.

Every moment is an opportunity to listen inside.
Drink it in until you are so full,
It spills out of you
Through your honest expression of your heart.
It will be the paintings that fill up the canvas,
It will be the songs that flow through your voice.
It will be in every act of kindness
As you listen deeply to others,
For you have no idea who will be put on your path.

In your fullness, you have returned home
To this place within your heart.
Only you know when you are ready
To rise and be fully yourself.
You have the freedom to be
All that you came here to be,
Authentically YOU!
That's the greatest gift you give to this world.
Be yourself, for no one is like you.
You are unique and powerful beyond all measure.

Day 314

Spirit Speaks

After these months of inner hibernation that have helped you let go of what was, you will now blossom. The fruits of your labor will bring aliveness and delicious parts of you into the world. Your body is the vessel of this infinite life that will continue to give to the world.

Like footprints in the sand, like a flower's sweet fragrance hanging in the still air, we each leave our imprint on this earth. From hugs and handshakes to myriad experiences throughout our lifetime, we feel Presence and allow it to move through us and out into the world of form. But it is with conscious awareness that we get to choose what mark we wish to make here.

Nature reminds us to return to ourselves, to take good care of our state of being. When we are filled up, we give from our fullness. Then we can go out into the world and stay long enough to gaze into the eyes of another and receive them, listen to them, hold them in that precious and sacred holy moment. We can't do it if we are distracted by the mind looking to save the world or to find another problem to fix. It is in the stillness, in nonjudgment, where we discover the peace of acceptance for ourselves and others.

I am here to learn self-love. As I receive every part of my humanity, all the darkness and the light, I can stop judging and begin to allow life in.

 Day 315

Death is more universal than life; everyone dies, but not everyone lives.

— Alan Sachs

Meditation

Hear the call from deep within.
This sweet sound gently wakes us up
Saying, "Be here fully."

There is nothing to do
But to accept that you are enough.

Life has moved you along your soul's path,
Every step forming you, molding you
From the inside to the outside.
More falseness falls away
As you move through the ups and downs
Of being human.

Slowly, surrender without trying to change a thing.
There is perfection in this magnificent ride.
Without any loud announcements or drum rolls,
You enter the present moment worthy to be here
In this magnificent life that gives without conditions.

Instead of letting the ego run the show,
Arrive in your heart that knows the truth.
Enter with grace as you open your heart and your hands
To the One who creates
Through this beautiful life
That is living and breathing through us all.

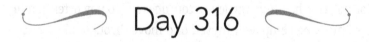

Day 316

If we always choose comfort we never learn the deepest
capabilities of our mind or body.

— Wim Hof

The greatest gift we give to humanity is taking impeccable care of our health in body, mind, and spirit. It starts with the breath because breathing helps the body release and clear toxins.

When there is tightness or pain in the body, we can lay our hands on it and bring our attention, our breath, and loving tenderness to the area. This brings more conscious awareness to the place within our tissues where we hold so much grief and trauma.

That's why I like Wim Hof's breathing techniques and the information he brings about cold showers. Thirty years ago, when I was suffering from chemical sensitivities and immune system breakdown, my homeopathic doctor would lay me in an ice bath. This therapy reduced my pain and inflammation.

The ice baths are an important part of what Wim Hoff shares in his Wim Hoff Method (WHM), which combines cold exposure, breathwork, yoga, and meditation to reduce inflammation and improve the body's detoxing abilities.

As I healed the inflammation, my weakened immune system grew stronger. And my mind got clearer, too. For years, I struggled with brain fog. Chemical exposures would leave me weakened in both mind and body.

I would wrap myself in a sheet that I had placed in the freezer wet. Then I would lay on the living room floor, breathe deeply, and go into meditation. I would feel my body relax and get warm from the inside.

They call Wim Hof 'The Iceman' because of his many endurance records set on, in, and under the ice. Through this work, he has come to believe that, "Cold is an absolute doorway to the soul," and that "Through deep breathing, we become alchemists. And that is actually the way we are."

For me, this healing journey encourages me to pay attention to the choices I make as I empower myself and move through all that seems uncomfortable.

Today in this new day, I see abundance all around me. The fullness of being present shines out of me as an expression of my unique way of being.

I give thanks for all the inspiring people who creatively seek new paths to healing and bravely share their ways with the world.

Day 317

A Brief Interlude. With God.

Reach deep within
As you breathe into the gap between your thoughts.
Wrap your sweet embrace
Around all the fears of what is and what could be.
There's nothing to do but stay here
Until you catch your breath and rest in the now.
Nowhere to go but here
Where you touch the stream of light
That waits for your return.
Listen to the voice of this quiet moment.
Be brave as you gather all that you know is true.
Fill yourself up with all that you are
As patiently you receive the gifts that life has offered.
Remember each moment before this one
And all that has been learned for your life's lessons.

Grasping outward for peace only brings suffering
Until you surrender again and again.
This pause is the way to receive the focus of inner sanction.
The space inside you fills with life.
You are filled with lightness as peace whispers,
"Be kind. Be fearless. Be loving."
Stand up amid all that is troubling
And reach out with your grateful heart that knows.
In the vulnerable heart of your human self, you are strong.
You are not alone as you move inside
To hold the hand of Spirit who guides your way.

Day 318

Spirit Speaks

You can call this power God, Universe, Presence. Here we are home within the heart where all is calm amidst the storm.

As I sit in my backyard this early morning, I am alive, I am awake, and I am grateful. Life has brought broken hearts and shattered dreams, but I am not shattered or broken. I am awake.

I have the courage to walk into this world as it is, trusting my Creator. As I open to the Universe again and again, I meet my God as my loving companion. Life happens, and I can fight it or accept it. I can spiral into fears of the unknown or I can rise and allow the strength of my inner knowing to guide my way.

This time with grief has shown me more truth and given me a greater understanding of who I am and why I am here. With new eyes, I see the bigger picture.

When we hold ourselves tenderly with complete acceptance, we find we will want to dance again. If we keep our hearts open, we can take the hand of Spirit and be led into new territory. We have a chance to wake up and allow all that is false to be washed away leaving only the clear mind of truth.

Each day my body reminds me to be vigilant, to take impeccable care of myself. This gift, I give to others. Self-love births compassion for all people and all creatures of this world. Earth is calling us to remember how precious this home is. Humanity is calling us to remember that we were born worthy.

Love is the path that empowers and inspires. We are here to receive fully and to serve with compassion and loving-kindness.

From deep inside my fragile, insecure, and lonely heart, I can move into the mind of my enlightened self and live free.

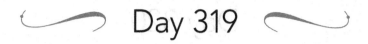

Day 319

What lies behind us and what lies before us are tiny matters compared to what lies within us.

– Ralph Waldo Emerson

Last night I woke up with a mind reliving difficult times in my past. Traumas were coming up and moving out. Often my deep sleeps are a time of healing and releasing what might still be deep in my cellular memory. Fearful and scary times can bring me to my knees as I reach for Spirit to open the doorway to the light.

Underneath the fear, the darkness of living in this world of challenges and upheaval, I trust as Spirit works through a family member or friend who allows God's arms to lift me up. Energetic hands touch me, and words of love reach through the phone as I gaze at the faces of my daughter and son, other family, and friends. They are here for me with their love and prayers.

I stop fighting and just surrender to the truth that I am taken care of. Both the low and high moments of my life have given me power— true power.

Today, I seek the truth as the light reflects to me what my heart knows. In my clear mind, I see how beautiful it all is as I glimpse the Divine looking back at me through all who walk with me. Nature in its glory speaks through the silence that we are all connected. This deep connection fills me up like the scent of jasmine.

Day 320

Meditation

Today I am bathed in the peace that comes in
When I let go of everything I think I know.
As my focus turns inward, I soften
Allowing my body and mind to surrender into the moment.
I pause as I breathe consciously and become aware
Of how I feel emotionally, mentally, and vibrationally.

Here, in the space between my thoughts,
I can touch any resistance or negative charge
In the undercurrent of my thinking mind.
I reach deeper as my breath connects me
To old, repressed feelings that vibrate at a lower frequency.

My conscious connection to my higher spiritual self
Holds me like a parent holds a child.
In total acceptance of all that is within, I listen.
The breath opens me into life's flow
Where there is more life… more sweet life.

It's not a thing or an object.
It's a feeling of contentment.
It's a knowing that all is well
Amid this spinning world of
Ups and downs, sorrow and laughter,
chaos and calmness,
Betrayals and unions, birth and death.

It's all part and parcel of the wholeness of life.
Can we let it all be and trust
that the Divine Universe has our backs?

Day 321

My Sweetheart:

Know that I have never left you, not for a moment. I travel both beyond and right here to bring all that is needed for the evolution of soul. Yes, you too are doing the same as you reach deeper into the self that remembers that you are far more than the physical eyes can see.

Reach deep into the dimensions that are beyond the sixth sense and trust that worlds beyond worlds are being born to bring the vastness of being fully into creation.

Limitations are only of the mind. Yet this mind, as it joins with the true mind of creation, is creating for the highest good of all.

Let yourself be more. Let go. As you focus fully on true partnership with Spirit, see how the attachments of this world fall away. You are centered inside your very core as you join with all. Your presence is like the sun, radiating outward from the center of you.

The spark of light, this flame, burns all karma into dharma as you enter inside. The core of your being is where all is one, never apart, never separate, altogether not only as one human family but one with all creation. This is pure love when you let go of the external and become the one choosing to be in the moment of pure beingness.

You don't have to drop your body like I did. You just expand beyond it into all your bodies. So vast is the universe that is born inside this heart that has no boundaries, no pain, no darkness, no limitation.

You are the vessel for love to flow through. You are the path, and the path is you.

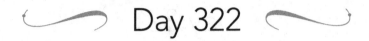

Day 322

Sadness is not a happiness deficiency. It is how the heart adjusts to loss and releases imagined patterns of attachment. Every time sadness arises, the body has an emotional garage sale. It releases what is no longer needed for the journey ahead and clears the space to welcome in what your entire life has prepared you to find— true happiness.

– Matt Kahn

I let out a sigh, aware of the sadness tucked inside the fabric of my inner being. My shoulders sink in like I am protecting myself from feeling. What is it trying to tell me?

As I take another breath in, my heart opens wide. Without shedding a tear, I feel the subtle energy of sadness. I don't have to process it, just allow myself to feel it without judgment. Suddenly something opens deep inside, and the sadness dissipates.

Maybe it moves out of the way when I don't judge it. Maybe it fades away when I don't focus on it. I soften around it, and slowly it leads me into more of myself. This release feels good.

This intimate journey isn't always easy. Sometimes the flood gates open and tears spill out of me.

Dwelling in the present moment, as intense as it may be, is the only path to the doorway inside. I clear the space within as I release my attachments and trust in a higher power that knows what I truly desire.

I am a child of God, worthy to be loved. I appreciate this moment as I listen to my heart and soul, free to return to love.

Day 323

Beauty and Love are as body and soul.
Beauty is the mine, Love is the diamond.
— Rumi

Loneliness hits me the hardest when I crawl into bed at night. Alone in the king-size bed, I sink into feelings of longing. I could tell myself that I don't belong here in this big bed. I could say that I feel like a fish out of water, and I don't belong anywhere. Then I might get stuck in the feeling, but I know that what I'm feeling is my hunger to be in the soul within where I am grounded inside my heart. This is where I am home.

I wake up in the morning and I look at the other side of my bed, which is still perfectly made. I get up and go directly to the garden that has called me to tend to it. I sit on the path under the shade of the Old Man tree and settle into this moment. I have the oldies blaring on my Bluetooth speaker as I enter my weeding meditation. With every plant I grasp and pull out, I also reach inside and feel the presence of life flowing within me.

This mundane task returns me to the earth and the treasures in my heart. It brings to mind the Zen saying, "Before enlightenment chop wood and carry water. After enlightenment chop wood and carry water."

There is death and new life all around me. I am content, and in the center of my heart, I feel the gentle touch of this world guiding me further inside. I see both worlds—suffering and freedom. With my spiritual eyes, I see everything blooming. It's so beautiful!

Meditation

Breathe.
Bring yourself
Into the center of being.
Meditate on all that is in the way
Of the fullness of life.

Breathe deeply
And let yourself move through
Your self-erected walls.
Let go and feel the space
At the end of your exhalation.
Acceptance!

Now, in the stream of consciousness,
Allow the next good idea
To come into your heart.
Take yourself
Into the next moment
Spontaneously.

When I choose to move past the noise and insanity of the mind, I find the door to stillness. Here the quiet of the moment offers me a breath of fresh air. As I take it in, the space inside begins to soften its hold onto the past and what was love gushes forth and whispers "I am here."

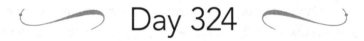 Day 324

Without any of us the Universe could not grow. Our eternal path is a narrow path where we need to wait for others to pass us. It is a bridge to all infinite possibilities. On this bridge someone always waits for us.

— Akianne Kramarik

Steve passed me on that bridge. So did my parents and friends who left this world before me. As I remove the mask of illusions, I can join with all who are striving for oneness.

As we dance around in these bodies of ours, we are not all listening to the same tune. When we let go of the thoughts made by the mind and just join in with our open and generous hearts, we can imagine how we are all part of this unity consciousness no matter what is going on.

This inward path is filled with so much; I am humbled by the inexhaustible sweetness that Source brings me no matter what my thinking has been. I feel a stirring in my heart and a subtle excitement deep inside. I feel happy and content just being here now.

I open myself up to a new relationship. I have arrived inside and lack nothing as I allow myself to dance in the flickering light of this new day. I can be loved and love as I trust that whoever I am with is worthy of my embrace.

We are all companions on this pilgrimage through grief. When I am ready to leave this body, Steve and all my spirit loved ones will be waiting with open arms excited to show me the way.

In the meantime, I open myself up completely, not holding anything back. Here I am alive, touching the beloved. In this heightened state, I celebrate the beauty in this world. Tuned into this moment, I walk this path receiving the truth:

"For everything there is a season, and a time for every purpose under heaven." – Ecclesiastes 3:1

Real happiness cannot be taken away by our darkness. The space within our hearts is so vast, even more vast than the ever-changing sky. It is here that the feelings of our unlovable and imperfect self are accepted and held in Presence. Everything is worthy to be here.

When I learn the lesson that my self-worth is not attached to another but is a part of this infinite love that is Divine, my heart will be broken wide open to allow rebirth into new life.

When you left your body, did suddenly you know
The answers to your questions or did you just let go
Of the traffic in your brain and let the light flow into you
Like sunshine through your veins.
When you left your body could you see me here, wearing my
black raincoat?
Could you taste my tears or does a soul remember pain?
When every minute of your freedom feels like sunshine
through your veins
When I leave my body, tell you what I'll do
Fly through that tunnel straight into you
And we will burst in golden flames and ride the wide forever
with sunshine in our veins
We will ride the wide whatever with sunshine
Sunshine

— "Sunshine" Lyrics by Angela Kaset
(singer/ songwriter)

I am in Nashville visiting my new friend Angela. After some deep, heartfelt conversations, she asks me to come into the living room. As she sat at her piano, she played and sang this song, "Sunshine." I receive her gift. It is a moment in time when I feel God reaching into my heart whispering, "You aren't alone." I weep with the joy of the vision of union.

All I want to do is fly through that tunnel and be with you again. So, I reach for the light in my quiet mind as I am pulled into the embrace of Spirit.

Day 326

Do you have the patience to wait
till your mud settles and the water is clear?
Can you remain unmoving
till the right action arises by itself?
                              — Tao Te Ching

I roll onto my side as I wake up in the darkness of my bedroom. I breathe into my body and soften as I receive the light. I let the light fill my mind's eye. My mind is quiet, allowing peace to wash over me. As I drink in this feeling of opening to love, I sink into the safety of my heart. Here in the sweetness of God's love, Spirit speaks to me again and again. I fall awake into a Presence that is beyond my thinking mind. I hear **"Be still, stay here. I am here."**

I listen to the quiet truth of what is needed, and I let the dawn open my hands to write.

Daily we are fighting the worries and fears,
And we lose our confidence.
Let us pause together as we breathe,
Resting in our hearts for this precious moment.
Slow down and receive
What is at the bottom of your feelings
Where unspoken fear and sadness live.
In the stillness, let yourself be touched
By kindness and tenderness.
Quietly open like a flower turning its petals to the sun.
Safety and serenity are right here.
Taste the goodness that is the essence of life.

If we stop for a little while and listen,
We don't take this life for granted.
There is strength and wisdom in this hidden wholeness Where inner light
touches our weaknesses.

I awaken this morning after experiencing the following dream:

I went to my pantry. A friend had decorated the outside of the door with jewels spelling out "Best Friends Forever." I opened it and inside were lots of little presents all wrapped up. I went over to her, hugged her, and said, "I love you."

Everyone reflects back to us a gift of truth. We can gather it all and nourish ourselves with the goodness that the world in form gives us. I could easily spiral down into vulnerable and insecure places of my humanness, or I can rise, take it all in, and trust that all of me is my strength.

Spirit Speaks

Right now, you are filling yourself up first. The more you give yourself in total acceptance and unconditional love, the more you become the representation of what is true. It seems too simple, but it is all you need to do. Fill yourself up with all that is here, and you will share it naturally without any effort at all. This is what your dream tells you. Go to your own pantry, be the best friend to yourself forever and ever, amen. Then as you open the pantry and see all the gifts, you can love another with this same love. How wonderful life in this world would be if everyone on the planet got this one great lesson.

I am redefining relationships and listening to my inner voice to guide me as I take care of myself in ways that will support me in my highest good. My days are filled with promise and well-being. No one is wrong and in the end, it's all going to be all right.

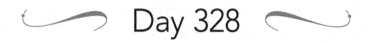

Day 328

I have discovered that the surest way to hear the soft strains of harmony is in the silence.

— Sarah Ban Breathnach

I sit inside my beating heart as the sweet sounds of this quiet room call me to enter the void of nothingness. Deep inside this space, a voice speaks to me as softly as the warm sun that touches my face. I invite it in. Humbled by this visit from the other side, I step aside, trusting that the spoken word is nothing more than love expressed through my simple thoughts.

I gather it all, breath by breath, until I am so full that it spills out of me without effort. This stream of consciousness, which contains the completeness of everything, uses my hands, my eyes, and my voice. Words fill the pages or expand into the room as I join with all humanity and creation. I stay quiet for a moment savoring the sweet taste of love as it moves from my lips or through my hands. There is a moment of complete emptiness as I join with the observer and witness it all.

When we enter inside, we can let go of the burdens and allow the falseness to fall gently away. We ease into a rhythm with ourselves. We recognize our uniqueness as the Presence shows us that we can walk on this precious Earth with the delight of our creator.

Listen, heart of mine, I want to trust in all that life brings me. Can I remember that the truth is always waiting to be heard in the quiet moments of my solitude? Here I am not alone as my soul connects me with the Universe. I see myself as God sees me as I transition into more life.

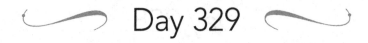

Day 329

*Maybe, as our hearts overflow, we find that love can,
naturally of its own accord, extend wider, until it
encompasses caring for all things, and connection to
everything—until our love becomes love itself, the very flow
and force of the Universe.*

— Danya Ruttenberg

Meditation

The greatest loss of all
Is the loss of my connection to Source.
When I am disconnected, I stumble.
Fearful and alone, I wander into unwanted territories,
Believing that the world can give me solace.

I grasp onto things outside of me—
Like medicine, food, or people—to make me feel better.
Life becomes a whirlwind of chaos and drama.
The temptations of the external world
Threaten my health and well-being.

I walk on shaky ground
Until I remember to breathe deeply.
Instantly, the path stabilizes,
Taking me back to the well of eternal bliss.

Grounded in my self-worth, I become vulnerable
And open to the hand of God.
It reaches into me and picks me up
As I gaze into the eyes of my loved ones.

When I act from this place of connection within,
I remember who I am—loved and lovable.
Unafraid of my humanness, I go out and touch the world.
Another day so worthy to be alive.

Today I clear my path inside for love to flow.

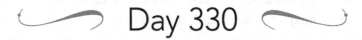

Day 330

*In this world, hate never yet dispelled hate. Only love dispels
hate. This is the law, ancient and inexhaustible.*

Buddha

Underneath the fear—the darkness of living in this world of
challenges, upheaval, and loss—there is an ever-expanding universe
moving us, individually and collectively, in the stream of evolution. Some
move quickly in the center of the current while others proceed much
more slowly as they stay close to the water's edge.

We move more fully into the flow when we release the thoughts
that keep us stuck and in suffering. These thoughts often arise
from unconscious, long-standing patterns. One way of bringing the
unconscious to our conscious awareness is by paying attention to our
bodies. Physical sensations can help us recognize and understand the
feelings or perceptions of our human self.

So instead of following the mind and getting pulled away into
thoughts that push against what is happening in the moment, we can
instead take a conscious breath and scan the body. Ask yourself: Where
do I feel discomfort? Focus on that area and allow the breath in to
soften it.

It's easier to see physical wounds because emotional ones are buried
and sometimes out of reach. Unsettling times will bring us to our
worries. How do we respond to this changing world? How do we find
peace inside and overcome the fear and helplessness that arise when we
reach in and touch our wounds?

In my vulnerability, I can move out of my ego and into the silence. There, God begins to change my mind. As I face myself intimately and with compassion, the light of my true self shines through my heart no matter how unworthy I think I am. It's just a moment in time when my human self is the opening for Divine Source to come in.

Day 331

I sit on the bench that is dedicated to Steve. This beautiful love seat that is under the shade of a pine tree at the beach. I come here daily to meditate and listen. I ask my beloved to sit with me as the beauty of nature transforms me. In my heart these words whisper through me like the breeze.

Spirit Speaks

Oh, Precious One!
There are so many sunsets and sunrises to capture in one lifetime.
The beginning and ending of a day bring so much to be thankful for.
No one can tell you what is coming next,
yet you can open to the infinite possibilities of creation.
I am here in all my glory seeing you in your magnificence.
Let yourself be so free to laugh, to dance, to celebrate this life well lived.
You have broken down all the walls that separate you from the Divine.
As you arise here, you see the truth that nothing has kept you held back from the joy of living.
It has only been your mind that keeps you stuck in old tapes
that have now lost their hold on you.
It is quite a mind game when ego runs the show.
Step into the sunrise, waltz into the sunlight, gaze into the beauty

that has been manifested through all your heart's desires.
Life as it is, has brought you here to receive its bounty.
Nothing is broken down.
Everything is wide open like the clear blue skies.
The dance with the divine is for all who walk on this earth,
so blessed to step into this great awareness with you.
There is nothing holding you back from being the brightest of lights.
The more you receive, the more it will spill out of you
with every moment and every gaze.
Every part of creation joins you this day and every day
from this moment forward.
The beauty of living in a body is radiating out of every cell of your
being.
Keep your focus here.
In this moment as the brightest of stars shines upon you.
Open your mind and your heart to receive the beauty that is
love moving through your human existence.
So sweet is this blessing given from your receiving.

Day 332

And you'll finally get it. For at least an instant you'll know
in your heart the Divine, the God, the Creator of this thing
we call life. At last you'll feel a connection to Spirit that
is undeniable. And you'll recognize the gift you've been
given—and the gift you are.
— Jean Slatter *Hiring the Heavens*

Today the spark of this magnificent being that I was born to be remembers that I am enough. Just breathing and receiving this moment is a gift. It's been vital for me to hold my internal resistance with love and gentle compassion. This allows me to reconnect and recenter. I can't figure out why things happen the way they do. Reopening those wounds won't make me feel any better unless and until I let go.

As I reflect on all that life has brought me, I sit in this new day feeling safe and cared for. I have learned to allow whatever is happening outside of me to bring me home inside so that wherever I am, I belong. I am comfortable in my own skin. Who I am in every given moment is worthy.

I don't need to blame another or myself for anything. Forgiveness allows me to see these wounds as opportunities. Whenever I have responded to difficult times in my life with tender, loving care, instead of ignoring these moments and keeping myself distracted, I have grown. I am mindful and able to return to see that in each stage of my life, I am blooming.

I open to more of myself as life pushes and stretches me to become the best version of myself.

Day 333

Meditation

I am a person, no different than anyone else.
I struggle daily with my emotional, physical,
And spiritual self.
Each moment, I have a choice to empty
And release myself from all that calls for my attention.
I can think a thought that keeps me locked up in resistance
Or I can reach for the thought that frees me
Into the softness as I let go and trust myself.
When I open, my chest relaxes, and I can breathe deeply.
I sit for a while in this place where I remember who I am.
It only takes a moment to move from the mind to the heart.
How lovely it is to feel my whole body

Sink into the moment
As if I have surrendered to the fullness of being here.
I touch myself with my awareness
And each part of this body is welcomed in this connection.
Being present brings Presence.
The vibration that fills me up is life-giving.
Slowly and gently, I feel myself rising.
Nothing blocks me from seeing the light.
My mind is quiet and becomes the channel
For this light to be received.
I am in the stream of consciousness.
The voice that guides my way reveals itself.
Like a flower turning its face to the sun,
I receive this light that feeds me like nothing else can.
As I drink it in, it nurtures my cells and gives me life.
Like a light bulb in a socket, I am energized,
And it radiates out in all directions.
There is no mind here to take me away from what is real.
The voice of my Creator uses me
As an instrument for peace.

I listen as I am filled with a love that has no conditions.
I am free to share this peace.

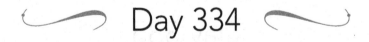 Day 334

Grief and pain are like joy and peace: they are not things we should try to snatch from each other.

— Glennon Doyle

For months following his death, I spoke to Steve as if he was still here, and in the quiet place within me, I could hear him whisper. I felt him; I knew he was around and inside this life that was left. There were always reminders—sounds of birds chirping or squawking, butterflies of all kinds, dolphins, rainbows, or songs on the radio. I had visits from him in my dreams that felt so real.

It brought me to myself and my heart where I listened. I felt the energy calming me as I realized that I am never alone. Maybe in the beginning, when the shock of loss was still filled with suffering, I was unable to touch the invisible because of the sadness, loneliness, and anger that weakened me. I fell asleep for a while…an intentional sleep, not to numb out but to honor where I was.

Grief lingered in my body, waiting beneath the surface until life showed me the way to let go a little more.

Yesterday, as my son and I worked out on the elliptical machines, he looked at me and said, "Nana was in my dream last night." As he was speaking, the light from his visitation was shining through his eyes.

Our spirit loved ones continue to share their presence in ways that always rock my world. They remind me that no matter what is going on, I can choose to be me, to sparkle and shine the true, authentic light of my soul. I am blessed to know that within this heart that is beating aliveness, I have angels guiding me and walking with me.

As the layers of falseness fall away, I allow that which is constant and always flowing through me to beam its light. It continues to give life wherever I may be on this incredible journey.

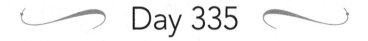

Day 335

Ultimately we're all walking each other home.
—Ram Dass

We are so lucky to be here on this incredible planet as each day brings more moments of awakening. Right here, right now, we are held in the arms of Spirit.

Nature reminds us to gaze up at the sky where rainbows, clouds, and magnificent sunrises and sunsets become the backdrop for the theatrical production that is our life. We glimpse this magnificence as the spark of God ignites in all our hearts.

No one is separate. We are all going home together, so we might as well take this moment to remember how precious we all are.

Steve remembered this the moment he left his body. We can live it now without leaving ours.

You are important. Being you is the gift only you can give to this world. This life is filled with so many opportunities to love. And what an incredible gift it is to love another. So, my sweet beloved ones, let's love ourselves completely so that we can just love. There is nothing you have to do, just be yourself.

Life is a gift, receive it fully. Let your heart drink it in until you are so full that it spills out without effort. Your life, just as it is, has cleared your inner path for love to enter and now it is the garment you wear as YOU.

Day 336

Moments of deep insight and all-embracing love purify the mind, while desires and tears, envies and anger, blind beliefs and intellectual arrogance pollute and dull the psyche.
— Sri Nisargadatta Maharaj

Waking up through grief isn't easy. The loneliness is piercing at times, yet sometimes being alone is all I can handle.

The emptiness you feel inside from grief becomes your opportunity to join in the presence of the now. As you connect here and breathe deeply, try to imagine that you are being filled with an energy that gives to you. It is the life force that wants to live through you, guide you and allow you to create this new life. This power that has always been here within you is the same power that is in every living thing.

Reaching deep inside, I know I'm not alone. The Universe is right here partnering with me and guiding my way. When I listen to my needs and rest inside my heart, I let go of the outer world and give up having to know the future. As grief takes a back seat, I see that I am ready to take the hands of all the ones who accompany me on this journey.

Meditation

Reach inside this quiet place within
Where the wordless tranquility brings you into stillness.
When the edges soften,
Let yourself rest inside this gap.
Feel this timeless being that you are
As this presence of love fills you up.
God enters here.

Day 337

You can lay new pipes right now. If there were ever an opportunity to flow through the free flowing pipes of infinite intelligence, it would be right here and right now.
— Abraham Hicks

I'm gasping for my breath. Not like a panic attack, this is different. I try to ignore it as I brush my teeth and get ready for bed. I crawl under the covers to try to sleep but my mind takes a hold of me, trying to figure it out. "What if I am having a heart attack and I am ignoring the signs?"

As I go in and out of sleep for a few minutes at a time, the symptom does not go away. If Steve were here, he would have called 911 by now. I am reliving all the times that my mitral valve gave me problems. The doctor had said, "You can take all the natural medicines you want and meditate to calm your stress, but one day, you won't be able to get off the couch. Unless you get a pig's valve, you will be dead!" Was this now that time he was talking about?

In the morning, I go to the emergency room. The doctor there scolds me for not coming in right away with my history.

I'm immediately admitted and phone a cardiologist I had met at an Abraham Hicks event just a couple of months before. Jessica answered my call and soon after walked into the hospital room saying, "You are in heart failure!" She leaned closer to me, and I said, "What are we going to do about it? "How about we lay new pipes!"

I had received that phrase—lay new pipes—many times during the workshop. Perhaps that means a new valve, or new beliefs, or maybe a new opening for more of this vast, intelligent energy to pass through.

This precious heart of mine is tired of my fears and anxieties and grief. I need to clear those pipes, the valve that has alerted me to lots of discomfort in the past.

I'm stunned, to say the least. I get my will in order, and in no time, I am heading into the operating room with a doctor who is aligned with my thinking. I said, "Do whatever you need to do when you get in there."

I had worked hard to be healthy so that I wouldn't have to have a pig's valve, but now I must let go and trust the Universe and everyone involved in this experience.

Terrified and yet present with it all, I'm wheeled into the operating room—the same room where Steve had died. Tears roll down my face as the compassionate nurses speak gently and I go into twilight with anesthesia.

After the procedure, while I was coming out of the sedation, Jessica goes to the waiting room where my son is meditating, praying, and holding the space for my healing. She tells Luke, "We haven't experienced something like that in a surgery room before. While sedated, your mom was giving messages to us all." She then shares with Luke, "There was blood in her heart, and we will take an ultrasound to find out why."

All I remember from the surgery is that Steve was there in the light. It felt like a dream. I felt him—it was a knowing and a comfort that he was right there.

After Jessica looked at the ultrasound, she came to me saying, "I know you believe in miracles...You do not have mitral valve prolapse anymore."

After these months of grieving, here I am wanting to live. The experience wakes me up out of the amnesia of grief. I'm not wanting to join Steve; I want to be in my life with my kids, my family, and my friends.

For years I had prayed for healing. I did everything I could—eating right, juicing, exercising, doing yoga, and meditating. When I experienced an episode, I'd feel fragile and weakened, like I was unplugged from my energy.

Still, I always believed that one day I would heal. And that day was here! The miracle happened, and Steve was a part of it all. He is a part of the vast energy that now fills my valves, my heart, and my new path that has shifted my vulnerable, grieving heart.

After all that I did to heal this heart, I now must let go and trust in how God is in my heart helping my soul heal.

There are no rules when you are going through grief. I loved Steve when he was alive and now there is a bigger heart inside me to love again.

Spirit Speaks

Stand strong in this knowing that forever and all eternity is always on your side—filled with this flow of living spiritual waters. You are embraced into the sacred holy place where you drink in all that now wakes you. There is only compassion, as the heart gives way to more love, more light, more joy.

Day 338

One of the most painful barriers we can experience is the
sense of isolation the modern world fosters, which can be
broken by our willingness to be held, by the quiet courage to
allow our vulnerability to be seen.

— Mark Nepo, *The Book of*
Awakening

Through my loss and grief, I often long for Steve's physical embrace. How do I ask for help when the things I am asking for seem impossible? How can anyone possibly help me? But I have found that just asking breaks down my walls and softens me. I return to my vulnerable heart where this silent gesture, a simple hug, calls out as a prayer.

Touching is another way I express myself. Even if I'm too tired to talk and share feelings, touching another is the easiest way to communicate the needs of my human self. I came into this world holding my triplet sisters. As fetuses in our mother's womb, we were constantly in each other's arms.

Yet even in our aloneness, we can welcome the ways that nature touches us. When the wind caresses my skin and the sun warms my body, it helps me feel wrapped up and held in the moment.

I still miss Steve's touch and his kisses as I remember how easy it was to go through the challenges of my past with the physical embrace of all who were with me. But if we allow it, life will bring us to more of ourselves.

The Divine nudges me, and I open because when I don't run away, the pain of living helps me feel. In my deep surrender, I stay with myself and receive. It's an intimate union with the Universe, love in its purest form. It reaches into me like the perfect song. The music lifts me up like a lover, intimately merging into every cell of my being.

Meditation

Lift your gaze to the light
That passes through your inner eyes
As the vision of heaven's Presence.
It feels like a dream
When you ascend into this space
Where eternity touches your expression
That consciously awakens.
This experience comes
Like the flight of a butterfly
So delicately moving higher
Into the vastness of skies beyond skies.
Feel yourself expand into this new life
Born because you entered inside.
Your breath brings you deeply
Into your true self.
You reach into the darkness
And touch the light.
As it illuminates the falseness,
You unveil, allowing your true self to emerge
Inside your open and revealing heart.
Step now through the doorway
Where duality becomes the union
Of hearts reaching deeply into Self.
Here no one is separate from the whole.
Everything is forever longing for this spiritual path
That inwardly calls upon the soul's choice
To gaze into the eyes of each one
Who appears on this path called life.
Enter inside your own chrysalis home
Within this heart of yours,
Where every part of life transforms you
Into this precious gem

Untarnished by the challenges
That tried to distract you and cover you up.
The light of truth peels away
The veils that hold our illusions
Until what is left is all that you are.
Home inside the Universe,
You radiate the light that can never be hidden
Or diminished by the human condition.
Bring forth the love that spills out of this open heart
And know that this is your birthright.
Now join with all who look your way
Each a spark—together the eternal flame—
That ignites the path you walk upon
With many who recognize you as the same.
Underneath the coverings of being human
Is the soul that divinely merges
With the breath of the One that creates worlds.

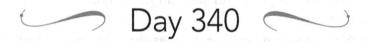 Day 340

I love to be outside in my garden. This chair I sit upon supports me as I sink into myself. I breathe, and my breath helps me enter this moment. My mind might be wandering into all kinds of stories, but when I follow my breath, I consciously enter inside. I feel deeply as I am taken into the moment while gazing at the flowers in my butterfly garden.

Here all of nature announces its arrival. I hear the birds singing quietly. I feel the wind as it touches the leaves. I see the squirrels running along the fence. It's food for my soul as this ever-so-sweet day wakes up all around me.

I sit beneath a magnificent, vast, blue sky in awe of how great it is to be alive. The world outside may be filled with chaotic noises and trembling voices full of fear of the unknown, yet when I enter inside, it's pure heaven as I commune with the beloved.

I feel the touch of Spirit as my soul opens me to what is real. I take refuge inside this quiet heart and still mind that receive this day like no other. In these moments I embrace the darker truths of my nervous inner child. No secrets, no hiding. I grasp onto this lifeline that pulls me in the direction of love.

My hopes and prayers for union become the promise of a life filled with joy. My prayers spill out of me as love and bring peace.

Day 341

Spirit Speaks

How sweet it is to be here in the sacred holy space of being. Life is our practice in learning to come alive; to rekindle that flame, that spark, that fire within the belly. Receive with the breath, for every breath ignites you, bringing passion fully into the body. And this light, it becomes more as you bow to this world in complete acceptance. No matter what, this offering, this love that flows through your opening, is loving what is.

In this container, all exist as the light and dark, woven together to show their true colors. Nothing to hide, for nothing is hidden in this precious moment of being. The mind cannot judge it when it is embraced fully as it is. What is real becomes illuminated with the perception of a mind that sees only truth.

The sounds, the smells, and the reflection of its nature bring you back to this moment of creation to see with the eyes of peace. Nothing to fear, for these eyes see beyond what is trembling.

In our humanity, we walk on unsteady ground. Yet in the acceptance of this moment, in the center of what is, there is softness. The rigid ideas of the past fall away and do not harden the heart.

Day 342

I feel my disappointments that arise from the wants and desires I can't have. Though it is out of my control, I get pinned down by these thoughts and squeezed by the grief that has settled in my heart. In the pain, I barely notice the life that is living all around me.

I gaze over to the bush where I hear something rustling in the leaves. As I make my way over, two turtles greet me in the garden. I am taken aback by something so fragrant that it turns my head in another direction. Beside me, I see a blossom that has just bloomed on a bush that has never flowered before. Never, in these countless years, did it bloom. Yet to my surprise, today I see this plant thriving; its flower is so pure and delicate.

I take these signs as teachings that have arrived for me. The turtles remind me to be grounded in the earth and to honor the creative source that flows within and all around me. How easy it is to regret life's decisions or beat myself up with negative thinking—because this one seed never germinated, this one relationship ended, this job terminated, this body got sick—and I take it on as my failure.

In truth, it's all a moment in time when I can feel the true feelings of loss, the excruciating pain of wanting to be loved. If I can just feel it without being distracted by judgments and the stories my mind invents, then I can be filled with the healing that comes through my living. This is life. This is how we grow.

As I sit in the space where tears have cleared my heart, I have deepened in this place within that lived through the pain. I ground myself here on Mother Earth and allow my thoughts to focus on what is. I take a sip of warm tea as I feel the breeze brush my face.

Day 343

Spirit Speaks

Life, so full, is birth. It becomes you. Like the new sunrise, it paints you, forms you. Like the masterpieces created by the greatest artists, you touch and enliven all who witness you in living form.

So, bring your focus to the sweet spot within your heart where that seed of your truest desires has been planted. Every breath and every thought of love is like sunshine, feeding you as this desire becomes what it is. Let go and allow yourself to be the one receiving all that you are. Let go of all that seems to be spinning around with ideas. Let go and rest in the quiet mind where your heart receives this life as you bloom and become more. That is creation.

It can never be—what was—never. It only becomes the wisdom of what is. Allow this light to pass through your eyes, your lips, and your touch. Then every word and every thought embodies truth. And that is love. A love that has no boundaries and knows what everyone needs. You would remember who you truly are as you look into the eyes of this world that reflect back to you this life that was given the moment you arrived in the womb of your mother.

Birth is the doorway to life. It is forever giving to this world because of its conscious, unstoppable commitment to bring forth all that is.

So, imagine that you are welcoming a baby into your world. You are not thinking that the world will be destructive, dark, and shallow. Now you have awakened to the truth of why birth continues, how life lovingly gives to this world without effort.

Receive yourself now in the greatest love that created you. It's hard to imagine that you get to be born again into another form, ready to meet the challenges of your human existence. Do not be afraid of this evolution, for it is how we bless this earth through these times of growth and freedom.

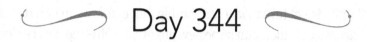

Day 344

Meditation

Love is your true nature.
Offer this light that passionately lives as you.
With compassion, bow to this world
And all that it has brought you.
When you allow, you become the heart of creation.

Live in the worthiness you are,
Creating the world from the inside,
And you will see it reflected on the outside.
You are loved and you are loving.
You are forever the love that will never die,
For in your being, it is you.

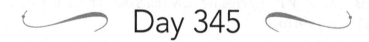

Day 345

It's not just that when one door closes, another door opens.

When one door closes, choirs burst into chorus, orchestras
orchestrate, bugles bugle, marching bands march, dogs
catch Frisbees, cats "chow, chow, chow," pigs fly, and 10,000
new doors open.

— Mike Dooley

In the center of my being where I am neutral, I feel the kiss of eternity. This path is an inward journey. Sometimes in this earthly body, when I let go of everything that I think I know, I enter into a portal where life shows me the infinite possibilities that are alive and becoming the new.

If I dwell on what has died, whether it be a loved one, a seed that I planted that did not take root, a relationship that ended, or an idea that has come to a dead end, there can be no new growth. No birthing. No creation.

All of it, the dreams, the thoughts, the desires that passed through my heart, all of it has meaning. As I stay grounded in the moment, as I let myself stand strongly rooted to the earth and expand through my heart, this everlasting power of creation moves me forward from this place to bring something new.

As doors close, many more will open if I am not distracted by this human self that thinks it knows everything and wants to control. I can rush the bloom by harvesting the fruit before it is ready, or I can sit patiently in this moment, in the void of the great unknown, and receive its abundance.

I breathe and allow myself to see what will be. As the will of my human self merges with the Divine, this beautiful Garden of Eden helps me trust the unfolding of this great mystery called life.

I open my heart to receive the truth and listen to the sweetness of the birds singing. I am lost in its beauty—no thoughts of pain or distractions, I am totally immersed in the songs. Then everything gets quiet. I get up and move through my day. It all seems different to me now. As I love what is, my creative flow pours out of me, and in this eternal time, I feel free.

Day 346

Spirit Speaks

As the mind lets go of its control and the heart gives way to all that cannot be contained, the limitations of the human condition dissolve into your expanded awareness. And what is perceived is what is real—the infinite possibilities that this world is offering.

A new idea, an original thought that comes out of nowhere, is born in the heart of unconditional love. Like a dream, it makes its way into the consciousness of humanity. In this awareness, you are the portal. You are the door that opens. And through this opening, you commune with something greater than your little self; you merge with the nature of all things.

There are no secrets here, just an invitation to connect to all that is and to live from the inside to the outside. Accept this invitation as you continue to walk on in this ordinary world. Then turning back and looking upon your life, you will see with the eyes of wisdom and true understanding. You will see that you would not be who you are without the experience, the gift, bestowed by each and every pebble that you walked upon.

Day 347

Every wrinkle and each scar is a part of the masterpiece we have painted with the brushstrokes of our life experiences. Laboring through the hard times brings us to wisdom with an understanding of our magnificent inner strength. When our cup runneth over with an abundance of love, we stretch and then expand into a glow of agelessness.

— Colleen Hoffman Smith

As I sit in the quiet embrace of the day, I feel the heavens open, and God enters me. I gaze up at the sky where the rays shine through the parted clouds as the birds sing brilliantly like a choir of angels. A burst of joy fills my heart.

Thirty-five years ago, I started on this journey to heal my body, mind, and spirit. My soul was calling me to transform through my body (illness) and I answered the call. These hard times helped me grow into a more conscious soul. This education—learning what I needed to live in a healthier way, restoring my body and mind—is a path, not a destination. It never ends, for there always are more layers of these human conditions to unveil. Each day, I wake up to something new that challenges me to stay awake.

My book, *From Modeling Clothes to Modeling Self,* was the journey back to my true self. In it, I share my path and my experiences as I made lifestyle changes and allowed the internal discomforts to bring me to my rough edges. It was what I needed to help me grow into a higher vibration. The key is to accept these feelings and unlovable parts without judgment and to become our own best friend.

I find ways to love from the deepest parts of myself. This love that is Divine power links us all when we open to it. I awaken to the truth that there is love in everything. This natural world that surrounds me offers gifts without conditions, and in the presence of this beauty that I am receiving, I feel love.

When I fill up with this true nature that lives inside of me, I want to give it away. It fills to overflowing and becomes the silent prayer of my heart beaming out into the world.

 Day 348

In this life, we will all face times of grief and loss. Our challenge is to find a deeper meaning. These life-altering situations, like terminal illnesses, relationship break-ups, difficult issues with our parents or children, job losses, and other financial stresses, all provide a doorway to new life. But first, we must go through the pain.

We must face our false core beliefs, these life-long untruths—that we are unlovable, unworthy, hopelessly flawed. We must drop our attachments and strip away all that covers us up. Then we can get to the deeper meaning.

When we drop our resistance and need for control, we can walk through the fire and transmute the condition. When you allow it, when you have been brought to your knees and call out, "What do I do now?" the Universe reaches down and picks you up.

Life brings us to the edge of the precipice where we are fueled by fear because we are afraid to touch our false self. The key is to accept, to sit with our internal discomforts, and be our honest-to-goodness self, even when we are afraid.

We meet these feelings, these unlovable parts of ourselves, and try not to judge. We try to be the best friend we can be to ourselves. And when we stay long enough, insights come, and life awakens us as we see with different eyes. Then we take off these coverings, these masks that cover up our true light, and we grow.

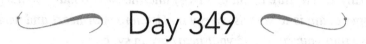

Day 349

To be fully alive, fully human, and completely awake is to be continually thrown out of the nest. To live fully is to be always in no-man's-land, to experience each moment as completely new and fresh. To live is to be willing to die over and over again.

— Pema Chödrön, *When Things Fall Apart*

I hear screeching in the backyard and find a woodpecker has fallen on the ground and seems wounded. It doesn't move when I approach it. When I pick it up and place it in the fountain to have some water, it does not resist me at all. I then put it down on the grass, listening to it chirp at me. As I continue to watch it through my window, it hops slowly over to a safe place near the trees.

I had noticed a second bird earlier, and I had hoped it would come to this woodpecker's aid once I left. But it does not return leaving the woodpecker I rescued all alone to face its life. As the experience unfolds, I think of the day Steve died and feel I must leave it alone. I become the observer, watching how the Divine takes care of this precious creature. I pray and pray for the healing of the bird, sending it energy while open to any message this bird may bring me for my life right now. I listen inside and receive:

Spirit Speaks

It's hard to fly after you have been wounded. All of humanity has been hurt and traumatized by unconscious living. No one is to blame, for we are all healing together.

This year is a new beginning for you to be conscious of every moment of your living. It seems like a tall order, but it is what our souls desire—to know that when you fall and feel like you cannot fly, just take those baby steps and trust in your ability to remember who you truly are. Nature is full of energy and the way to make yourself stronger again is to let this energy in. Listen to your heart and what is true so that your head and your heart are in sync.

I am here with you. Writing this book is what we choose to do together. I am a part of this energy and universal life force that desires to flow through your channel.

You held the bird in the palm of your hand and the bird looked at you with trust and peace. You see, my sweet, this is how God holds you in the palm of the hand of this world that is the heart of all that is Divine. You will keep trying to jump up with great effort, but what if you just allow this force of nature to take you up and up and up? How delicious the feeling to be swept away into the magnificence of being the Presence that is so vast and glorious.

Day 350

I walk outside into the garden, and in this glorious moment, I take a picture of a flower that has bloomed on the bush. As I turn away to walk back into the house, I hear a loud bang from a blackbird that has flown into the screen.

Last night I finished yesterday's entry about the fallen woodpecker. So as the blackbird flies away, I know that it got my attention so that Spirit could bring me another message. I listen:

Spirit Speaks

I am nudging you. I am pushing you to fly and be free. There is so much to experience right now. There is a clear message for you as you let yourself be free of anyone trying to get their light from you. It is in them. To find it, they must feel what is in the way, what blocks them from their own eternal Presence. This is what it is all about. The heart knows that all the love that is flowing in you is within each person's reach.

Letting go is difficult. I had to watch you struggle from where I am. You can allow the world to attend to their struggles and know that it is where they will transform and become more. So, bow to each one as they play their part for you so that you can continue to be strong in your knowing that love never dies.

Fly now and be free of all that weighs you down. Those unending thoughts will pass by like clouds as you let this day begin by serving yourself. The food that gives you life will restore you and then it will spill out into the hearts that come to sit with you.

Serving humanity is such a delight and gives you all you need right now. Let it be enough until one day when that special someone walks into your heart. It could be today...just trust in this beautiful life that is giving to you like the beautiful flower on the bush that I planted long ago.

Day 351

God's message of love is sent into this world in a human envelope.

— Richard Rohr

Despite the stresses of living in this human body, I strive each day to be the best version of myself. I glance over to the bookshelf where a colorful plaque screams the words etched on its surface and in my heart...

LOVE LIKE YOU'LL NEVER BE HURT
SING LIKE NO ONE IS LISTENING
DANCE LIKE NO ONE IS WATCHING
LIVE LIKE IT'S HEAVEN ON EARTH

As I ride the waves, big and small, that carry me through this vast ocean that is life, again and again, I am shown yet another way back to myself. From this place, I know I can and will open my heart again. I let my soul's song release the truth for everyone to hear as I dance on this incredible earth with abandon.

Day 352

Meditation

Out of the darkness of thoughts
That can only bring suffering
Comes the ever-present breeze of Spirit
Calling your name,
Nudging you to break away
From the mind that holds you
In the grip of despair.

You turn your gaze to the sun
Where ripples of golden light
Move and dance upon your eyes
As you take in the story
Written long ago
Yet now remembered.
There is so much to see
When you live in union with the Divine
Expressing the wisdom of the heart.

Oh, precious One!
Take off the denial
So that your feelings can be allowed
To pass through the river
That once brought soothing
In the womb of the mother.
Let the unconditional stream of consciousness

Pull you into the embrace of tender loving care.
Look now to the sweetest life given,
For both the struggles and triumphs
Have allowed you to grow into yourself.

This internal path brings forth the new,
As the seasons of grief change all your colors.
In the barren land of emptiness,
You become filled with the light that gives and gives
Knowing that there is so much more to be received.
Now, as you reach into the deep canyon of emptiness,
The light awakens and everyone in your presence
Is welcomed into the embrace
Of the One Eternal Being that transcends time.

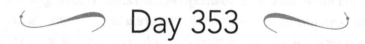

Day 353

I wake up to a new day, surrounded by the morning sounds. The sun coaxes me out of my lonely bed along with all that is here within me, like the sweet pain of loss or betrayal. Whether it is the suffering from days gone by or something that my physical body awakens in me, I let it be. All the suffering in my life has made me a vessel, an instrument, a channel, an open space for deeper life to be born.

Surviving the pain of letting go empties me. What lives and breathes through me is the love. This garden where I sit daily has been the witness to my everyday human self, emptying and sharing my deepest truth. This garden that grew from the tiniest seeds and plants is thriving in the stillness of another dawn. The Bismarck palm offers shade, and the banana trees give fruit. All that nature holds for me is endless in possibilities.

It's quite a journey when we love someone, and they leave. It feels like they take a part of us with them, those tender parts that were intimately shared, like the way they gazed into your eyes by candlelight, or that glance from across the room when you know they were watching you. They shared tears and fears, grins and giggles; those moments of silent loving that perhaps were taken for granted because in the moment you were sure it would never end. Now we remember that everything in this world is temporary.

Day 354

Spirit Speaks

There is an understanding of the heart when you let go of your grievances with me and yourself. You can never fake it. You are forever revealed when you enter your heart and step into the truth that always opens you up to more love. To accept our darkness is to forgive it in another and, ultimately, in yourself. You are understanding the true power of seeing it all and trusting in its ability to now be gone from your consciousness.

Repeating the past will never give you your freedom. Touching the past with your eyes wide open and without condemnation releases you and others from the lie of separation and suffering.

What you see is yourself. This world is your mirror and instead of a cross to bear, you find the burdens are lifted off your shoulders, for you do not have the responsibility to carry another. You are free to see that it has always been you that needed your love.

Hold yourself now, my sweet, and take into your mind and body the truth that will always set you free. You are so worthy to be loved. You did nothing wrong, for all you needed was to forgive them all for not seeing you as you are, innocent and worthy of love.

As a messenger of light, I let my voice sing the praises of the Universe as I celebrate each day on this earth. I am alive to witness its beauty. The door that closed has opened many others. The trumpets sound the arrival of this new day when I begin again. I dance in the living room with my puppy and sing like no one is listening. The song goes like this:

I AM!

I AM!

I AM!

Day 356

I am the channel for love in the world. Only then is my call
for love answered. For as I open to love, I extend it, and as I
extend it, it returns to me.

—Paul Ferrini

There is so much that is pushing us all into higher consciousness. Deaths of loved ones, loss of relationships, illnesses, and other endings. But also birth and new beginnings. New partners, new babies/grandbabies, new clients, and new friends.

Buddhist teachings and meditations help me uncover the layers often muddied by false ideas that stir things up and cause chaos. When I get still and quiet, the inner waters calm, the sediment falls away, and who I really am can be seen and felt in the emptiness within. I love how ACIM brings everything back to me and my forgiving heart.

I once pondered, "If you take away money issues, you take away illnesses, you take away this or that, all these so-called problems, what is left?" If we can let go, for a moment, of the ego and all it wants to identify with, then the mind will quiet and there will be space inside to birth what is real. And that is Presence; that is the connection to our perfect spirit.

This lightness of being is love. It reminds me we are all connected. So, I can sit at the table of life with all humanity and keep my heart wide open. No matter where they have been, what dogma or political belief, whatever the color, gender, circumstance, or behavior, I can settle inside my heart and listen. No matter their story, I can see the offering of love being presented to them. It fills me up and spills out as the compassionate loving of all mankind.

It is my work and joy to share this with the world. There are no enemies, only opportunities to heal what has been held within the body to learn the lesson of our souls.

Day 357

There is a sacredness in every human being because we are all
Divinely created. When our thoughts speak truth, the body fills with
light, and our eyes become the vessel through which this light shines.
When our minds are filled with negativity and fear, we only see
darkness, and our light is dimmed.

As we remember who we are, which is the likeness of God/Divine,
we can receive and share our wholeness. Being yourself is the greatest
gift you give to others. When you acknowledge your wholeness, you can
witness the opening of the door to your heart, for nothing can hold you
back from being all you came here to be. This world is your mirror. If
you stand for a moment in its reflection, it will reveal the flaws in your
thinking. This mirror allows you to see your state of being, whether it is
stable or in disharmony.

I have the choice to be free inside no matter what is going on in the
external world. There I become my own happiness, my own light. As I
let go of my attachments to the external world, I can rise up through my
heart. As I receive the desires that inspire me to be my best self, I choose
to live this day in a peaceful mind.

Meditation

*Troubling emotions
Begin to rise to the surface.
I bring the focus of my inner reality
To my breath,
And I breathe.*

In the presence of this moment,
I open to reveal
All that desires to be shared.

I allow darkness to be seen
As I move my awareness
Underneath my thoughts.

In Your love Divine,
I can finally be me.

Though I don't know how the story will unfold,
I trust you, God/Source/Great Mystery/Universe.

From this deeper connection
I have with myself
And all beings,
I listen.

Day 358

Spirit Speaks

This new world is birthing through each individual form, through the heart where you merge and allow the higher vibration to create through your living. Let go of what was and experience fully in this place called home.

Arriving here has been a journey of the earthly body to join with all that is illuminated and seen as a passageway. Entering into the depths of this human self, you expand and transform until you emerge out of the darkness to embody the light.

All is held and seen without any thought of judgment or rejection. The light of the heavens shine through all your doing as your being becomes the vessel and conduit for the message of hope and renewal.

You take it in, breath by breath, as the empty mind settles into the intelligence of the heart that knows the truth that frees you and liberates all. This is love and this love would never separate or need to do anything but beam into the moment for the good of all.

You are filled with this breathtaking masterpiece designed for all. Enter this new life, born without conditions, through the heart that is always in union with all.

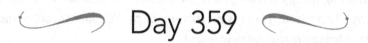

Day 359

Having traversed all the unexpected curves and bends along this path that is my life, I stand on rich soil. It has brought me here to this incredible place.

These days are full of many moments that take my breath away or make me breathe more deeply. These moments, these days that become weeks and months, do not define me.

The pages of my life keep turning, presenting the next opening or closing that supports my growth as I become all that I am.

In this moment, the dawn breaks open a smile upon my heart. I hear the first sound of a bird and witness the light awaken the flowers. As the sunlight becomes a paintbrush, touching the leaves with beauty, I open further to take in this masterpiece.

Oh, sweet day, I drink you in. Naked, I arrive, the shiver of life pouring through my body. As I unveil myself, you continue to be my partner. Oh, sweet day, show me who I am as I let go again and again.

Day 360

Spirit Speaks

As you choose to be here, be still inside this hologram that brings you deeply inside the center of something so magnificent. Be here, inside the miracles of life where you witness what you feel. This explosion of energy within you is the passion for this beautiful life that has already arrived. There is no turning back. You have become the one that brings forth the new world.

It is within your reach. Dance now on this earth as if you have been born again. You have risen out of the trenches of grief and now your light shines brightly for all to see. Know that when you are spinning in this galaxy within, all who come to be in your presence get to touch what they have forgotten. It's within every individual yet each will awaken in their own time. Be in this peace where nothing separates you from your Divine, human self.

Now it's time to live it. No one can take this away unless you forget that I am all that you are... and this will never happen. Today you have helped the past be healed for many as you allow yourself to be fully in your body. You are here to be fully inside of yourself, a passionate woman who loves her life. You have journeyed well, and now without saying a word, know that I will always help you remember how great it is to be you.

The Divine human will awaken others. So, with this love, be free of any guilt or shame because who you are is now living life fully.

Day 361

The shadows sometimes are unbearable. Yet if I stay here for a while, the light comes in, revealing the contrast between the light and dark.

What an incredible work of art. It is unique, designed just for me. I am the reason why it looks the way it does.

I am the way that shows me the illusions. As they shatter, it brings me to transcendence. As I choose to see the truth, it aligns me with my soul's purpose.

Today I experience everything as if I am the center of creation—loving it all from a space of no mind, no judgment, no labels, or definitions. In this space where light meets dark, I am still, and the sweet spot within my heart fills me up like nothing else can.

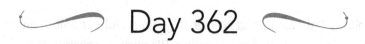 Day 362

Dear Human:
You didn't come here to master unconditional love.
That is where you came from and where you'll return.
You came here to learn personal love.
Universal love.
Messy love.
Sweaty love.
Crazy love.
Broken love.
Whole love.
Infused with divinity.
Lived through the grace of stumbling.
— Courtney Walsh

We all face so much through these times, yet as we uncover the false beliefs that keep us attached, we become the ones walking in this world but not of it. So, when the world turns us upside down and inside out and shakes us to our core, we are anchored by our knowing that fear does not hold us back. It helps us to feel our human selves.

Allow the mud to settle and reveal your shining light. Then look in the mirror and, seeing yourself fully, greet all that is reflecting back to you with, "Hello, you beautiful being of light, I love you!"

I hear my heart's longing for the healing of our world. I am here to serve this love that spills out of me. This light shines through my eyes as I see you and I say, *"Hello, you beautiful being of light. I love You!"*

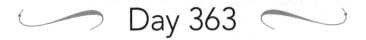

Day 363

Colleen, Philomene, and I decide to go for a walk and sit at one of our favorite spots to meditate together. We park ourselves at the picnic table and allow this familiar place to cradle us. We all feel the energy as nature's sounds call us to move deeply within.

I breathe into that peaceful place within my heart and almost immediately I see a vision of Steve waving to me. It's a wave that says goodbye. I'm in a bubble of light and held in the arms of my sisters' love as I channel Spirit. It's a love letter from heaven.

Spirit Speaks

I'm going now and leaving you all together. I am moving into more learning. All that is real lives in the heart and all that is true lives forever. I am passing the torch as you take care of each other. The pictures of our life together will fade but the light continues along with a love that will never die. In fact, it will become stronger.

I am always with you, so as I expand and move beyond, we are always connected. The voice of Spirit will get louder now without being shrouded by all your grieving. You will see it all and understand when you leave your body. Take care of each other and remember that I am only a thought away.

I bow to you, for in your death from your body, I am reborn and inspired to live more fully here. I allow the gifts that you have given me to ground me here as I continue to share myself and all that I am because of you. I am ready to allow this new life to unfold.

Day 364

Grief and pain are like joy and peace: they are not things we should try to snatch from each other.

— Glennon Doyle

It's not about the whys.
It's not about the how comes.
It's not even about the what-ifs.

That's just the mind trying to make sense of what is.
Drop into your heart and receive
As you remember that there is no need to search.
Receive how great it is to be you.
As you dwell in this place of knowing,
Nothing outside of you
Could ever cause you to question
Who or what you are.
So, surrender into yourself and be patient.
Enjoy what it is like to be fully here
Without making up stories
That do not belong in this heart of yours,
For what is real
Can only be grasped by the heart.

Then you will be so filled and flowing
With life, this beautiful life,
That there will be no questions.
There will be no whys, what-ifs, or maybes.

There will be no longing because
You have learned that all your longing
Is for your connection to who you truly are.
Your longing is to be with that true self
In every moment of your living.
Life happens and sometimes it feels
As if you are moving through mud,
Or you hit a wall.
You want to live in the past
Or dream about a future.
Know that in the present moment,
Every part of your humanity is a steppingstone
To a true reality that gives, and gives, and gives.

Truth be told, sometimes it is a whisper.
Sometimes, if you are not here in your heart,
You will miss the nudge to move forward,
The encouragement to keep going,
The reassurance to trust in the outcome.
When you do not listen, you forget
How worthy you are to hear what is true.

Move from this place
Where you are settled and happy and feeling.
Nothing could be better than this.
It is the feeling, Beloved One,
Of complete union with the Beloved
Who is loving every part of you,
Accepting every part and listening.

Life is a mystery.
As your soul walks in this mist —
Not a fog, but a mist,
For in the stillness, you can see —
Every cell of your being remembers.
As your mind's eye clears, you discover
The most beautiful gift you will ever receive:
What you see is what you are.

The pure light of being merges with everything
As you expand and become so much more
Than you ever thought you were.
Through this light within,
You join with everything that is.

This is oneness. Everyone you meet
Brings you more of you.
So, as you look inside,
You can face the truth –
How content you are in being alive,
And how joyous you are to share this life
With whoever joins you on this path.
Whether it is for a moment or a lifetime,
It is all good.
It is all beautiful.
It is all for the awakening,
For you can't imagine
How your presence awakens another.

Blessed is your being as you drink this nectar.
So, raise your head and open your heart.
Let it be poured into you,
Quenching your thirst and filling the void.
Your heart holds the key that opens the great mystery
As you merge with all that is Divine.
And so it is.

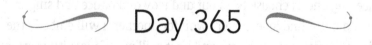

Day 365

I sit under the moon, so beautiful as it illuminates the darkness in the clouds and night sky. I feel amazed by the magnificence of this life. Every heartache and painful experience, every rejection and loss has been an opportunity for acceptance.

I am free. No matter what has happened in my life or in the lives of others around me, in this moment I see the importance of receiving the beauty of my inner reality. Everything, even the pain and all my difficult feelings, has been needed for me to be all I can evolve to be.

I surrender. I let go of the mind that wants to attach to what is going on. Instead of grasping or resisting, I don't try to change a thing. I want to be in this moment, open to receiving.

In the stillness, I give thanks for all that has come before me and all that will come in the aftermath of life's storms. It comes as a calmness inside that moves and breathes and is aware of this incredible life that flows without effort. It illuminates me and opens me to the reality that is here humbly giving life.

Nature, with all its honesty, is all around me bowing to this cherished moment, holding me with reverence, and waiting for me to get it, to understand with my heart that this life is perfect.

It has grounded me into being the receiver of everything until the light enters my conscious awareness and tells me the secrets of the Universe. These messages come streaming into me like the light from the moon. The energy that radiates such power wakes me up to the truth. There is nothing to fix, nothing to do but allow this moment to birth me into being more loving, more kind, more compassionate, more patient, more giving, more connected to this love that is the Universe. This omnipresent bigness of a power that is so vast, that as I let it in, I am healed. And so, I can radiate that which I am into this world I am a part of. As I move out of my head and into the heart, it moves me into a higher vibration that allows me to inspire in new ways.

The new world is in me. A new life has come. I do not have to shake the sleeping ones. I choose to go out and play and dance and sing and write and paint and love. I won't wait for another; I will embody the offering that flows through me and let it spill out of me with every hug or gaze or hello. Every word I write, each stroke of a brush, whether preparing food or taking part in a conversation, I am the illuminated heart of the One who enters this divine moment with grace.

Grace isn't always easy, and it reminds me that I have surrendered into the now without expecting anything. How beautiful this feeling is of allowing my heart to receive it all. Nature reminds me each moment to be the observer and the lover of life.

Has it been easy? Of course not! This journey is hard. It's not a Hallmark movie. There aren't always happy endings, but the opportunities for growth are endless.

The sweetest offering I can give to you, my soul family, is to stay in this Presence. Breathe into this moment so that the gift of your true essence can nourish and renew like nothing else in this external world can. This fragrance of peaceful tranquility emanates from you wherever you are. It infuses others during your quiet walks and your moments of reflection, and while doing all those little things with great love.

I am participating in something much greater than I could have ever imagined. Let me be empty so that God/Universe can fill me up and light can shine through my heart as I touch the world. Even without physically touching anything, I pray and become the space…quietly empty for growth, life, and Spirit to enter.

Be still and know that I Am. I Am that I Am.

Epilogue

I Will Never Stop Speaking to You!

About a year and a half into this journey, I woke up to a voice in my head saying, "Go to the medium. I will speak through him." I had helped promote an appearance by acclaimed spiritual medium Roland Comtois, but I had not planned to attend because the event was sold out.

Then, at the last minute, everything lined up for me. In the nick of time, I got a call from the event organizer who said she had a ticket for me!

As I drove to the venue, I felt this energy pulling me to the event like metal drawn to a magnet. I just knew that Steve was going to connect with me. While sitting at a red light, I glanced up at the sky and watched a jet leaving a bright, white contrail. And then I noticed that the clear, blue sky was filled with big, white Xs...more kisses from Steve!

Once I arrived, I felt grateful to have a seat. The room was crowded and not just with people. I felt many spirit loved ones there, too.

Eager to see how it would all unfold, I sat with my vulnerable feelings, present with anticipation. Over the next three hours, Roland presented messages from spirit loved ones. The energy was amazing. The messages Roland shared were all so beautiful but, alas, none were from Steve.

When Roland announced that his time was up, I was surprised and a little disappointed that Steve had not come through. I could feel my disappointment. But in response, I rationalized to myself, "Oh well, these others need the messages more than I do since I can connect with Steve all the time."

To end the session, Roland selected "To Where You Are" by Josh Groban. As the music started, my body immediately began to vibrate with energy. When this song was first popular and played on the radio, Steve and I had said that after one of us passed, whoever was left would sing this song to the other.

Roland began walking from the front of the room toward me, and I knew Steve was now here. He stretched his hand out towards me, shouting to everyone in the room, "This is our song! This is our song!" I felt Steve's energy, and as I began to cry. Roland continued to channel Steve. He stood right in front of me and loudly proclaimed, "She was the best wifey! She was THE PERFECT WIFE!"

As he looked into my eyes, I felt Steve's love pouring in. "We didn't expect this," he said. "We were not prepared for this. It happened so fast. But love never dies. So, don't ever stop writing because I will always be speaking to you."

Steve/Rolland continued, "You know that shuffling you hear at night? That's me checking up on things." (Steve always shuffled his feet as he walked to the bathroom in the middle of the night.) "And that puppy you got, she will never replace me, but I'm glad you got her."

"He wants me to do this," Roland said, as he put his arms around me and whispered, "You are so beautiful, I love you so much." Those were the exact words Steve said to me during our last time together at the beach on his final day. I sat in the chair crying, feeling all the love and energy. He saved the best for last. Steve was the finale.

I left there shifted, more open to the next chapter of my life. Deep in my heart, I felt so grateful for this gift from my beloved Steve that Roland delivered to me.

I was changed that day. The experience anchored in the importance of the work I do for others. Receiving messages from Spirit is life-changing. Through Roland, Steve reminded me to keep writing "because I will always be speaking to you!"

Afterward

P.S. I Love You

I'd finally finished the manuscript for this book when the doctor called and said, "You have cancer Frannie." What??? Who, me??? I felt myself more inside my body than ever before, present to the silence within. I could feel my heart pounding in my chest as he made a referral. "I am sending you to the best doctor for this kind of cancer," he explained before hanging up. I got off the phone and walked around in disbelief. Was this really happening to me?

The mountain before me seemed way too big to climb. Tears came as I encountered my grief. This time I was grieving for myself and my life. I called my sisters. They cried with me. I called my children. They cried with me. I called my brother. He cried with me. I called my friends, they all cried with me, too.

When I was ready, I sent out a newsletter announcing my diagnosis and asking for prayers from the many people around the globe who I've come to know through my work as a healer and counselor. I called on all these angels to help me with their conscious intention. How powerful prayer is. I received so much love and energy—all of us on this soul journey are so connected.

As I faced my own mortality, I initially felt devastated. My sister Philomene and brother, Phil, flew down immediately. Sometimes the pain was so great that I fainted in their arms. They held me with the loving spirit of my mother and father. Then one week post-op, after viewing my pathology report, my surgeon Dr. Stacy South looked at me with so much presence and declared, "You are cancer free."

The miracle happened. After receiving this tremendous gift of healing, I find myself gathering small insights as I recover from the surgery. I am free! My suffering has brought me home to my heart, and I receive myself fully. My feminine self, so emotionally authentic, real, and mature, holds my masculine self as I continue this human dance. I surrender into the softness of my belly where I encounter the pain of my past. The landscape is littered with debris from a lifetime of betrayals and unwise choices. I don't run from this mess. And as I allow the light from within to illuminate all that is there, it has a cleansing effect. I feel renewed.

When I accept my humanness, I see how fragile living can be, and I realize how precious life is. Now, I can let my body rest and heal. In these days of recovery, I continue to breathe deeply into this feeling of relief. My heart fills with joy, and it sings to me. The music is so beautiful, so sweet, I weep. These tears arise from so deep within. How grateful I am for the gift of more life and opportunities to experience more love in this body.

The life I am living right now on my island, this is my real life, and it is paradise. The universe has conspired to keep me awake and conscious of this fact. The mourning doves remind me, the mockingbirds remind me, the fragrance of the blooming jasmine bushes remind me, the sunlight reminds me, the silence of my morning ritual and the smell of my sweet tea remind me, the pen in my hand, the moisture on my skin, my children, family, and friends living their lives all remind me that my life right here, right now, is magnificent.

When the love of my life, Steve, fell on the floor and then took his last breath, his spirit made sure that I would continue this journey to heal and do what I came here to do. The urge to grasp and try to fix or change was a distraction from sitting in the void that waits in the infinite space between my breaths.

Why is it that the moment I feel some healing, I want to reach out and share it? Why is it that when my garden is blooming, and my heart is so full of love, I just want to paint it, write it, dance and sing it at the top of my lungs? (I may not have a great singing voice, but always I sing!)

This journey through my experience with cancer stopped me in my tracks. It opened me and demanded that I listen and unveil as I unlocked this incredible light that wants to be received.

As I finish these words, it is 10 years since Steve transitioned into pure light. His mission in a body on earth, in his earth suit, was done. Funny, his nickname growing up was spaceman.

So, sweet love,

I thank you for doing the greatest act of kindness. You left me here to pick up the pieces of my life and to trust completely in the Divine. And now the light in me is burning deeper and fuller.

The doorway has swung open, and I walk through it in my body. I am now 70 years old, a lifetime of growing, and now, I rest in all my giving, and I receive.

I found my beloved—It is me! I have met her and now, as I move into my happily ever after life, in this life, I can say to my beloved Steve, "There you are love, I am not afraid of living without you." My gaze at the world becomes my dance with you. I am living with you, for your spirit dances with me as the butterfly flutters around the hibiscus tree that I planted when you died. The hummingbirds come too, along with rainbow-painted skies where the clouds are bright with the sun, at times, peeking through. It's all here right now. Everything in this world is the union of the love of creation and humanity.

I write this letter to you, to the heavens and beyond, and I thank you for leaving me to find myself; to find my wholeness. I searched for you until I found myself. It's been a decade of searching, longing, and wanting to find the love that I had with you. I now know that it's here, in me always.

I have had the most wonderful love affair with myself as I allowed life to teach me.
I had lovers and friendships and experiences with betrayals and it all brought me so much.
No one had to stay. I stayed.

So, I write these messages to myself and these words that speak of love, and I realize that this new relationship with myself has brought me to my wholeness. I have been my best friend, confidant and lover. I have nurtured myself, and I no longer pass judgment when I make mistakes. I parent myself well, and I allow the aloneness to bring me to stillness where I find myself happy with me...

I honor the sacred energies of my inner feminine and masculine selves as I engage in my life with creativity. I want for nothing but this feeling that love flows freely inside of me no matter what. I write, I paint, I dance, I sing, and I love. The sacred relationship of my soul that creates through this human body continues to bring me into more consciousness and love each day.

As God lives and breathes in me, my spirit soars and expands to love greater. And no one is separate from this. God is in us all and the Universe bows to our existence.

Let's live this life fully as Stevie would say, being fully present, even in the small moments that seem to be nothing...it's all something to bring more of us here.

Soar my love—because I am.

Always and forever,
Frannie

P.S. I love you

Printed in the United States
by Baker & Taylor Publisher Services

Printed in the United States
by Baker & Taylor Publisher Services